THE ABOLITIONISTS

The Growth of a Dissenting Minority

Minorities in American History

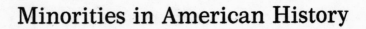

THE ABOLITIONISTS

The Growth of a Dissenting Minority

Merton L. Dillon

Northern Illinois University Press

DE KALB

Merton L. Dillon is professor of History at Ohio State University, Columbus, Ohio.

The illustrations on pages 5, 17, 51, 85, 115, 143, 177, 201, 221, and 249 were taken from *The Anti-Slavery Record* for 1835 and 1836, and reproduced through the courtesy of The Newberry Library, Chicago.

The illustrations on pages 37, 41, 65, 96, 125, 154–55, 185, and 207 were taken from the Prints and Photographs Division of the Library of Congress and reproduced through the courtesy of the Library of Congress.

Library of Congress Cataloging in Publication Data

Dillon, Merton Lynn, 1924–
    The abolitionists: the growth of a dissenting
minority.
    Includes bibliographical references.
    1. Slavery in the United States—Anti-slavery
movements. I. Title.
E449.D58   1974   322.4'4'0973   73–15096
ISBN 0-87580-044-0
ISBN 0-87580-513-2 (pbk.)

Copyright © 1974 by Northern Illinois University Press
Published by the Northern Illinois University Press,
DeKalb, Illinois 60115
Manufactured in the United States of America
Designed by George Lenox

For Mary, Helen, and Jim

Contents

Foreword

Minority History, once a euphemism disguising unpleasant or intractable social realities, has come in our time to be viewed as a source of American vitality and self-illumination. In an era when American society has been undergoing a vast realignment of its human resources, institutions, and habits of mind, Americans are more prone than ever to see that the experiences of ethnic, regional, social, economic, occupational, political, religious, intellectual and other well-defined groups have spotlighted and personalized strategic problems in the American past.

The Minorities in American History series will encompass a whole range of such group experiences. Each is intended to illuminate brightly a critical event, movement, tradition, or dilemma. By so doing, these books will individualize the problems of a complex society, giving them both broad pertinence and sharp definition. In addition, the special insights afforded by the increasingly sophisticated methodology of the "new history" will be reflected in an expanding list of ethnohistory studies where sociological theory and quantitative analysis will further inform, document, and shape the dramatic narrative.

Few themes have engaged as much fervid attention and historical controversy in recent years as has the role of the abolitionists in affecting the drift of events in pre-Civil War America. Indeed the impressive volume and high quality of the historical literature devoted to that dissenting minority and to related themes has created an acute need for an authoritative synthesis that would integrate and assimilate the latest scholarship in the field.

Now Merton Dillon has provided us with such a work. A ranking authority, he is saturated in the literature and in the sources of the abolitionist era. He has written a book that in its sustained narrative sweep captures the spirit of his protagonists and of that age. At the same time, he retains a balanced appreciation of the limitations of the abolitionists no less than their virtues. Their relationship to other reformers, to black abolitionists, to the full spectrum of abolitionism, to a developing racism, and to the changing psychology and temper of succeeding decades is spelled out with quiet eloquence and rare scholarly breadth. While this study conveys the immediacy of the universal contemporary involvement with the race question, a mood revived for the first time in nearly a century, at no point does Dillon invoke the past as simple witness to the prevailing scene. Although his work speaks to us with unusual power and depth, ascribable in part at least to his own sober but passionate involvement with the current scene, in no sense does he pretend to directly link the abolitionists with their putative counterparts in the present.

The anniversaries of the Civil War and of the American Revolution do contribute a unique perspective. Professor Dillon, however, judiciously refrains from attributing profound significance to this singular historical coincidence. The renewed concern with the problems of liberty and equality for Blacks has its own parameters and an agenda for which abolitionists showed little prescience. The enlightenment-inspired abolitionism of the Revolutionary era and the religiously-inspired antislavery ethos of the pre-Civil War years provide the framework for the age of abolition. It is an era that is instructive on its own terms.

MOSES RISCHIN, Series Editor
San Francisco State University

A Preview

On 23 March 1965, at one of the most dramatic moments in the civil rights movement, the *New York Times* reported that the Reverend Martin Luther King, Jr.'s huge protest march from Selma to Montgomery, Alabama, would soon be joined by at least twenty prominent historians. Included in the list of those about to depart for Alabama were some of the best known students of the Civil War and the Reconstruction. In this manner men whose careers focused on the study of past crises concerning race announced their intention to plunge into what many then regarded as the very eye of the twentieth century's racial storm.

The incident, instructive on a number of counts, is perhaps most noteworthy for its vivid illumination of the links that so closely bind the social concerns of the present with those of a century and more ago. It hardly needs observing that the explosive problem of race, which was central to the Civil War and Reconstruction period, is central also to our own, and that questions and policy decisions surrounding it engage the present generation much as they have engaged Americans throughout nearly all our history.

Events of the 1950s and afterward gave to the abolitionists, the group chiefly responsible for bringing racial issues to public consciousness in pre-Civil War America, a degree of contemporaneousness not often achieved by figures of the past. While acknowledging the differences that inevitably distinguish men and circumstances in widely separated historical periods, present-day students of the antislavery movement can detect in events since the 1950s, echoes of nineteenth-century developments as similar arguments, similar agitational devices, and similar conflicts reappear. Because of these imperfect parallels the antislavery movement can now be studied with greater perception and depth of understanding than could easily be achieved before. For some persons contemporary involvement has reached back to illumine the past, and acquaintance with the abolitionists has made more comprehensible some of the events of recent times.

A continuity of ideals, premises, goals, and methods extends from the abolitionists of the eighteenth and nineteenth centuries to their modern successors, who likewise see in the peculiar form race relations have taken in America a danger to the survival of the Republic. Viewed in that way, the American Revolution, the Civil War and Reconstruction, and recent civil rights struggles may be seen as occupying positions on a continuum, originating in 1619 with the appearance of Blacks at Jamestown and whose stopping point is not in sight.

From the seventeenth century, when the first American critiques of slavery appeared, through 1865, when the Thirteenth Amendment abolished it, the active opponents of slavery and the advocates of racial equality constituted a minority in American society. Their ideas and programs never were fully accepted, save perhaps briefly during the American Revolution and for a still more fleeting moment during the Civil War. On the contrary, the majority of their countrymen continued to adhere to the venerable conviction that the welfare of society demanded subordination of Negroes.

Yet the most obvious of the abolitionists' goals—the ending of slavery—eventually came to be public policy. The changing relationship between the abolitionist minority and the rest of society, and the process by which a portion —but not all—of the abolitionist program gained northern majority acceptance are the main themes of this book. Every reader should understand that in a sense the book is unfinished, as all accounts of the abolitionists must remain unfinished: The last chapter in the history of their struggle for freedom and justice cannot be written because it has not yet been lived.

Yet the account that follows should not be read as glorification or judgment or as a call for action. The abolitionists' bravery seems beyond dispute, for only men and women of great moral courage and independence of mind venture to subvert the dominant practices and values of their age. That they adhered more faithfully than their contemporaries to the principles of justice and freedom associated with one of the great western traditions seems equally certain. Nonetheless, objections can validly be raised. Abolitionists were as humanly flawed as the rest of us. In particular they were prone to be unattractively censorious, self-righteous, and bellicose. Further, it can be charged, their agitation perhaps helped generate that American spirit of international moral responsibility which is alleged to have been a prime source of human misery in this century as well as a means for its relief. An ultimate effect of their crusade also may have been not to subvert—as some of them had hoped—but to strengthen and lend legitimacy to institutions and values whose ultimate beneficence is in doubt. But such considerations, compelling though they are, are not matters of central concern here. Understanding is.

While the sympathies in the account that follows are not hidden, its purpose is neither to identify heroes nor to expose villains. The abolitionists' record is clear and immutable. They do not need us for their defense; we cannot come to their aid by changing the past if we would. Neither is it likely to prove useful for us to try to summon them and their tradition in support of causes we ourselves favor. We stand alone on our own resources as they did; we bear full responsibility for our errors and failings as they do for theirs. And no more clearly than they can we foresee the full consequences of our acts.

THE ABOLITIONISTS

The Growth of a Dissenting Minority

CHAPTER ONE

Riding the Wave of History

ABOLITIONISTS IN THE REVOLUTIONARY ERA

Slavery was an institution whose growth in modern times was inseparable from the development of European empires in the New World. It first came under heavy and sustained attack when revolutionary upheaval racked the unity of one of those empires. This coincidence was not merely accidental.

For a few English colonials in America the intellectual currents that swept the Atlantic community in the mid-eighteenth century brought visions of a new and better world. Moral progress, those optimists believed, eventually could remove every age-old obstacle to happiness and virtue. Faith in human progress stimulated political revolt. While most of the Americans who chafed under English rule after the French and Indian War doubtlessly had the easing of political control and the ending of economic restriction as their chief goal in opposing English policy, some took a larger view. They saw revolution as a more comprehensive process than merely the cutting of political ties and the removal of economic hobbles. Also encompassed within the term "revolution" was the dream that society could at last be freed from all those remnants of a less enlightened past that hampered the development of human potential. No American institution more strikingly belonged to that category than slavery.

It may be that white Americans in the 1760s were made more sensitive to English encroachments on their rights by their daily observation of what they themselves did to black men. Slavery was not simply a theoretical possibility, not a mere figure of speech. It was a state into which men actually had fallen. It was a condition observable within their own communities.[1]

Although Americans profited from slavery and had long taken its existence for granted, many now agreed that slavery violated natural law. This conclusion presented slaveholders of the Revolutionary era with a troublesome problem, because natural law had come to have for them much the same force that divine law exercised in earlier times. It was a rare politically-conscious American in the late eighteenth century who did not view slavery as conflicting with the natural-rights principles from which the Revolution was derived and as clashing with the Revolution's goals. That generally held assumption appeared unmistakably even in the rhetoric of the age.

By verbal association and analogy, discontented Americans compared their relation to England with the relation existing between slave and master. England, Americans charged, aimed to reduce free-born colonists to "slavery"; the political and economic regulations imposed by English officials "oppressed" Americans and threatened to "enslave" them. In justifying rebellion against such prospective dangers, Americans emphasized their inalienable right to freedom, drawing upon a venerable English radical tradition in the process. "We hold these truths to be self-evident," wrote Thomas Jefferson, "that all men are created equal; that they are endowed by their Creator with certain inalienable rights...." By implication, Americans of the Revolutionary era extended the rights they claimed for themselves to all mankind.

A colonist needed no unusual degree of perception to note the embarrassing contradiction of a slaveholding people rebelling against "slavery." The crusty eighteenth-century English writer, Dr. Samuel Johnson, took delight in asking

Toussaint L'Ouverture—the George Washington of St. Domingo

the obvious question: "How is it that we hear the loudest yelps for liberty among the drivers of negroes?"[2] Americans too were uncomfortably aware of the irony in their situation. Some pious colonials construed the troubles they experienced with England as God's punishment imposed upon them for their own transgressions. Among those sins, it sometimes was said, slavery loomed the most prominent.

Thus in the Revolutionary era, a religiously inspired sense of guilt joined with a belief in the natural rights of man and faith in the dawning of an age of reason and benevolence to produce a home-grown critique of slavery.

Throughout America increasing numbers of the conscience-stricken, in the 1770s and afterward, freed their slaves, a procedure made easy even in the South when the legislatures of Delaware, Maryland, and Virginia removed restrictions that previously had either discouraged or prohibited such acts of generosity. In New England, slaves themselves shared the liberating enthusiasm of the time and petitioned the state legislatures to grant them freedom. Not surprisingly, their efforts in Massachusetts apparently were aided by Samuel Adams, one of the earliest and most consistent advocates of colonial rights. In several Northern states and in Virginia, antislavery legislators introduced bills providing for gradual emancipation. Only in South Carolina and Georgia were evidences of advancing antislavery sentiment for the most part lacking.[3]

On account of such events, opponents of slavery during the Revolutionary era understandably viewed themselves as forming part of the great army of Americans whose activities in behalf of liberty were combining to usher in a more enlightened age. They had no reason whatever to consider their antislavery program as being out of harmony with the main developments of their time. On the contrary, society everywhere was apparently moving toward greater freedom and the loosening of bonds. Accordingly, abolitionists might reasonably anticipate that the continued working of moral progress would soon accomplish their aims with minimal opposition and conflict.

The most prominent figures of the American Revolution were also leaders in the expression of antislavery sentiment. Benjamin Franklin was founder and president of the Pennsylvania Abolition Society. Alexander Hamilton wrote powerful statements asserting the natural equality of Blacks and their right to freedom. John Dickinson, Thomas Jefferson, George Washington, Patrick Henry, John Adams, Henry Laurens, George Mason, James Otis—all those Revolutionary leaders and others of lesser fame—let it be known by words and sometimes by their actions that they gave at least some support to the movement against slavery.[4]

Abolitionists of the Revolutionary period thus enjoyed the assurance that comes to those who know they have friends and partisans both in high places and scattered generally throughout the land. It had not always been so, and, as we shall see, the relation between active opponents of slavery and the rest of society would soon undergo drastic change.

When, toward the end of the seventeenth century—several generations before the outbreak of the American Revolution—opposition to slavery was first conspicuously voiced in America, it obviously was minority sentiment that could find no means to influence the direction of events. Antislavery in those early years was the expression of individual dissent. It did not represent the considered views of significant portions of the population; moreover, no channels then existed by which such minority sentiment could exert influence or even be widely heard.

In the early colonial period it was an unawareness that slavery presented any moral problem rather than an active resistance to antislavery ideas that provided the chief obstacle to the spread of antislavery sentiment. There was as yet no imperative to act, for no widespread dissatisfaction with existing social practices and institutions had developed. Concepts of liberty seldom appeared in the writings of a people who did not yet feel themselves oppressed.

Quakers alone among religious groups in pre-Revolutionary America developed an ethic that demanded antislavery action. They alone grasped the dimensions of the problem. As craftsmen, merchants, and planters, Quakers had yielded to the same allure of profit and ease that led other Americans to own slaves. Quakers too became slaveowners. This fact appalled certain sensitive members of the sect to whom slaveholding seemed a betrayal of the ideals upon which the sect was founded. For the most impassioned of those early critics—Ralph Sandiford (1693–1733) and Benjamin Lay (1677–1759)—slavery was the epitome of evil. It symbolized for them all the cruelty and despotism, all the violations of the religious ideal of love and brotherhood that marred the earthly order. Providence had designed the new world, such antislavery Quakers romantically believed, as a garden of virtue and abundance, but men had defiled it by introducing slavery. God's wrath must be anticipated if the evil were not soon removed.[5]

Such warnings, vivid though they were, went little heeded, even by most Quakers, until near the middle of the eighteenth century. At that time, certain political troubles besetting the sect led Quakers to subject themselves to intensive self-examination in the hope of discovering the cause of their ordeal. Out of that crisis of conscience came a strengthening of the original Quaker commitment to loosen worldly attachments and to aid the poor, the downtrodden, the distressed.

Now feeling themselves persecuted on account of secular involvement, Quakers at mid-eighteenth century made the difficult and costly decision to remove part of their worldly ties. First they ceased participation in the slave trade. Soon they required all members of the sect to free their slaves. At the same time, they intensified their humanitarian commitment to aid victims of hatred and persecution. None of the oppressed who came under their observation were more victimized than freed Negroes and Negro slaves.

Thus, by the time of the American Revolution, Quakers had freed themselves from direct involvement with slavery, and some had dedicated themselves both to active antislavery work and to philanthropy among Blacks. Their movement in this direction was powerfully stimulated by the work of two able Friends, who expanded the abolitionist tradition established earlier by Sandiford and Lay. Anthony Benezet, a schoolmaster of Philadelphia, crusaded against the slave trade and also established a school for Blacks. The saintly John Woolman, an itinerant Quaker preacher, carried the antislavery message beyond the bounds of the Quaker sect by warning Americans generally of the impending divine wrath they must expect to suffer if slavery was not soon abolished.[6]

Until well into the nineteenth century, Quakers dominated the antislavery movement, furnishing an important part of the rank-and-file membership as well as some of antislavery's most effective leaders. Even after actual anti-slavery leadership had passed to other hands, traditions that were closely associated with Quaker thought and practice—especially the doctrine of nonresistance—continued to exercise significant influence among abolitionists.[7]

The tides of antislavery sentiment that swept America during the Revolutionary era suggested that influential segments of the population had come to share at least part of the Quaker hostility to slavery. In the North, antislavery ideology became strong enough to counteract the economic interest some Northerners had in slavery and to overcome the racially inspired apprehensions commonly felt about the results of freeing Blacks. Although in New York and Pennsylvania, efforts for abolition aroused strong and stubborn resistance, gradual emancipation was accepted even in those states. In 1804, the process was completed in the North when New Jersey, the last to fall in line, enacted a gradual emancipation law.[8]

No legislature south of Pennsylvania passed such a measure. Yet this fact did not signify a dearth of antislavery sentiment in the South. Especially in Maryland and Virginia the numbers of freed Negroes rapidly increased as individual owners manumitted their slaves, themselves voluntarily doing what the legislatures of their states refused to require.

Religious institutions, like the political institutions, were beginning to take antislavery stands. By emphasizing the worth and potential of every individual—whatever his earthly status—and his equality before God, the revivalism of the Great Awakening of the 1740s encouraged antislavery thought and action within the churches (though it hardly required them). Revivalism as a process provided a model for the personal decision and commitment that came to characterize those abolitionists whose inspiration was predominantly religious. Further, the theology that developed in several Protestant groups in the middle of the eighteenth century counseled "disinterested benevolence toward mankind," a duty that some converts expressed in antislavery action. The church organizations themselves, however, while often officially condemning slavery, were extremely reluctant to impose sanctions against their slaveholding members.

By the late eighteenth century, enlightened opinion everywhere supported antislavery movements, and antislavery sentiment had been channeled into both politics and religion. Thus, at the end of the Revolutionary era abolitionists anticipated the future with confidence. Both religious principle and political ideals had been marshaled to the support of their program. Abolitionists understood very well that the victories they had achieved were far from conclusive and that much entrenched interest and inertia with respect to slavery still needed to be overcome; nevertheless, impressive evidence suggested that the nation was moving steadily toward the ultimate elimination of slavery. It would have been easy to conclude that continued work for that end, following lines already established, could achieve success.

Reformers might have tempered their optimism had they recognized the import of two forces that emerged soon after "independence" to work powerfully against their efforts. One of these was economic—a growing absorption with the accumulation of wealth and a strengthening attachment to individual property rights, rights often considered fully as "natural" and "inalienable" as any other secured by the Revolution. Abolitionism was sometimes opposed as being in conflict with such economic rights and interests.[9]

The other force countering abolition was cultural—a sharpening awareness of the significance of racial differences. Race consciousness, perhaps never absent from Anglo-American culture, had contributed to the ease with which Blacks in America were enslaved in the seventeenth century. Historians Winthrop Jordan and David Brion Davis have demonstrated that at the end of the eighteen century it also worked against their emancipation.[10] White Americans, struggling after independence to develop a national identity, embraced the conviction that America was intended exclusively for Whites. Despite the fact that they had never been alone on the continent but from practically the first day of settlement shared occupation with both Indians and Blacks, Anglo-Americans assumed that Providence designed America to be a white man's country. The possibility that Blacks would be incorporated into American society as free men, thereby "debasing" it and destroying its homogeneity, must accordingly be resisted; above all, racial amalgamation must not be allowed to occur.

While some critics of slavery fully shared such views, abolitionists invariably rejected them. When Thomas Jefferson in his *Notes on the State of Virginia* (1785) expressed carefully qualified and tentative doubts about the intellectual potential of Blacks and about their fitness to remain in America after emancipation, advocates of abolition vigorously contradicted him. They denied that the alleged inferiority was inherent.[11] But these strong, twentieth-century-like assertions of human equality had little effect in countering the more widely held and more deeply ingrained contrary views.

Early abolitionists at first underestimated the power of such racist ideas and economic interests to obstruct the progress of antislavery principles. They expected to persuade southern political majorities to enact the same kind of gradual emancipation laws that had ended slavery in Pennsylvania, New York, and New Jersey. Gradualism and moderation would characterize both their program and their mode of operation before 1830. Though they mercilessly condemned slavery and slaveholders and looked forward to total abolition, they seldom proposed drastic, immediate change in master-slave relations. They were more likely to regard slavery as an evil to be ameliorated and very gradually ended through slow and painless changes than as a sin to be abandoned immediately. As men of the Enlightenment, they were conscious of the fragility of the ties that bind men and institutions together. As observers of contemporary events they were dismayed by the violence that accompanied the French Revolution and the slave upheavals in Santo Domingo. Thus they feared the violent disruption of the entire social order that might result from precipitate change in any part of it. Accordingly, in developing their programs they were more likely than their nineteenth-century successors to consider the interests and prejudices of slaveholders and to weigh the consequence of abolition on the whole of society.[12]

Even great evils, they assumed, should be remedied by good will and moderate efforts and through mutual consent. They had confidence in gradualism, in the efficacy of piecemeal reform. Patience was a virtue many of them deliberately cultivated, for they confidently expected Providence eventually to provide solutions for problems that then seemed beyond the powers of man to resolve. Meanwhile, through rational accommodation, mankind could gradually progress in social relations and thereby move step-by-step toward a better world. He could ameliorate such evils as slavery and gradually, with minimal disruption to the social order, eliminate them altogether. That goal could be reached through rational persuasion and mutual adjustment without resorting to the clash of conflicting interests.

Such caution and restraint and such conciliatory attitudes were not qualities for which nineteenth-century abolitionists would be noted. The dramatic transformation that soon took place in abolitionist temper and mode of operation resulted in part from a change in world view from the rationality of the Enlightenment, with its sense of corporate order, to the more impatient and emotional Romantic age, with its emphasis on the needs, aspirations, and worth of the individual. In part, the changed attitudes and tactics of the abolitionists can be accounted for simply as resulting from their own prolonged, frustrating experience as reformers.

Notes

1. Bernard Bailyn, *The Ideological Origins of the American Revolution* (Cambridge, Mass.: Harvard University Press, 1967), pp. 230–46.
2. Samuel Johnson, "Taxation No Tyranny; an Answer to the Resolutions and Address of the American Congress, 1775," in *Political Tracts* (Dublin: W. Whitestone, W. Wetson, 1777), p. 259.
3. Mary Stoughton Locke, *Anti-Slavery in America from the Introduction of African Slaves to the Prohibition of the Slave Trade (1619–1808)* (Boston: Ginn, 1901), pp. 69–70.
4 For a collection of their views see George Livermore, *An Historical Research Respecting the Opinions of the Founders of the Republic on Negroes as Slaves, Citizens, and as Soldiers* (Boston: A. Williams, 1862).
5. David Brion Davis, *The Problem of Slavery in Western Culture* (Ithaca: Cornell University Press, 1966), pp. 306–16, 330–32, 483–87.
6. Sydney V. James, *A People Among Peoples; Quaker Benevolence in Eighteenth Century America* (Cambridge, Mass.: Harvard University Press, 1963), pp. 268–334.
7. Thomas C. Drake, *Quakers and Slavery in America* (New Haven: Yale University Press, 1950), pp. 167–200, and *passim.*
8. The process is detailed in Arthur Zilversmit, *The First Emancipation: The Abolition of Slavery in the North* (Chicago: University of Chicago Press, 1967).
9. Staughton Lynd, *Class Conflict, Slavery, and the United States Constitution* (Indianapolis: Bobbs-Merrill, 1967), pp. 181–83.
10. Winthrop D. Jordan, *White Over Black: American Attitudes Toward the Negro, 1550–1812* (Chapel Hill: University of North

Carolina Press, 1968), pp. 542–69; Davis, *Problem of Slavery,* 446–82.

11. William Stanton, *The Leopard's Spots: Scientific Attitudes Toward Race in America, 1815–1859* (Chicago: University of Chicago Press, 1959), p. 12; William Linn, *Serious Considerations on the Selection of a President* (New York, 1800), pp. 6, 11, 13; Gilbert Imlay, *A Topographical Description of the Western Territory of North America . . .* (London, 1792), pp. 185–86, 191–92, 194–201; Thomas Branagan, *A Preliminary Essay on the Oppression of the Exiled Sons of Africa . . .* (Philadelphia: John W. Scott, 1804), pp. 100–101; *Selections from the Writings of the Late Thomas Hedges Genin* (New York: E. O. Jenkins, 1869), pp. 102, 109–11.

12. The foregoing remarks do not apply to evangelically oriented abolitionists, who maintained a little-noticed agitation throughout these decades; for the most influential example, see George Bourne, *The Book and Slavery Irreconcilable* (Philadelphia: J. M. Sanderson, 1816). For the evangelical record of the South during part of the period see James B. Stewart, "Evangelicalism and the Radical Strain in Southern Antislavery Thought During the 1820s," *Journal of Southern History,* 39 (August 1973); 379–96.

CHAPTER TWO

Disenchantment: The Forging of a Minority

1780–1830

At the close of the Revolution, abolitionists, still confident in the progress of enlightened principles, believed they might be able to persuade the Confederation Congress to abolish the slave trade and perhaps even end slavery itself. But Congress soon demonstrated that it was unwilling and perhaps incompetent to do these things. Thus abolitionists welcomed the convening of the Constitutional Convention at Philadelphia in 1787 as a new opportunity to implement antislavery ideals.

The convention was filled with men who had been identified with the Revolutionary movement and its ideology and who had gone on record as opposing slavery. Since little had yet occurred to suggest to abolitionists that their views on human rights were not still shared by American leadership, they imagined that a convention of enlightened patriots could be depended upon to write into the new framework of government Revolutionary ideals with respect to slavery. Of course they were too optimistic and took too much for granted. Certainly they seemed unaware that they themselves might try to use the available channels of power to influence convention delegates to act in accordance with their wishes.[1]

Not until the end of the summer of 1787 did the New York Manumission Society, of which the future Chief Justice

John Jay was president, appoint a committee to memorialize the convention "to promote the attainment of the objects of the Society." But the New Yorkers had acted too late. The convention completed its work and adjourned before the New York committee could even present its memorial.[2]

The Pennsylvania Abolition Society had moved more speedily than its New York counterpart but with no greater effect. It prepared a memorial asking the convention to abolish the slave trade—a major aim of most early abolitionists—and requested Benjamin Franklin, the society's president and one of the convention's most distinguished members, to present it. This Franklin declined to do, reportedly because in his opinion the memorial would "do more harm than good by exciting the suspicions of Southern members."[3]

This was an ominous development. It was one of the first indications voiced by a prominent American that influential parts of the population were now judged not to adhere to the antislavery ideals of the Revolution, which all Americans supposedly shared. Further, Franklin's refusal suggested that national policy with respect to slavery henceforth would be shaped to a large extent by the needs of slaveholding interests rather than by scrupulous adherance to principle. Just as significantly, the incident demonstrated that Northern political leaders, even while retaining their reputation as opponents of slavery, would sometimes be tempted to sacrifice antislavery ideals in order to conciliate the South and gain the support of their slaveholding colleagues. Nothing could more clearly indicate the disadvantagous position in which antislavery proponents would be placed in the new government nor more sharply forecast the difficulties antislavery programs henceforth would encounter.

The final product of the convention's deliberations could only further have disappointed abolitionists who, but a short time earlier, had envisioned the nation as following a smooth and straight course toward abolition. It may be true, as has often been claimed, that some of the men who

"Cruelties of Slavery"

framed the new constitution viewed their creation as an instrument that eventually could be used in the antislavery cause; perhaps too, the framers shared the rosy view that slavery must soon disappear under the force of increasing rationality and benevolence and therefore needed no positive action against it.[4] But whatever basis in truth such assumptions may have, the fact remains that in their deliberations at Philadelphia the Founding Fathers did not seize the opportunity that then was theirs to implement Revolutionary ideals by acting against slavery.

On the contrary, their compromises with slaveholding interests secured a strong foothold for slavery in the new government. "When our *own* liberties were at stake we *warmly* felt for the *common rights of man*," commented Luther Martin, one of the most radical members of the convention, but with such danger passed, "we are daily growing more insensible to those rights."[5]

Of the greatest consequence was the fact that by providing for political representation of three-fifths of the slave population the new constitution gave to white men in the slave states larger influence in setting the policies of the new government than their own actual numbers would have allowed, thereby creating a powerful political motive for perpetuating and extending slavery. Because of the three-fifths compromise, the eradication of slavery by peaceful, constitutional means was made exceedingly difficult and unlikely to occur. Thus if the Constitution gave the new government potential power to destroy slavery, as has been asserted, it also created obstacles against the exercise of that power.[6] Furthermore, while the Constitution did not recognize political parties, it nevertheless created the potential for control of the nation by a political party dominated by slaveholding interests.

Few abolitionists could have been aware of such possibilities in 1787, for only time would reveal them. Neither could they then know that the westward movement of the American people, about to enter an enlarged phase, would contribute to widespread popular attachment to slavery, rather than to revulsion against it.[7] Soon such developments would force abolitionists to reassess their belief that the majority shared their hostility against slavery. They abandoned their faith that history would inevitably carry the nation toward freedom. Eventually some of them would conclude that slavery formed such an essential part of American government and economy and society that only a revolution could dislodge it.

With the rapid spread of cotton production across the lower South after 1800, slavery attained still more widespread economic importance than before, and fewer voices were raised against it. Instances of antislavery success became infrequent, even while abolitionist rhetoric grew more intense. Antislavery appeals in the North aroused diminishing response, and in the South, antislavery sentiment was in fast retreat.

Rhode Island abolitionists observed as early as 1806 that members of what they called "the young and rising generation" felt less repugnance against slavery than did older men who had lived through the inspiring days of the American Revolution.[8] Apparently the same was true in the South. At one time Jefferson had put his trust for eventual antislavery action in young men whose ideas were formed during the Revolutionary period, but he lived long enough to become as disappointed in the new generation as he was in his own. When in 1814 his youthful and idealistic neighbor Edward Coles disclosed to him his hopes that slavery could be destroyed, Jefferson responded with the amazing statement that "your solitary but welcome voice is the first which has brought this sound to my ears."[9]

A stumbling block to antislavery action appeared everywhere in the form of racial prejudice. Proposals for abolition were always countered with questions about what would be done with the supposedly inferior and dangerous Blacks after emancipation. Few indeed could accept as anything less than madness proposals to incorporate them into American society on terms of equality. Instead it was generally taken for granted that freed slaves ought to be sent to Africa or otherwise removed from close contact with Whites.

In 1816, a group of reformers who sought the end of slavery as a great evil—but who at the same time rejected as a similar evil the prospect of the Blacks' remaining in America—formed the American Colonization Society.[10] Its program of transporting free Blacks to Africa, although from one point of view a drastic solution to the problems of slavery and racial adjustment, may be regarded as conservative because it made no effort whatever to alter the racial prejudices of white Americans, accepting these as unchangeable.

The 1820s was the heydey of the colonization movement, the decade when it won endorsement from an array of prominent clergymen and of such influential statesmen as Henry Clay. But backing by great personages proved insufficient to accomplish the Society's purpose. The success of its ambitious plan required a degree of organizational effort and financial support that only the national government could supply. Such a large undertaking, even if it were otherwise feasible, ran so counter to the decentraliz- ing tendencies of the time that it could not be adopted.[11] Southerners would never agree that slavery and racial problems came within the sphere of federal power. Fur- thermore, most free Blacks resisted the prospect of removal to Africa, though there were conspicuous exceptions; a number of Blacks at this time, as in every subsequent gen- eration, viewed their prospects in white America as hope- less and accordingly sought some form of separation.

Despite the inability of the Colonization Society to carry out its program, it did succeed in spreading information about slavery and the oppression of free Blacks into com- munities where these matters were not objects of daily observation.[12] In that respect the work of the American Colonization Society may be regarded as a constructive pre- lude to the widespread abolitionist campaigns of the 1830s. But it had a negative effect as well, for by incessantly em- phasizing the degradation of free Blacks, it probably strengthened the hold of racial prejudice on the minds of white Americans. On that account alone, most abolitionists came to regard the American Colonization Society as work- ing against their own program and against the welfare of the Blacks.[13]

Clearly unable to reverse the economic and social forces that so powerfully supported the growth of slavery, the early abolitionists believed they could at least help to re- move racial bias, one of slavery's strongest buttresses. Ac- cordingly, they devoted much of their effort before 1830 to extending humanitarian aid to the black population that already constituted a conspicuous minority in nearly every Northern city. The ending of slavery in the North had not been accompanied by change in the racial attitudes that for so long had supported it.[14] If anything, prejudice increased as the numbers of free Blacks grew and as the insecurities resulting from rapid economic and social change were felt throughout white society. Prejudice was not expressed in verbal slurs and social slights alone. Far more serious was the fact that custom barred most Blacks from economic and educational opportunity. Although striking examples can be cited of Blacks who overcame all such obstacles, the majority were shut out by prejudice from sharing in the profits and advantages of the growing American economy.[15]

Abolitionists resolved to change that situation. A prerequisite to emancipation and to the elevation of free Blacks, so they believed, was the elimination of racial prejudice. Blacks must be recognized as men and brothers. If they were proved to be the equals of other Americans in capacity and accomplishment, abolitionists reasoned, the only justification for enslavement and discrimination would disappear. Accordingly, as early as 1800, abolitionists expanded their program to embrace educating free Negroes and otherwise helping them to rise above the lowly position most of them then occupied. Such endeavor would satisfy the obligations of philanthropy—always a prime consideration for Quakers and other religious reformers—but its more significant function would be to demonstrate the abilities of Negroes and thereby prove current racial practices unwarranted. With the walls of prejudice shattered, reasonable men would stop scorning Blacks and begin to treat them in every respect as equals. Slavery itself, it was thought, could not long withstand that development. It should be noted that the reformers who held such expectations hoped to eliminate prejudice among Whites by working with Blacks. They would "improve" and "elevate" the Negro until he reached a level Whites found acceptable.

In order to make a start toward those goals, several early abolition societies—including some in the Upper South—founded schools for free Negroes and tried to find employment for black youths. The abolitionists's schools supplemented instruction that Blacks already supplied for themselves under the guidance of the Negro churches and mutual benefit societies that emerged in black communities at the end of the eighteenth century.[16]

Abolitionists launched their educational efforts with all the energy that optimism can lend to a cause, yet none of the experiments succeeded to the degree their backers had anticipated. Neither black children nor abolitionists were responsible for the failure. Abolitionists' schools provided ample evidence, if more were needed, of the Negro's intellectual capacity. According to numerous reports, black children learned to read and to compute about as well as white children; their accomplishments in craftsmanship were commendable. Yet none of those attainments helped very much to elevate Blacks in the eyes of the white majority.[17]

Racial prejudice proved stronger and more stubborn than abolitionists had realized. Although many white persons learned of the achievements of Blacks both in schools and outside of them, they seldom allowed such knowledge to alter their bias. The effect of that stubborn prejudice on black children was often discouragement. The sunny predictions that education opened the door to opportunity were false. When black children came to understand this fact, their eagerness for such training was likely to diminish. The Negro's successes in education confirmed the optimism of philanthropists but did little to alter the majority's racial views. All available evidence suggests that despite the efforts of white humanitarians and of Negroes themselves, racial restrictions and discriminations increased rather than diminished after 1820.[18]

In the all-important area of achieving recognition of racial equality, the early abolitionists for the most part failed. But in the political arena they achieved occasional success. Their most conspicuous legislative accomplishment—after passage of gradual emancipation laws in the North—was the decision of Congress in March 1807 to end the foreign slave trade, a measure supported by American statesmen, including President Jefferson, as well as by little-known antislavery reformers. In the same month that Congress outlawed the African trade, the English Parliament passed a similar law. Those victories, important though they were thought to be, were in a sense hardly more than symbolic, for while they significantly limited the African slave trade, the prohibition was but imperfectly enforced and still left the extensive domestic slave trade undisturbed. Further, enactment of the laws had the effect of causing some reformers to relax their antislavery efforts for a time because they believed that the end of the African trade had put slavery itself on the way to extinction. In a sense, those optimists were not mistaken, for a long debate preceeding the measure's passage brought into the open for the first time the cruelties inherent in slavery and in that way stimulated a humanitarian controversy over the institution that not even the most determined opposition could ever quite still.[19]

Antislavery failures were more frequent than successes after 1800, however, and probably more important in their consequence. One of the earliest of these defeats, and the one that most severely shocked abolitionists, was the refusal of Congress in 1820 to halt the admission of Missouri as a slave state. Even though later abolitionists would interpret the exclusion of slavery from the rest of the Louisiana Purchase north of 36° 30' as a major achievement, in 1820 they viewed the restriction as trivial compensation for the fact that slavery had been allowed to expand into new regions. "Hell is about to enlarge her borders and tyranny her domain," was the despairing comment of the Quaker abolitionist editor Elihu Embree, when he received the news.[20]

The Missouri Compromise convinced opponents of slavery that they could not depend on Providence to achieve their goals for them but that they must themselves act forcefully in the antislavery cause. An opportunity to test their strength and resolution soon appeared on the northwestern frontier of the American settlement. In 1823, in the infant state of Illinois, carved from the Northwest Territory from which slavery supposedly had been forever excluded by the Ordinance of 1787, ambitious settlers of Southern origin laid plans to call a state constitutional convention whose members, they hoped, could find a way to legalize slavery.

A full-scale antislavery movement was soon underway in

Illinois as preachers, editors, and politicians combined forces to persuade the electorate to vote down the proposed convention. From his office in Tennessee, Benjamin Lundy, the Quaker editor of the *Genuis of Universal Emancipation,* sent antislavery arguments to Friends in Illinois as ammunition in the campaign. From Philadelphia, Quaker humanitarians, including the illustrious Nicholas Biddle, who as president of the Second Bank of the United States would a few years later gain notoriety as an object of Andrew Jackson's wrath, supplied the antislavery forces with money and pamphlets. In Illinois itself, John Mason Peck, a Baptist preacher, traveled up and down the state organizing church members and clergymen against the proposal. Presiding over the entire coalition was the Virginia-born associate of Jefferson, Governor Edward Coles, who a few years earlier had freed his slaves and moved to Illinois.[21]

The outcome of the political campaign was one of the few antislavery triumphs of the decade, as aroused voters soundly defeated the convention proposal at the polls. The victory over pro-slavery forces in Illinois had been achieved by using the safe and prudent means early abolitionists believed would be sufficient to end slavery everywhere—peaceful, rational persuasion and conventional political action. But the victory could not be repeated. Never again would such moderate means suffice to defeat the proponents of slavery, because at no other point of conflict were antislavery forces ever more than a minority. That fact in part accounts for the growing frustration of abolitionists and for their willingness by 1830 to abandon their earlier expectations and to adopt more extreme goals and tactics than those advocated by eighteenth-century antislavery partisans. The situation that confronted them must now be examined if the extent of their problem is to be understood.

The dominant political fact in the United States by 1830 was the creation of the Jacksonian party, democratically based and singularly attentive to pro-Southern, pro-slavery interests. The new party's implication for the abolitionist cause was ominous, for Jacksonian democracy represented, among other things, obedience to popular will. In the South, popular will generally supported slavery; in the North, it tolerated the debasement of the free Negro. For those reasons, the growth of political democracy damaged the antislavery cause rather than aided it.[22]

Although Jacksonian leaders disagreed on numerous issues of public policy, they could unite behind the determination to maintain silence on slavery and thereby, in effect, to safeguard it. In many parts of the North the rise of the Jacksonians brought to office men whose ties with the South were intimate and whose prospects for continued political success depended on retaining the approval of Southern party leaders. And a few years later, the Whig party, developed in opposition to Jackson, also often looked to Southern votes to help carry its candidates to office. Neither party dared sacrifice support by taking antislavery stands or even by tolerating them. A tacit agreement among party leaders kept slavery out of politics. Public discussion of slavery, politicians understood, would tend to weaken the institution of slavery itself as well as disrupt party structure. An antislavery political policy would assure the loss of Southern votes and risk Northern votes too. For while Northerners held practically no slaves, the North's involvement with slavery was only slightly less complete than that of the South.

Northern involvement was primarily economic. Much of the profit of Northern business derived from Southern trade and hence ultimately from slavery. This tie grew ever closer. Powerful Northeastern interests—especially shipping, textile manufacturing, and the cotton trade—flourished because of their Southern connections. Much the same thing was true in border areas of the new Northwestern states, where businessmen soon developed lucrative trade relations with the South. The economic welfare of the entire nation, in a sense, became tied to slavery. The bulk of American foreign exports consisted of slave-grown cotton. From its sale abroad came those credits that supported

American purchases in Europe. Hence, American imports of manufactured goods and American international finance likewise heavily depended, in the final analysis, on slavery.[23]

For those reasons, the abolitionists' program to destroy slavery appeared to run counter to progress and to the national interest. With some justice, abolitionists might even be considered subversive or "un-American," for by 1830 the United States had become a great slaveholding republic. Only an American blind to the events of his day could fail to see that American social and economic development was taking place with slavery at its base and that the nation's future growth apparently was pledged to its continuance.

Further, quite apart from their economic interest in slavery, a majority of Northerners were as intent as any Southerner to maintain white supremacy. Slavery kept most Negroes securely in the South. Its abolition presumably would leave them free to move to the North, a prospect that much of the Northern population dreaded. The dictum of the influential historian of the South, Ulrich B. Phillips, that the central theme of Southern history was the determination to keep the South a white man's country might, with accuracy, be recast to read: "A central theme of *American* history was the determination to keep the *United States* a white man's country."[24] Slavery and its corollary of white supremacy were thoroughly enmeshed with American political and economic institutions. Abolition, it appeared, could not be accomplished without unparalleled disruption of the entire social order.

The problem facing abolitionists thus was staggering. The problem was not, as Stanley Elkins has suggested,[25] that the United States lacked institutions through which slavery might have been ameliorated or abolished but rather that most of the institutions it did have were heavily involved with slavery.[26] The ending of slavery would require such a vast reconstruction of the American system as to constitute revolution. Few aspiring businessmen and few clergymen in the national denominations—whose mem-

bership was in large part Southern—could support abolition. No politician whose election depended on more than
a small, homogeneous constituency dared advocate such a
program or even allow it to be advanced within his district.

By any index that might be applied, abolitionists appeared to be losing the contest with slavery. Slavery was a
stronger, more widespread institution in 1830 than it had
been ten years earlier. Its spread into the Southwest continued unimpeded as cotton production increased. The domestic slave trade flourished, bringing renewed prosperity to
the Upper South, where cotton and the plantation system
had little hold. The influence of slaveholding states in de-
termining national policy had in no way declined. Northern prejudice against free Negroes had not lessened, and
sympathy for abolitionist programs had not appreciably
increased. Economic interest and racial bias had moved the
nation still further from the Revolutionary ideals upon
which abolitionists believed it had been formed. Politicians
and patriots continued to assert attachment to the noble
and venerable ideals of liberty, equality, and opportunity,
but the words uttered so easily in Fourth of July orations
only partially corresponded to American reality.

Early nineteenth-century reformers—among whom abolitionists were only one group among several—seized every
opportunity to warn against what they regarded as a dangerous decline in the nation's moral standard. Intensely
religious persons in particular detected from certain recent
changes in popular outlook and emphasis evidence of
American degradation. A decline in the influence of clergymen and churches accompanied the new, all-absorbing
popular interest in secular politics. Growing materialism,
loss of spiritual values, and neglect of the ideals enunciated
in such documents as the Declaration of Independence,
seemed to some persons to constitute an emergency which
called for the utmost in exertion if the nation were to avoid
destruction. A deepening anxiety was experienced in certain ecclesiastical and political circles, especially those of
New England and New York, as they watched control of the

nation falling into the hands of Western and Southern interests who neither accepted Northeastern leadership nor shared Northeastern values. To such Easterners, the nation appeared to be in the grip of forces oblivious to any principle transcending the acquisition of wealth and power. America was losing its spiritual purity in an all but universal grasping for material advantage.

Out of that sense of crisis—and supported by humanitarian and benevolent impulses—was born a general reform movement designed to save the nation by reasserting clerical influence and by removing some of the grossest of its moral lapses. In a sense the movement was highly conservative in its effort to shore up old values and to restore old authority. But contributing to it was a new evangelical fervor which had potential for taking reform out of the hands of philanthropists, censorious clerics, and a backward-looking upper class and transforming it into a genuinely radical enterprise.[27]

By the 1820s, a romantic spirit, less concerned for the welfare of society than with the well-being and happiness of individuals, largely replaced Enlightenment attitudes in the thinking of younger men in the United States as well as in Europe. Perhaps its most striking manifestation in America was the wave of religious revivals that swept the West in the late 1820s. Christian teachings had long provided powerful stimulus to criticism of the existing order. Now the evangelical Christianity that spread across America supplied youthful reformers with attitudes toward social change that fostered an unyielding campaign against slavery.[28]

Unlike rational religion and Enlightenment philosophy, the Christianity of the revivalists was marked by violent disjunctions. It presumed discontinuity in history. It did not foresee continuous progress throughout infinite time. In the life of the individual, it sought the event of conversion. That event was likely to be sudden and devastating, often marking radical change in the individual's relation to God and to society. Its theology described creation out of nothing. It forecast judgment upon man and all his works. It anticipated the end of the world.

Evangelical Christianity embodied a spirit that was compatible with radical thought and action because it did not itself shrink from extremes. By no means all evangelicals became radical reformers. Indeed many of them continued to hold conservative social views. But for those persons who already were critical of their society and whose sympathies lay with reform, evangelical Christianity offered a theology and world view that both justified and encouraged programs for fundamental change.

The connection between evangelicalism and abolitionism soon became all but explicit. The evangelical abolitionists saw themselves as participants in a cosmic drama of sin and redemption. The nation had fallen from grace by embracing the sin of slavery; it could be redeemed, they believed, through the conversion and moral regeneration of individuals. Some abolitionists, especially those whose religious roots lay in the revivals the fiery evangelist Charles Grandison Finney had fostered in western New York, looked forward to the Second Coming. Part of their task, as they conceived it, was to renovate the earth in preparation for that event. The elimination of slavery, which they viewed as the sum of evil, was therefore crucial, and the church must be made an instrument of the abolitionist cause. Their enthusiasm becomes more comprehensible when it is understood that they had undertaken something far more significant in their eyes than secular reform. They were concerned with what theologians call "eschatology"— that is, the last things that are to be accomplished before the Last Things when Christ comes again and men and all their works are judged.[29]

The radical spirit that marked American religious life in the decade after 1825 came also to characterize a portion of its most important reform movement. The abolitionists who put forward appeals for immediate emancipation had no patience with those who wished to end slavery slowly and by degrees. As evangelicals, they believed that immediate renunciation of sin was both possible and necessary. If their program of immediatism should destroy the slaveholders' power and rend the very fabric of American life, they could face that prospect as righteous judgment and find metaphors for it in Christian doctrine. If the men then living did not themselves purge the nation of its most conspicuous sin, abolitionists believed, they assuredly might expect God himself to do so. The theme of retributive wrath runs through much early antislavery literature. Even Jefferson, not ordinarily given to celebrating a vengeful God, had trembled for the nation when he remembered that "God is just."[30]

It was, then, a complex set of circumstances that moved abolitionists in the late 1820s into a new phase of their movement against slavery. Frustrating experience had combined with cultural influence to encourage them to re-examine their tenets and programs. Against this background, a new stage of the antislavery movement developed. Far more strongly than their predecessors, abolitionists of the late 1820s and 1830s were moved by a sense of religious duty. While they were as aware as earlier men of the difficulties that stood in the way of emancipation and of the dangers that would accompany it, they swept aside every objection as irrelevant. Duty canceled all considerations of expediency. "Let Justice Be Done Though the Heavens Should Fall" was the motto that regularly thundered forth from the masthead of the *Genius of Universal Emancipation,* the antislavery newspaper edited by Benjamin Lundy from 1821 to 1839.

Notes

1. Betty L. Fladeland, *Men and Brothers: Anglo-American Anti-slavery Cooperation* (Urbana: University of Illinois Press, 1972), p. 46.
2. "Minutes," 16 September 1787, Papers of the New York Society for Promoting the Manumission of Slaves (New York Historical Society).
3. "Memorial," 2 June 1787, Papers of the Pennsylvania Abolition Society (Philadelphia: Historical Society of Pennsylvania); Mary Stoughton Locke, *Anti-Slavery in America from the Introduction of African Slaves to the Prohibition of the Slave Trade (1619–1808)* (Boston: Ginn, 1901), pp. 136–37.
4. For a sampling of contemporaries who so argued, see Amos A. Phelps, *Lectures on Slavery and Its Remedy* (Boston: New England Anti-Slavery Society, 1834), pp. 191–95; "Minutes of the Illinois State Anti-Slavery Society," (Chicago Historical Society), pp. 186, 190; American and Foreign Anti-Slavery Society, *Report . . . 1851* (New York: the Society, 1851), p. 106; *Radical Abolitionist,* 1 (1855): 24.
5. Max Farrand, ed., *The Records of the Federal Convention of 1787* (New Haven: Yale University Press, 1937), III: 212.
6. Dwight Lowell Dumond, *Antislavery: The Crusade for Freedom in America* (Ann Arbor: University of Michigan Press, 1961), pp. 63–73; John Kenrick to Francis Jackson, 17 March 1829, *Liberator,* 18 December 1846.
7. John Hope Franklin, *From Slavery to Freedom, a History of American Negroes* (New York: Alfred A. Knopf, 1947), pp. 166–67.
8. "Minutes," 1806, American Convention for Promoting the Abolition of Slavery (Philadelphia, 1806), p. 22.

9. Merrill D. Peterson, *Thomas Jefferson and the New Nation* (New York: Oxford University Press, 1970), p. 999; Thomas Jefferson to Edward Coles, 25 August 1814, in *The Life and Selected Writings of Thomas Jefferson,* ed. Adrienne Koch and William Peden (New York: Modern Library, 1944), pp. 641–42; Robert McColley, *Slavery and Jeffersonian Virginia* (Urbana: University of Illinois Press, 1964), pp. 124–32; Edward Coles to Martin Van Buren, 12 October 1848, in *Letters and Literary Memorials of Samuel J. Tilden,* ed. John Bigelow (New York: Harper Brothers, 1908), I: 55–56.

10. P. J. Staudenraus, *The African Colonization Movement, 1816–1865* (New York: Columbia University Press, 1961), pp. 19–22.

11. George M. Fredrickson, *The Black Image in the White Mind: The Debate on Afro-American Character and Destiny, 1817–1914* (New York: Harper and Row, 1971), p. 25.

12. Eliphalet Gillet to R. R. Gurley, 5 January 1828 and Samuel J. May to James Dunn, 5 July 1828, American Colonization Society Papers (Manuscript Division, Library of Congress).

13. Dumond, *Antislavery,* pp. 127–28.

14. Alexis de Tocqueville, *Democracy in America,* ed. Phillips Bradley (New York: Alfred A. Knopf, 1945), I , chap. 18.

15. "Minutes," 1824, American Convention for Promoting the Abolition of Slavery (Philadelphia, 1824), pp. 12–13.

16. "Minutes," 1801, American Convention for Promoting the Abolition of Slavery (Philadelphia, 1801), pp. 6–7, 13; "Minutes," 1812, American Convention for Promoting the Abolition of Slavery (Philadelphia, 1812), p. 6; Trustees of the African Free School to the Manumission Society, 4 November 1817, Papers of the New York Society for Promoting the Manumission of Slaves.

17. "What avails it, that we educate our children, seeing that having bestowed every attention to meet this end, we find them excluded from patronage suited to their attainments?" *Freedom's Journal,* 30 March 1827.

18. Northern racial prejudice is detailed in Leon F. Litwack, *North of Slavery: The Negro in the Free States 1790–1860* (Chicago: University of Chicago Press, 1961).

19. Fladeland, *Men and Brothers,* p. 79; William W. Freehling, "The Founding Fathers and Slavery," *American Historical Review,* 77 (February 1972): 81–93.

20. *The Emancipator (Complete), Published by Elihu Embree, Jonesborough, Tenn., 1820* (Nashville: B. H. Murphy, 1932), p. 89.

21. Merton L. Dillon, *Benjamin Lundy and the Struggle for Negro Freedom* (Urbana: University of Illinois Press, 1966) pp. 72–74;

Merton L. Dillon, "John Mason Peck, a Study of Historical Rationalization," *Journal of the Illinois State Historical Society,* 50 (Winter 1957): 385–90.

22. Richard H. Brown, "The Missouri Crisis, Slavery, and the Politics of Jacksonianism," *South Atlantic Quarterly,* 55 (Winter 1966): 55–72.

23. Douglass C. North, *The Economic Growth of the United States, 1790–1860* (Englewood Cliffs: Prentice-Hall, 1961), pp. 40, 67–68, 189–98.

24. Ulrich B. Phillips, "The Central Theme of Southern History," *American Historical Review,* 34 (October 1928): 30–43.

25. Stanley Elkins, *Slavery, a Problem in American Institutional and Intellectual Life,* 2d ed. (Chicago: University of Chicago Press, 1968), pp. 27–80, 141, 143–44.

26. This became a common observation. For examples see Massachusetts Anti-Slavery Society, *Nineteenth Annual Report ... 1851* (Boston: the Society, 1851), pp. 81–82; Gerrit Smith to Wendell Phillips, 20 February 1855, *Liberator,* 16 March 1855; Lydia Maria Child to W. P. Cutler, 10 July 1862, Lydia Maria Child Papers (William L. Clements Library, Ann Arbor).

27. Bertram Wyatt-Brown, "Prelude to Abolitionism: Sabbatarian Politics and the Rise of the Second Party System," *Journal of American History,* 58 (September 1971): 316–41; Clifford Griffin, *Their Brothers' Keepers: Moral Stewardship in the United States, 1800–1865* (New Brunswick: Rutgers University Press, 1960), *passim;* Lois Banner, "Religious Benevolence as Social Control; a Critique of an Interpretation," *Journal of American History,* 60 (June 1973): 23–41.

28. The classic statement of the relation of the revivalism to abolitionism is Gilbert H. Barnes, *The Antislavery Impulse, 1830–1844* (New York: D. Appleton-Century, 1933).

29. Dumond, *Antislavery,* pp. 154, 158–59; Ira V. Brown, "Watchers for the Second Coming: The Millenarian Tradition in America, *Mississippi Valley Historical Review,* 39 (December 1952): 451; see also the remarkable antislavery sermon preached by the Presbyterian Thomas Lippincott, *Edwardsville Spectator,* 9 November 1824.

30. *Genius of Universal Emancipation,* 1 (March 1822): 136; ibid., (April 1822): 151; ibid., 2 (July 1822): 10; *Edwardsville Spectator,* 9 November 1822; for an earlier example see *American Museum,* 1 (March 1787): 239; a relatively late expression is in *St. Louis Observer,* 16 April 1835.

CHAPTER THREE

Garrison Enters the Scene

1829–1831

Diminutive in stature, partially deaf from childhood, and only slightly educated, Benjamin Lundy, founder and editor of the *Genius of Universal Emancipation,* nonetheless permitted no opposition or adversity to deter him from pursuing the antislavery goals he set for himself in youth. On the day he first saw manacled slaves making their way from Virginia to plantations in the lower South, he pledged his life to the antislavery cause.[1] Whatever he may have lacked in native talent and worldly advantage found ample compensation in the steadfastness with which he conducted his various antislavery enterprises. Alone among contemporaries in the 1820s, he made abolition his career and his all-absorbing interest, giving up a promising business and sacrificing the welfare of his wife and children in the process. But not even such extraordinary devotion to duty brought success. He moved his struggling newspaper from Ohio to Tennessee and then to Maryland in a search for more generous support and a more receptive public. The effort was in vain, for by the late 1820s few residents of the slave states, whom he had hoped to win as allies in the antislavery cause, were any longer willing to patronize his paper, which, after all, aimed at the downfall of their society. Subscriptions fell off so drastically that in the winter of 1828–1829 he had to shut down his print shop.[2]

By the time he managed to scrape together enough money to resume publication of the weekly *Genius* late in 1829, he had found two able assistants to share his labors. Elizabeth Margaret Chandler, a young Quaker writer who rivaled the later poet Emily Dickinson in shyness and self-effacement, agreed to supervise the paper's "Ladies Department" from her wilderness home near Adrian, Michigan.[3] More important, as it proved, was the fact that Lundy was joined at Baltimore by an editorial partner, a zealous twenty-two year old native of Newburyport, Massachusetts, named William Lloyd Garrison.

By the time Garrison began work at Lundy's office, he already had been associated with several New England newspapers that dabbled tentatively in various reforms. As the slavery issue attracted wider notice, Garrison's interest had been drawn irresistibly toward it. He became an admiring reader of the *Genius,* the principal organ of the antislavery movement in the 1820s, and when Lundy visited Boston in the summer of 1828, the two men met. Garrison was captivated by the Quaker's earnestness and devotion to the cause that was assuming ever greater importance in his own mind. At that time he still thought gradual emancipation a wise program and still supported the American Colonization Society, as many other antislavery advocates did. But in the months before joining Lundy in Baltimore, he followed the path already taken by a growing number of other New England reformers. He too became an advocate of immediatism. The free Blacks he met in Baltimore encouraged him further in his decision to agitate for the immediate end of slavery and to renounce colonization. Under his co-editorship, the doctrine of immediatism came to dominate the pages of the *Genius,* where previously it had appeared as only one among several possible solutions to slavery.[4]

Exactly what Garrison and other advocates of immediate emancipation meant by the term was as uncertain to the general public then as it is to students now. The term understandably misled many persons who naturally sup-

Anthony Benezet Instructing Negro Children

posed from its literal meaning that the abolitionists were as extreme in their program as they were radical in spirit and choice of language. The truth was otherwise. "Immediate emancipation" was always a doctrine to be endorsed rather than a program to be implemented. It was a statement of what *ought* to be done rather than of what *could* be done. It was designed to arouse complacent persons to their duty with respect to slavery.[5]

The slogan also implied an opinion about slavery that slaveholders, most of whom felt themselves to be moral, God-fearing people, found intensely galling. Slavery, abolitionists charged, was always and under every circumstance a sin that, like other sins, ought immediately to be abandoned. Of course this idea did not originate with Garrison. A number of earlier writers in the *Genius* and elsewhere

had presented similar views.[6] Their most influential exponent was the Reverend George Bourne of Virginia, an En-
glish-born Presbyterian, whose antislavery sentiments,
later set forth in *The Book and Slavery Irreconcilable*
(1816), led to disciplinary action by the church and to his
flight from the South.[7]

Garrison learned much from Bourne's book, adopting as
his own both Bourne's view that slaveholders were mon-
strous sinners guilty of "manstealing" and his stance of
merciless condemnation of error. Yet even Garrison on occasion explained away some of the apparent extremism of
the words "immediate emancipation." "Immediate abolition does not mean," wrote Garrison in 1832, "that the
slaves shall immediately exercise the right of suffrage, or
be eligible to any office, or be emancipated from law, or be
free from the benevolent restraints of gradualism." What
the phrase did mean, he went on to explain, was that the
arbitrary power Whites then exercised over Blacks should
be ended at once and that immediate steps should be taken
that would eventually end slavery.[8]

But apparently most persons paid no attention to the abolitionists' scrupulous explanations of their new slogan.
Thus they acquired a reputation for being rather devious in
their use of language and for being both impractical and
dangerous in their demands. So far as the substance of their
doctrine was concerned, immediate abolitionists of the
1830s were scarcely more extreme than the gradualists who
preceded them. Yet slaveholders—and many Northerners
too—thought they were. And in one crucial sense they were
correct, for given the importance of slavery in the United
States, anyone as determined as the religiously dedicated
abolitionists interfering with slavery in any manner at all
was radical and dangerous indeed.

Garrison's forthrightness in helping to edit the *Genius*
soon embroiled him in legal difficulty when a thin-skinned
slave-carrier from Garrison's home town in Massachusetts
accused him of libel. A Baltimore judge found him guilty of
the charge and since he could not pay his fine, sentenced

him to jail. With the young editor thus confined and subscriptions to the *Genius* still lagging, Lundy and Garrison
decided their efforts to publish an abolitionist weekly must
be abandoned as a failure. Lundy would try to keep the
Genius alive as a monthly magazine, but for that he would
need no partner, nor could the enterprise any longer support two men. Accordingly, the Lundy-Garrison partner-
ship was amicably dissolved. Shortly afterward, the New
York philanthropist Arthur Tappan paid Garrison's fine
and secured his release from the Baltimore jail. Garrison
then moved back to Boston and started his own antislavery
newspaper while Lundy continued the *Genius* alone.[9]

Garrison's *Liberator* began publication on 1 January
1831, advocating a program of immediate emancipation
without compensation to the slaveholder and without colonization of the freedmen, the last point being a doctrine
that Garrison's close association with free Blacks in Baltimore had convinced him was correct. In retrospect, the
appearance of the *Liberator* constituted a milestone in the
progress of abolitionism, but at the time it hardly seemed
to be so. Subscribers were no more plentiful nor easy to
come by than they had been for the *Genius.* With the exception of the wealthy Tappan brothers, Arthur and Lewis, of
New York and the aristocratic lawyer Ellis Gray Loring of
Boston, the newspaper had the backing of only a few persons, and most of those enjoyed little access to power or
influence. Its chief support during its first years came from
the free black population of New York, Boston, Philadelphia, and Baltimore, who saw in the efforts of such white
abolitionists as Garrison and Lundy the Negro's only hope
for achieving freedom and equality.[10]

But the significance of Garrison's newspaper should not
be measured by its limited subscription list. One of the most
important aspects of the founding of the *Liberator* was that
it was located in Massachusetts rather than in a Southern
state. From the late eighteenth century, when Jefferson
wrote his critiques of slavery, until the day Garrison established his newspaper at Boston, the Upper South was a

chief center of the antislavery movement and an important source of antislavery argument. Now all that had changed. So great was the power of slaveholders by 1831 that the South would no longer harbor abolitionists or tolerate their message. The focus of the antislavery movement shifted to the North. Even Lundy, who continued stubbornly to believe that an antislavery movement could be created in the South, soon transferred the *Genius* from Baltimore to Washington, D.C., then to Philadelphia, and eventually to Lowell, Illinois. Antislavery, like slavery itself, had once been national. By the 1830s it became, for the most part, a purely sectional concern. A more fateful change than this for the continued peace and unity of the country could hardly be imagined.

Abolitionists were sometimes charged by their critics (most conspicuously by Catherine Beecher, elder sister of the author of *Uncle Tom's Cabin*) with having abandoned their responsibility when they avoided working in the South but instead, like Garrison, concentrated their activity among Northerners who owned no slaves themselves and who apparently had no way to reach into the South to end slavery.[11] The observation doubtless had some merit, although Northern abolitionists, as we shall see, did sometimes try to circulate their writings among slaveowners. Yet in another important sense, the critics were wrong and betrayed serious misunderstanding; for if slavery and the racial prejudice that supported it were national rather than sectional failings (as abolitionists generally understood them to be), and if Northerners were as much implicated in slavery as were Southerners themselves and benefited from its earnings just as Southerners did, then antislavery efforts to change Northern attitudes were as necessary and appropriate as were efforts to reform the South. The campaign to convince Northerners that they did indeed "have something to do with slavery," that it was not a remote institution which did not concern them occupied abolitionists until the Civil War.[12]

"Negro Expulsion from Railway Car, Philadelphia."
Wood engraving from the *Illustrated London News,* 1836,
shows Europe's view of the American treatment of Negroes

Another possible view of the matter, as adopted by a few abolitionists, assumed Northern virtue rather than Northern guilt with respect to slavery, and yet on grounds of duty still demanded a Northern crusade against slavery. Theirs was a sense of obligation, of mission, and of self–righteousness that when later identified not with a geographical section but with a virtuous nation cast in a sinful world could generate reforms and imperial enterprises on a scale as spacious as the globe:

If there is, upon the farthest isle of the ocean [ran an essay in the first volume of the *Anti-Slavery Record*], a tribe of robbers, murderers, and cannibals, we, here in America, have something to do with them. It is not consistent with the welfare of the human race that there should be robbers, murderers, or cannibals, anywhere. . . . [As Christians], we are entrusted with a set of principles, which go to abolish crimes, and are commanded by the Redeemer of the world to promulgate them. We have something to do, then, as long as there is upon the earth a single man who has not been reached and won to righteousness by these heavenly principles.[13]

While Garrison and other northern abolitionists forged ideological weapons for carrying out their crusade to spread the doctrine of immediatism, Lundy sought more direct means to end slavery. Always more pragmatic than Garrison and more eager actually to free slaves than he was to develop and proclaim antislavery argument, Lundy now concentrated on projects designed to demonstrate the superiority of free over slave labor. He developed a plan to establish free Blacks in a colony in Texas, which was then a Mexican state. He hoped in that way to improve the lives of a limited number of Negroes by removing them from the damaging effects of prejudice, but his purpose went beyond that narrow aim. His grand motive was to found a black free-labor colony whose prosperity would convince planters that they could make more money by emancipating their slaves and hiring them as free workers than by retaining them in bondage. Southerners, he believed, would be prompted by the profit motive to end slavery voluntarily and with no disruption of the social order.[14]

Lundy's plan had about it an appealing simplicity, but it ignored the all-compelling fact that slavery involved much more than economics. Lundy seemed not to realize that slavery formed the basis for a way of life and for class and sectional power and thus would be defended even if account books proved some other labor system more profitable.[15] Lundy spent years in Texas in the 1830s, futilely negotiating with Mexican authorities for a land grant on which to make his free-labor experiment. By riding his fruitless hobby, he removed himself from participation in some of the most critical abolitionist developments. His antislavery achievements were not yet finished, and before long he would emerge from the obscurity in which his Mexican enterprise placed him to help once again in shaping the antislavery movement; but for the moment, younger, more ideologically oriented abolitionists—of whom Garrison was the archetype—dominated the antislavery scene, while Lundy and his free-labor projects were lost sight of.

In publicizing the antislavery program, abolitionists decided to pursue the policy Lundy had followed throughout the 1820s before he embarked on his free-labor plan. They would appeal primarily to the consciences of Americans, rather than to their greed. They would publicize the cruelties to which slaves were subjected. They would instruct the religious in the ways slavery violated each of the Ten Commandments. They would explain to patriots the points at which slavery contradicted the ideals of the Declaration of Independence. On every occasion they would confront Americans with the vast gulf that separated their pretensions to virtue from their practice of slavery and oppression.

Since presumably slaveholders were reasonable and potentially virtuous men, they could be expected to free their property as soon as the enormity of their offense had been exposed. Lundy, as well as other early abolitionists, had shared Jefferson's doubts that this would ever happen, but evangelical abolitionists were more hopeful. Slaveholders, they believed, would be neither able nor willing to resist the moral influence of a public opinion aroused against slavery.

Neither the antislavery arguments abolitionists used nor the measures they employed in the early 1830s differed fundamentally from those of previous years. If Southerners reacted more shrilly and with a greater degree of unanimity against Garrison's *Liberator* than they had reacted against Lundy's *Genius*, it was not because Garrison had hit upon more effective argument or because he employed more vivid and persuasive language than his predecessors had used; it was simply because the growing ease of communication in the 1830s and the increasing number of newspapers willing to take note of Garrison's writings gave his words wider circulation than had previously been possible. Thus, slaveholders learned that a small minority in the North had resolved to destroy slavery, to make absolutely no compromise on the issue, to offer no concessions whatever, to accept no excuse from those who persisted in holding slaves. Understandably such resolution and inflexibility struck Southerners as being ominous for their future.

Perhaps still more important, Southerners, by the early 1830s, had at last awakened to their peril. Whatever sense of security slaveholders felt earlier had disappeared. They now responded to every antislavery threat with a degree of urgency commensurate with the danger which they believed they faced. Slavery had become more obviously the basis of Southern power at the very time when attacks against it became more frequent, more adamant, better coordinated.

Slaveholders occasionally had reacted to earlier criticism just as strongly as they reacted to Garrison.[16] But by 1831, they could afford to let no challenge to their system go unmet. They now realized that their way of life rested on an anachronism. Slavery once had been accepted nearly everywhere. That was no longer true. Now antislavery movements could be seen bearing down against the South from every direction, threatening to confine slavery to a cramped corner of the American continent. The former Spanish colonies in South America had abolished slavery; an antislavery movement gained strength in England; Congress had barred slavery from much of the Louisiana Purchase; and in the North, abolitionist voices continued their bold and strident denunciations.[17]

Negroes themselves rankled in their bondage. In Boston in 1829, David Walker, a free black dealer in old clothes, published his *Appeal,* a passionate condemnation of white America and a proclamation of the justice of black resistance. To the dismay of slaveholders, the pamphlet circulated even in the South.[18] Still more shocking events would soon occur. In Virginia in 1831, only a few months after Garrison founded the *Liberator,* Nat Turner led a band of slave rebels on a bloody march through Southampton County, and in the same year news of a slave rebellion in Jamaica spread further terror in the South.[19]

Southerners might reasonably conclude in the early 1830s that they faced disaster. They reacted accordingly, with unrestrained denunciation of abolitionist activities and with both legal and extra-legal acts to prevent abolitionism from obtaining a hearing within the South.

Slaveholders were hardly incorrect in their understanding of the general movement of the nineteenth-century Western world toward fostering individual freedom, but they much overestimated the extent of abolitionist power and influence in the United States. Therefore they exaggerated their immediate peril. Because abolitionist influence even in the North was still slight, a different, more patient response on their part might have delayed emancipation for many years.[20] If the Southern conscience was able to bear the moral burden of slavery while in daily contact with the institution, it is hardly surprising to discover that the Northern conscience made its own accommodation. The number of persons in the North willing to see slavery ended at once and the freedmen incorporated into American society, as abolitionists proposed, still were few. Abolitionists remained the minority they long had been, advocating a doctrine and a program unacceptable to most Americans. Garrison's *Liberator* reached the reading tables of few Northern Whites. Even in Boston, where the newspaper was published, it at first created hardly a ripple. When late in 1831 Mayor Harrison Gray Otis received frantic Southern appeals to take action to silence the *Liberator* and its young editor, he responded, no doubt truthfully, with the admission that he had not previously even known of their existence.[21]

Notes

1. [Thomas Earle], *The Life, Travels and Opinions of Benjamin Lundy* ... (Philadelphia: W. D. Parrish, 1847), p. 15.
2. Ibid., pp. 15–26.
3. Merton L. Dillon, "Elizabeth Margaret Chandler," in *Notable American Women, 1607–1950*, ed. Edward T. James and others (Cambridge, Mass.: Harvard University Press, 1971), I: 319–20; a comprehensive obituary is in *Liberator,* 29 November 1834.
4. Wendell Lloyd Garrison and Francis P. Garrison, *William Lloyd Garrison, 1805–1879; the Story of His Life Told by His Children* (New York: Century, 1885), I: 124, 140; William Goodell, *Slavery and Anti-Slavery; a History of the Great Struggle in Both Hemispheres; with a View of the Slavery Question in the United States* (New York: W. Goodell, 1852), p. 401; *Genius of Universal Emancipation,* 10 (2 September 1829): 8; (25 September 1829): 19.
5. Anne C. Loveland, "Evangelicalism and 'Immediate Emancipation' in American Antislavery Thought," *Journal of Southern History,* 32 (May 1966): 172–88.
6. See especially Elizabeth Coltman Heyrick, *Immediate Not Gradual Abolition* ... (London: Hatchard and Son, 1824), a small pamphlet widely circulated in the United States in the mid-1820s.
7. John W. Christie and Dwight Lowell Dumond, *George Bourne and The Book and Slavery Irreconcilable* (Wilmington: Historical Society of Delaware, 1969), pp. 28–65.
8. *Liberator,* 7 January 1832.
9. Walter M. Merrill, *Against Wind and Tide; a Biography of Wm. Lloyd Garrison* (Cambridge, Mass.: Harvard University Press, 1963), pp. 32–45; Merton L. Dillon, *Benjamin Lundy and the*

Struggle for Negro Freedom (Urbana: University of Illinois Press, 1966), pp. 140–64.

10. August Meier and Elliott N. Rudwick, *From Plantation to Ghetto, an Interpretive History of American Negroes* (New York: Hill and Wang, 1966), p. 102.

11. Catherine E. Beecher, *An Essay on Slavery and Abolitionism, with Reference to the Duty of American Females* (Philadelphia: Perkins, 1837), pp. 11–13, 56–58, 87–88; Angelina E. Grimké, *Letters to Catherine E. Beecher, in Reply to an Essay on Slavery and Abolition Addressed to A. E. Grimké* (Boston: I. Knapp, 1838), pp. 63–64, 65–90.

12. For examples see *Freedom's Journal*, 13 April 1827; "Slavery: The Right of Northern Interference," *Anti-Slavery Record*, 3 (April 1837): 1–11; reports of lectures by William T. Allan, *Western Citizen*, 23 February 1843 and *Illinois Statesman*, 19 February 1844.

13. "What Have the People of the North to Do with Slavery?" *Anti-Slavery Record*, 1 (April 1835): 40.

14. Dillon, *Benjamin Lundy*, pp. 175–83.

15. For this aspect of slavery see two works by Eugene D. Genovese, *The Political Economy of Slavery: Studies in the Economy and Society of the Slave South* (New York: Pantheon Books, 1965) and *The World the Slaveholders Made: Two Essays in Interpretation* (New York: Pantheon Books, 1969), esp. pp. 118–244.

16. For examples see U.S., Congress, *Annals of Congress,* 1st Cong., 1789–1791, pp. 1184–91, 1198–1205, 1452–65 and William W. Freehling, *Prelude to Civil War; the Nullification Controversy in South Carolina, 1816–1836* (New York: Harper and Row, 1966), p. 116.

17. *Christian Spectator,* quoted in *Freedom's Journal,* 23 March 1827; Goodell, *Slavery and Anti-Slavery,* pp. 383, 385–90.

18. Clement Eaton, "A Dangerous Pamphlet in the Old South," *Journal of Southern History,* 2 (1936): 323–34.

19. Betty L. Fladeland, *Men and Brothers: Anglo-American Antislavery Cooperation* (Urbana: University of Illinois Press, 1972), pp. 190, 191n; for a full account of the Turner revolt, including sources, see Henry Irving Tragle, *The Southampton Slave Revolt of 1831* (Amherst: University of Massachusetts Press, 1971).

20. Freehling, *Prelude to Civil War,* pp. 356–59.

21. Merrill, *Against Wind and Tide,* p. 54.

CHAPTER FOUR

Goading the Monster

THE 1830s

While vague disapproval of slavery became commonplace in the North by 1830, willingness to take strong stands against it remained rare. Thus it was not surprising that when in November 1831 fifteen men—the earliest and most earnest of Garrison's white friends—met with him in Samuel E. Sewall's law office at Boston to consider founding an antislavery society, only nine admitted that they were ready to join a society based on immediatism. Since immediate abolition was the principle Garrison considered essential, formation of the New England Anti-Slavery Society waited several weeks until the twelve adherents that Garrison decreed to be the required number had declared themselves.[1]

Only an alarmist could see in the new organization an immediate threat to the status quo. Though a few of its early supporters came from the ranks of the prominent and influential, most did not. About a quarter of the seventy-two names eventually affixed to the constitution of the New England Anti-Slavery Society were those of free Blacks.[2] But this feeble outward appearance sharply contrasted with the dynamism and intensity of purpose of the movement whose leadership Garrison had assumed.

Garrison's crusading zeal was reflected in his rhetoric. An imperiousness not unlike that of the revivalists' ser-

mons characterized his writings. He condemned slavery
and slaveholders as relentlessly as revivalists condemned
sin and sinners. The revivalists called for total commitment to Christ; Garrison demanded total commitment to
the abolitionist cause. For Garrison, there was no middle
ground. In effect he held that those who did not join him in
the abolitionist camp were against him and thereby supported slavery.

An antislavery advocate who did not accept the abolitionist doctrine in its totality, and exactly as Garrison defined
it, was likely to see himself condemned in the *Liberator* as
a minion of slaveholders. So doctrinaire a position inevitably antagonized moderates and lost some potential support.
But for the most part, the loss was of lukewarm adherents
of the sort Garrison believed might profitably be sacrificed.
As a consequence of this winnowing process, Garrison soon
surrounded himself with a tightly knit circle of men and
women as intense and as single-mindedly devoted to abolition as he himself was. Dozens of abolitionist reformers
recalled in later years Garrison's influence in awakening
them to the failings of American society and in giving
meaning and direction to their lives. "I remember very distinctly the first time I ever saw Garrison," wrote Lydia
Maria Child, one of the most self-analytical of his converts.

I little thought then that the whole pattern of my life-web would
be changed by that introduction. I was then all absorbed in poetry.
. . . He got hold of the strings of my conscience and pulled me into
reforms. It is of no use to imagine what might have been, if I had
never met him. Old dreams vanished, old associates departed, and
all things became new.[3]

Young men and women ardently seeking a cause commensurate with their capacity for passion found it in abolitionism, as Garrison opened their eyes to the hideousness of
slavery. Persons who, for whatever reason, were not content
with existing practice and values were likely to seize upon
his program as the means for renovating the nation.[4]

"The Desperation of a Mother"

Garrison's call for immediate emancipation met especially eager response from free Negroes, from certain young people caught up in the widespread religious revivals of the late 1820s, and from a number of older persons, many of them Quakers, who already had established for themselves a record of antislavery persuasion. Such kindred spirits might be found anywhere, but they appeared earliest and most plentifully in parts of New England and western New York, where revivalism was common; in Ohio, particularly on the New England-dominated Western Reserve; among established antislavery groups of Southern origin in Ohio and Illinois; and among Quakers, especially in Pennsylvania, Ohio, southern Michigan, and Indiana.

Important and influential though the converts to abolitionism came to be, their numbers remained relatively few, simply because the number of persons capable of sustained moral commitment at the level of intensity demanded by that stage of the antislavery movement is always limited.

Not many members of any generation are likely to see themselves as a saved remnant set apart to rescue a lost society from the consequence of its own folly, and not many will wish to subject themselves to the hostility and ridicule such a position ordinarily calls forth.

The abolitionists' appeal was religious, moral, and intellectual. It therefore was self-limiting in scope, except perhaps among free Blacks, who, whatever their attitudes on other matters might be, were likely to share the white abolitionists' determination that slavery and racial oppression must end.

The converts to abolitionism never expected to pursue their activities as solitary reformers. Even before the New England Anti-Slavery Society was formed, Garrison and other abolitionists, especially those in New York and Philadelphia, made plans to coordinate antislavery action on a nation-wide scale. "The guilt of slavery is national, its danger is national, and the obligation to remove it is national," explained Garrison. Black abolitionists played a large role in the developing project.[5]

When the First Annual Convention of People of Color met at Philadelphia in June 1831, a number of white abolitionists attended as guests. These included Garrison, Lundy, Arthur Tappan, and Simeon S. Jocelyn, a young Congregational minister who had Tappan's financial support for his plans to found a college for Negroes at New Haven, Connecticut. During the sessions, these men joined with Philadelphia Quakers and with Samuel Cornish, a black Presbyterian preacher, to discuss founding a new national antislavery society.

Apparently a good many members of the convention agreed to support the project, for a few weeks later Lundy announced in the *Genius* that an association to overthrow slavery would shortly be formed "upon an enlarged and extensive plan." But the "association" did not immediately materialize. Nat Turner's slave uprising in Virginia in August 1831 brought a nearly hysterical response from Northerners and Southerners alike, terrified by the prospect of

Blacks taking up arms in their own behalf. Garrison and the *Liberator,* together with David Walker's *Appeal,* were commonly alleged to be responsible for inciting the rebellion, even though Garrison had consistently opposed the use of force in the antislavery cause and uncategorically repudiated Turner's action. Soon afterward, violence having racial and anti-abolitionist overtones broke out in New Haven. At the conclusion of a mass meeting held to protest the plans of Jocelyn and Tappan to establish a black college in the city, vandals broke the windows of Tappan's summer home and wrecked the property of a Negro family.

Although Garrison was still eager to proceed with the proposed national antislavery society, these events made Tappan and other New York abolitionists uneasy about the consequences of further antislavery action. They agreed that national organization in so unsettled a time would be hazardous. Even though convinced of their duty to end slavery, they nonetheless were apprehensive of the results of defying majority opinion on so sensitive an issue. Philadelphia Quakers, with their long record of principled opposition to violence, had their own reasons for proceeding cautiously. Confirmed opponents of slavery though they were, they decided to withhold support from a project that they feared might encourage other slaves to follow Turner's example. "The Southampton affair has paralyzed our Philadelphia friends," Tappan noted.

But it was not alone the dread of slave insurrection that deterred some abolitionists from action. Antislavery men from the beginning disagreed among themselves on some of the goals of the movement, particularly on the future they envisaged for the Negro. William Jay, the New York lawyer, for instance, worried that certain abolitionists accepted Negroes on terms of equality—Garrison's New England Anti-Slavery Society had even admitted black members—and that they went very far in advocating Negro rights. Was it true, Jay asked, that some abolitionists intended to call for black suffrage? Justice and humanity required emancipation, he agreed, but those principles did not also require abolitionists to endorse the explosive proposal of extending political privileges to Blacks. Jay later moved considerably to the left of his early position on these matters, but for the moment he agreed with other conservatives that insistence on full implementation of the principles of racial equality would arouse unmanageable hostility to the abolitionists' entire program. It was such solicitude for public opinion and such readiness to accommodate to popular prejudices that most clearly distinguished moderates within the antislavery ranks from such radicals as Garrison.

Not until December 1833, after the British Parliament had emancipated the West Indian slaves to the accompaniment of much favorable publicity throughout the North, did the three most active antislavery groups—Philadelphia Quakers, New England Garrisonians, and New York reformers—finally join with representatives of the free Blacks to call a convention at Philadelphia for the purpose of organizing the American Anti-Slavery Society. Garrison had long urged such action, only to be rebuffed by the New York group. Only after Evan Lewis, a respected Quaker philanthropist from Philadelphia, journeyed to New York in support of the project, did the New Yorkers agree that the time for organization had come and should not be further postponed.

Of the sixty-two persons who assembled at Philadelphia in an atmosphere heavy with local suspicion and hostility, twenty-one (including four women) were Quakers. Three of the signers of the new society's constitution were black: James G. Barbadoes, Robert Purvis, and James McCrummell. Although the best known person at the convention was Garrison, the proceedings were dominated by the New York associates of the Tappan brothers, a group that outnumbered the delegates from New England.

After several better known men had shied away from the assignment, the delegates selected one of Garrison's early converts, the Reverend Beriah Green, president of Oneida Institute in western New York, as presiding officer. They chose Garrison along with two of his circle—Samuel J. May, a Unitarian clergyman who had helped found the New England Anti-Slavery Society, and John Greenleaf Whittier, the young Quaker poet—to draw up a Declaration of Sentiments, which would serve as a platform for the new Society. As is characteristic of committees, one man did most of the work: the document presented to the convention was essentially Garrison's.[6]

The declaration breathed a spirit at once militant and pacific. The abolitionists, Garrison wrote, were uniting in order to complete the unfinished work of the American Revolution. Their ancestors had "waged war against their oppressors" and spilled human blood "like water in order to be free." Yet the colonists' grievances against England "were trifling in comparison with those of the slaves." This statement, which seemed to promise advocacy of violence, might well have caused apprehension among those convention members who were pacifists and nonresistant Quakers. But Garrison went on to assure them that abolitionists renounced "all carnal weapons for deliverance from bondage." Unlike Americans of the Revolutionary era who took up arms against oppression, abolitionists would seek "the destruction of error by the potency of truth—the overthrow of prejudice by the power of love—and the abolition of slavery by the spirit of repentance."

The abolitionists would take their stand, Garrison continued, on a platform demanding immediate, uncompensated emancipation without colonization. He then added, in defiance of moderates within the movement and of all but universal prejudice, that they also would seek "to secure to the colored population of the United States, all the rights and privileges which belong to them as men and as Americans. . . ."

The declaration pronounced all laws supporting slavery to be "before God utterly null and void," but at the same time, in an apparently contradictory statement, it recognized the right of each state to legislate on slavery within its own borders. It conceded that Congress "under the present compact" had no power to interfere with slavery in any state. Such a restrictive view of national power and of constitutional limits was to be expected in the early 1830s; but by the late 1840s, it would be recognized as an obstacle to antislavery accomplishment and therefore rejected by an important group of abolitionists.

Despite the inability of Congress to interfere with slavery in the states, political antislavery action still was possible, Garrison said, for Congress did have unquestioned power to end the domestic slave trade and to abolish slavery in the territories and in the District of Columbia.

Then, after establishing such general principles, the declaration went on to describe the mode of operations abolitionists planned to use in their proclaimed crusade. They intended to persuade residents of the free states to endorse the abolition of slavery "by moral and political action." To accomplish this goal, they would organize antislavery societies "in every city, town, and village in our land." They would send out antislavery agents and circulate antislavery tracts and periodicals. They would try especially to convert preachers and editors to the abolitionist cause, since these were the men thought to be the effective molders of public opinion. In particular abolitionists would "aim at a purification of the churches from all participation in the guilt of slavery." As a practical device to weaken slavery and also to end their own involvement with it, they would urge all abolitionists to adopt the old Quaker tactic of abstaining from the use of goods produced by slave labor.[7]

The American Anti-Slavery Society would focus its efforts on groups thought to be particularly receptive to the abolitionist message. In practice, this meant that it intended especially to work among the evangelicals, who presumably would be sympathetic to abolitionism. Given the close ties the antislavery movement had long had with religion, such a policy probably would have been followed in any event, but it was encouraged by the fact that the headquarters of the new Society was established in New York City. There the antislavery movement was dominated by

the Tappan reformers, most of whom were themselves pro-
foundly religious men and whose connections with nation-
ally prominent evangelical churchmen were close.[8]

If clergymen and church members could be persuaded to
accept the Society's program, the evangelical churches
would be transformed into powerful agencies of abolitionism. Except for the political parties and government itself,
the Protestant denominations were practically the only institutions that functioned in every part of the nation. Their
power, though not yet thoroughly tested, presumably was
enormous. Their endorsement of the abolitionist program
would virtually assure its success because, it was thought,
slavery could not long withstand such a concentration of
moral power arrayed against it. Churches thus would
become the institutions by which American society would
be renovated.

It was the policy of addressing its efforts primarily to
clergymen and to church members, as well as the fact that
so many prominent abolitionist leaders were themselves
evangelicals, that accounted for some of the chief characteristics of the antislavery movement throughout the 1830s.
The abolitionists' message typically was presented as a religious appeal. Slavery was shown to be a sin. Rarely was it
any longer analyzed as an economic, social, or political lia-
bility.[9] The rhetoric and the arguments used against slavery were familiar to persons accustomed to listening to
sermons and to thinking in theological terms. Church
members and clergymen made up the majority of the abolitionists' converts during the early and middle 1830s. But
even such people did not always find acceptance of abolitionist doctrine easy.

The revivalists' plea for the immediate abandonment of
sin strikingly resembled the abolitionists' demand for the
immediate end of slavery. Immediate emancipation generally was presented as a religious imperative. But the
strength of the obligation to accept the doctrine ignored the
difficulty of doing so. Religious persons, when confronted
with the abolitionist call to commit themselves to immedia-

tism, often went through an observable agony of spirit. Just as the process of religious conversion involved dramatic readjustment of values that might be accompanied by inner torment, so desperate soul-searching and spiritual anguish might accompany conversion to immediatism. For many, acceptance of the doctrine was itself a climactic spiritual act resembling baptism into a new faith. For such persons the decision to identify themselves with the abolitionist cause came only after tortured self-examination. Those who successfully completed the ordeal felt themselves dedicated soul and body to a holy crusade. Their commitment then knew no limit.

Theodore Dwight Weld, perhaps the West's leading antislavery evangelist, described his winning to abolitionism of William T. Allan, son of an Alabama Presbyterian preacher, while both young men were students at Lane Seminary. Weld labored with the youth through many prayerful sessions exactly as a nineteenth-century revivalist preacher would have labored with an occupant of the "anxious seat." Only "after some weeks of inquiry and struggling with conscience," as Weld triumphantly recorded, did Allan's "noble soul [break] loose from its shackles." Then he proclaimed his conversion from his former support of gradual emancipation and colonization to the doctrine of immediate abolition. Like many another young man in similar circumstances during that decade, he resolved to devote the rest of his life to the antislavery cause.[10]

A number of abolitionists who took part in the most tumultuous phase of the movement, the 1830s, reported the profound spiritual effect such participation had on them. They felt themselves altered; as a consequence their values changed. Abby Kelley, one of Garrison's Quaker converts and a strong exponent of women's rights, remarked in 1838 that abolitionists had "good cause to be grateful to the Slave for the benefit we have received to *ourselves,* in working for *him.* In striving to strike *his* chains off, we found most surely, that *we* were manacled ourselves." Wendell Phillips, the Boston patrician who became one of abolitionism's greatest orators, explained many years later what those manacles were. "My friends, if we never free a slave, we have at least freed ourselves in the effort to emancipate our brother man," he said in 1851. "From the blindness of American prejudice, the most cruel the sun looks on; from the narrowness of sect, from parties, quibbling over words; we have been redeemed into a full manhood—taught to consecrate life to something worth living for."[11]

For such persons participation in the antislavery movement seemed a duty quite apart from the objective benefits it might render the slave and society. The Garrisonian view of the imperious demands of individual conscience was perhaps more widely shared than has sometimes been supposed. Even James G. Birney, sometimes considered the epitome of the practical abolitionist on account of his commitment to antislavery politics, once remarked that "God has, at no time, told us ... that we are responsible for the country; but he has told us ... that we must *individually* give a good example. He has given us only our *own selves* to be responsible for."[12] If such a position led Birney into hopeless but morally rewarding presidential candidacies in 1840 and 1844, it led Henry David Thoreau to spend a night in jail for refusal to pay taxes to a government whose policies he repudiated, and to write an essay on "Civil Disobedience"; and it led Garrison to a stubborn refusal either to vote or to recognize the legitimacy of the United States government.

There can be no doubt that many opponents of slavery underwent emotional upheaval in the early 1830s as they struggled to achieve total commitment to the abolitionist creed and then went on to attempt to win others to similar conviction. Their turmoil at such moments was thoroughly justified, for in accepting abolitionism they were setting out on the hazardous path of opposition to entrenched institutions and prevailing values. They proposed to defy the course of American development which seemed to be moving the nation toward ends that denied the ideals upon which it had been founded. In such a setting a man who joined the abolitionist crusade was likely to do so in a spirit of resignation, consciously facing the prospect of tragedy and sacrifice, but undertaking a holy obligation that could not be shirked. "I am the one," an abolitionist may be imagined as saying, "And there is no way not/ To be me[.]"[13]

Despite their crusading efforts and considerable success in gaining converts, abolitionists failed to win the churches to their cause. In 1837, the Presbyterian General Assembly "excised" from the church its most thoroughly antislavery synods.[14] No major denomination endorsed abolitionism. This reluctance on the part of clergymen and church bodies was to have profound consequences for the course of the antislavery movement. It helped push Garrison and others into taking militant anti-clerical stands, and it caused the movement in the later 1830s and 1840s to adopt increasingly secular policies.

While the abolitionists were attempting to secure converts, they also engaged in a war against certain of their rivals who had once been thought to form part of the antislavery alliance. Essential to their success, abolitionists believed, was the discrediting of the rival programs of gradual emancipation and colonization. The older notion that slavery could be ended in easy, gradual stages and that free Negroes must be transported out of the country still exercised a stubborn hold on many philanthropists. Until reformers were made to understand that such ideas were erroneous and harmful to the antislavery cause, the doctrine of immediatism would seem radical, dangerous, and wholly impracticable.

Thus one of Garrison's first undertakings after launching the *Liberator* in 1831 was a campaign to destroy support for the American Colonization Society. In doing this, he found himself in opposition to a highly respected project which enjoyed the support of powerful and prestigious men. It seems likely that this campaign, rather than the doctrine of immediatism itself, was the source of much of the hostility directed against him.[15] Colonization had nearly achieved the status of being a national goal. The fact that free Blacks and abolitionists had long opposed it did little to lessen its esteem in the public mind. But Garrison was never deterred from his attacks merely by the respectability of his target.

Soon after the New England Anti-Slavery Society was founded in 1832, its agents began speaking against colonization to audiences in southern New England. Garrison delivered a series of anti-colonization addresses and in May 1832 published *Thoughts on Colonization,* a long and heavily documented work exposing the American Colonization Society as a pro-slavery, anti-Negro organization.[16]

Garrison's pamphlet brought together a large number of anti-colonizationist resolutions passed by meetings of free Blacks and numerous excerpts from the speeches and writings of colonizationists demonstrating their racial bias and their lack of sympathy for ending slavery. Thus, in the eyes of abolitionists, the advocates of colonization were convicted by their own words as Garrison proved them to be supporters of slavery and hostile to the aspirations of free Blacks. Garrison's technique of assembling quotations to unmask a hitherto respected institution would later be used in exposés for many causes. Theodore Weld probably modeled his famous abolitionist tract, *American Slavery as It Is* (1839), after Garrison's *Thoughts on Colonization,* published seven years earlier.

Neither Garrison's pamphlet nor the other anti-colonizationist works that soon appeared succeeded in destroying interest in proposals to deport the black population. Agitation against the colonization program was necessarily a continuing one.[17] As late as 1853, Giles Stebbins, a Garrisonian abolitionist, felt called upon to expose the society once again in his *Facts and Opinions Touching the Real Origin, Character and Influence of the American Colonization Society.*

The American Colonization Society recognized Garrison and the new American Anti-Slavery Society as enemies. War between the two societies was soon underway. The most conspicuous and significant incident in the long battle occurred at Lane Seminary in Cincinnati in the spring of 1834.[18]

The New York reformers had recently established Lane as a training school for evangelists. Its graduates were expected to convert the West, whose unchurched population, Easterners feared, risked falling into unbelief. It was a measure of the project's importance that Lyman Beecher, perhaps New England's most distinguished clergyman at that time, was willing to resign his pastorate in Boston to become president of the new Western institution.

The reformers expected much from Lane; they received more than they anticipated. Gathered at Lane from many parts of the country, including the South, was a student body composed of pious and highly competent young men who had committed themselves to something more than books and lectures. Their evangelical ideals did not allow them to retreat from secular concerns; rather, evangelicalism thrust them directly into the tumult of their time. The students took for granted their duty to participate actively in helping decide the great issues of the day. They would use their talents to shape the course of American development. Shortly, under the leadership of Theodore Weld, perhaps the most able member of the seminary, the students began a public discussion of immediate emancipation.

After debating the subject for nine days, they agreed by nearly unanimous vote to endorse immediatism. For nine more days they argued the merits of the American Colonization Society. Then, as one of them wrote, "like men whose pole star was fact and truth, whose needle was conscience, whose chart was the Bible," they voted to reject colonization. They then proceeded to organize an antislavery society on the principle of immediatism. All this talk and promise of action proved disquieting to residents of Cincinnati who feared that such events would antagonize their slaveholding neighbors across the river in Kentucky. But even more disturbing things were to come.

Having accepted immediatism with its implied requirement to abandon racial prejudice, the students began to work among the local black population. Shocked Cincinnatians soon saw that the students were advocates and practitioners of racial equality. They had begun associating with Negroes as partners, friends, and fellow workers. Two students, Augustus Wattles and Marius Robinson, dropped out of the seminary to spend all their time conducting a school for free Blacks. Others organized black churches and in various other ways tried to aid members of Cincinnati's black community. They established a lending library and conducted lyceums, an evening class in reading, Sunday schools, and Bible classes.[19]

The Negroes of Cincinnati, many recently arrived from the slave states, were generally poor and oppressed and eager for all the help they could get. But however great the social needs may have been, the students' interracial activities could only arouse old antipathies in the city, where scarcely five years earlier white citizens had rioted against the black population, forcing many of them to flee to Canada.[20]

An influential Cincinnati journal, the *Western Monthly Magazine,* did its best to awaken hostility against the youthful abolitionists. It worried that the students were "perverting seminaries of learning into political debating clubs" by discussing issues "which do not concern minors who are at school." Students, declared editor James Hall, should "mind their business and their books," and leave public policy to older, wiser men.[21] The seminarians were uncowed by Hall's dictum, but such evidence of community displeasure persuaded Lane officials that they must restore local confidence in the institution. During the summer of 1834, while President Beecher and most of the faculty were absent from Cincinnati, the seminary trustees ordered discussion of slavery to cease on the campus and the abolition society to disband. Thus was ended freedom of speech and association at Lane. A large part of the student body rebelled at such coercion and withdrew from the seminary. Many of them soon made their way to Oberlin College, a new institution in northern Ohio, financed, as Lane had been, largely by Arthur Tappan. The majority of the Lane Rebels, as they came to be called, remained active participants in the movement against slavery. From that group of dissident students came a number of the men Weld soon recruited and helped train in 1836 as members of "the Seventy"—the antislavery agents who as evangelists of abolitionism under commission from the American Anti-Slavery Society toured the North in the mid-1830s preaching the doctrine of immediatism.

Their goal, like Garrison's, was to win Americans—slaveholders and nonslaveholders, Southerners and Northerners—to the principle of immediate emancipation. As might have been anticipated, they made little headway in changing Southern views. It was no doubt naïve for them to expect slaveholders to surrender some three billion dollars worth of property and the institution upon which their political and social power depended simply because abolitionists declared that slavery was rooted in sin; yet as evangelicals these men considered the power of the gospel irresistible, a universal solvent of earthly obstacles. Their expectation of mass Southern conversions, however unrealistic a later generation may consider it, was nonetheless consistent with evangelical faith. But of course they were disappointed. As early as 1835, James G. Birney, himself a native of the South, concluded that the South's conversion to immediatism was unlikely—"repentance is far off," he wrote, "if at all likely to be expected."[22]

With a fair amount of success, slaveholders sealed off their section from exposure to antislavery argument.[23] Southern legislatures made it illegal to circulate or possess antislavery publications. It became most hazardous for abolitionist agents to venture into the South, and almost none did. When Lundy passed through the Southern states in 1832 on his first trip to Texas, he thought it prudent to travel under an assumed name. Officials in Charleston warned Angelina Grimké not to visit her old home after she became identified with abolitionism, and she never tried to do so. Birney's father informed him that to return to Ken-

CAUTION!!

COLORED PEOPLE

OF BOSTON, ONE & ALL,

You are hereby respectfully CAUTIONED and advised, to avoid conversing with the

Watchmen and Police Officers of Boston,

For since the recent ORDER OF THE MAYOR & ALDERMEN, they are empowered to act as

KIDNAPPERS

AND

Slave Catchers,

And they have already been actually employed in KIDNAPPING, CATCHING, AND KEEPING SLAVES. Therefore, if you value your LIBERTY, and the *Welfare of the Fugitives* among you, *Shun* them in every possible manner, as so many *HOUNDS* on the track of the most unfortunate of your race.

Keep a Sharp Look Out for KIDNAPPERS, and have TOP EYE open.

APRIL 24, 1851.

tucky would cost him his life. William T. Allan, one of Weld's converts at Lane, was told that his former neighbor at Huntsville, Alabama, had threatened to cut his throat should he reappear there.[24] During the summer of 1835 Amos Dresser, another of the Lane Rebels, journeyed into Tennessee to sell Bibles and probably also to do some private antislavery work. He was arrested by city authorities in Nashville, charged with being an antislavery agent, tried by a vigilance committee, publicly whipped, and ordered out of the city.[25]

Such Southern reaction was predictable. After all, as Garrison observed, no oligarchy willingly gives up power or unprotestingly allows the subversion of its institutions. Less readily understandable was the fierce hostility that met abolitionist efforts nearly everywhere in the North. The anti-abolition mobs and the riots that occurred in the North with such frequency during the 1830s become comprehensible only if one remembers that while slavery was practiced only in the South, it nonetheless was sustained as a national institution. Abolitionists demanded the destruction of a system that had become interwoven with the very structure of American society.

The aspect of the abolitionists' program that particularly antagonized persons in the North, who otherwise quite readily conceded that slavery was evil and destructive, was the demand that the Blacks, when freed, remain in the United States, be elevated in status and condition, and be allowed to participate as equals in society.[26]

It is true that many abolitionists, especially those in New York and the West, attempted to reassure the timid by explaining that they expected the Negro's freedom to be hedged with restrictive laws—that "immediate emancipation" did not really mean what it seemed to mean. But the explanations were never very persuasive, for it was obvious to anyone who thought seriously about the matter that even abolitionists who supplied such assurances (and these became less numerous as years passed) did not intend restrictions on the free Black to be more than a temporary expedient. Equality of status, abolitionists insisted, right-fully was his. He was to be prepared for it, and eventually it would be granted. Soon most abolitionists abandoned the effort to explain away the immediatist slogan.

Similarly disturbing to white Northerners was the abolitionists' inability to give satisfactory assurance that emancipation would not cause one of their strongest apprehensions to be realized—the emancipated slaves would be free to move into the North. There they would settle in vast numbers among the Whites, compete with them for jobs, and marry their daughters. For many Northerners a more frightful prospect could scarcely be imagined, and they recoiled at the thought of it. Economic fears and racial prejudice warred in Northern minds with religious and political principle. More often than not principle was the loser.

In 1836 Theodore Weld estimated that "at least 3/5ths of the northerners *now* believe the blacks are an *inferior* race."[27] It seems unlikely that the situation changed very much over the next thirty years. In a few places, especially in parts of New England, prejudice eventually came to hold less sway; yet all available evidence suggests that for a great majority of persons in the North racial bias and racial fear remained deep and fundamental.[28] Prejudice formed part of their culture that most found impossible to relinquish. It may even be that the widespread discussion of the slavery issue occasioned by the abolitionists' campaign strengthened and confirmed racial prejudice rather than diminished it. Certainly Blacks as well as abolitionists were held responsible for increasing sectional tensions during the 1830s and afterward, and they were accordingly resented.

Abolitionists did not modify their program in order to accommodate the prevailing racial bias. Instead they confronted it squarely. The ending of prejudice, they insisted, was prerequisite to the abolition of slavery. As soon as the Negro is "felt to be in *fact* and in *right* our own country-man, the benevolence of the country will be emancipated from its bondage," predicted an early abolitionist. "It will flow out to meet the colored man ... it will proclaim his rights—and the fetters of the slave will fall asunder."[29]

While readily granting the fact that prejudice was rampant and all but universal, the abolitionists denied its inevitability. As radical reformers they refused to recognize any view or institution as unmalleable under the blows of religiously inspired emotion and logic. "They contended," as Henry B. Stanton, an official of the American Anti-Slavery Society, explained in 1834, "that this prejudice was vincible; that being a sin it could be repented of, being a folly it could be cured." Stanton further announced, in 1837, that the Society's lecturing agents had been instructed "to wage the same warfare against prejudice which they do against slavery, and if possible to kill them both at one blow."[30]

Abolitionists in the 1830s became convinced that belief in the Negro's inferiority more than anything else caused Northerners who otherwise accepted the abolitionists' view of slavery to hesitate to endorse their program to end slavery. Prudence Crandall, whose integrated school for girls in Canterbury, Connecticut, was closed by public pressure in 1833, concluded that racial prejudice was "the strongest, if not the only chain that bound those heavy burdens on the wretched slaves."[31] Birney agreed: "Whilst the poor black is treated so contemptuously in, what are called, the free states ... it is not to be wondered that the cause of negro-emancipation moves so slowly." Unless racial prejudice could in some way be destroyed, the antislavery crusade was not likely to succeed, for adherence to the idea of the Negro's inferiority, abolitionists discovered, had the effect of producing not ardent crusaders but, as one of them said, half-hearted antislavery men "who would abolish slavery only in the abstract, and somewhere about the middle of the future."[32]

In their effort to counteract such prejudice, abolitionists used varied appeals. Naturally, they cited Scripture to prove the brotherhood of all men. But they put forward other arguments as well. As early environmentalists, they pointed out that the blighting effects of slavery and prejudice explained the free Black's apparent shortcomings. They cited the numerous instances of accomplishment by Blacks to disprove allegations of their innate inferiority. They especially dwelt on the genius of Frederick Douglass, the outstanding fugitive-slave orator and editor, whose talents outshown those of many other Americans of his time, whatever their color. They continued the efforts begun by their predecessors to help free Blacks improve themselves. Any evidence of progress in this area, they believed, would help eliminate bias.[33]

Abolitionists joined free Blacks in campaigns—mostly unsuccessful—for repeal of the restrictive legislation against Blacks that had been passed by most Northern states. Such laws, they argued, were not only unjust but had the effect of stimulating prejudice and of hampering efforts of free black persons to improve themselves. Ohio, Indiana, and Illinois were the most notorious for their legal discriminations, although all Northern states outside New England had some legislation of this kind.

Soon after the New England Anti-Slavery Society was founded in 1832, it appointed standing committees charged with apprenticing black children to learn trades, ending school segregation, and improving the existing schools for black children. In 1834, the Society looked far into the future when it observed that "emancipation would be a very imperfect measure, if provision were not at the same time made for the intellectual, moral, and religious education of newly emancipated slaves."[34]

In its first years the American Anti-Slavery Society concentrated more on spreading information about slavery and on winning white converts than on work among black people. But in 1836, Weld proposed to the Society that it reconsider its priorities and "turn more of its attention to the education and elevation of the *free colored* population." Besides helping to relieve prejudice, such activity, he believed, also would have the important result of convincing Southerners, who delighted in accusing abolitionists of hypocrisy, that "*real* benevolence," and "not politics, sectional feeling, *party*ism," or any similar motive was at the bottom of the antislavery movement.[35]

Weld understood that kindly feelings on the part of white persons toward Blacks were not enough. He urged the importance of education and economic opportunity for the advancement of the black population. Special agents should be appointed, he advised, to recruit talented black youths to study at such colleges as Oberlin. The agents should also encourage abolitionists to find jobs for Blacks, and they should try to persuade mechanics to accept black apprentices.

By 1837, the American Anti-Slavery Society had followed Weld's advice in part, if not in every detail. Yet its success in solving so vast a problem was slight. Individual abolitionists seem not to have given free Blacks much economic aid. Numerous instances can be found of antislavery farmers who furnished them jobs. Occasionally, as in the instance of Gerrit Smith, a wealthy and eccentric antislavery landowner in New York, such aid was given on an extensive scale, but in Northern cities less was accomplished.[36] Business establishments run by abolitionists often employed no black workers, except perhaps in menial positions, a fact that came to be greatly resented by certain black spokesmen. Many leading abolitionists, however, were clergymen, writers, and professional reformers who commanded no labor force and thus had no jobs to give. Their efforts to help Blacks necessarily were confined to education and moral uplift.[37]

As it turned out, abolitionists in the 1830s worked less intently than their predecessors had done in the 1820s to aid free Blacks and thus to demonstrate the truth of their assumptions of racial equality. They tirelessly proclaimed such equality, but for most of them projects directly aimed at improving black people became only a side issue, if they were interested in them at all. This relative neglect did not result from wavering determination or from abandonment of principle, but only from their conclusion that demonstration of Negro abilities no longer was either essential or effectual. Ample evidence already was at hand to prove the capacity of the Negro for achievement. Helping him to make still more progress would be a commendable act of benevolence, but it would not solve the problem of prejudice. What was needed was not further improvement of Blacks in the hope of thereby making them more acceptable to Whites. Instead, the requirement was to improve Whites so that they would renounce their racial prejudice and anti-Negro practices.

For that reason, abolitionists after 1830 more often worked with Whites than they did with Blacks. The key point in their program was their call for a change of heart —the shedding of racial pride—and this was an event more likely to come through faith than through reason. White Americans already had observed abundant demonstrations of the Negro's capacity, but more often than not they remained blind to their import. Abolitionists in the 1830s were content to rely on the evidence of things *not* seen. But this made their program in no way more acceptable to the white majority.

Black abolitionists attended antislavery meetings as full-fledged participating members, served on committees of antislavery societies, wrote pamphlets and delivered speeches for the cause; yet it probably is true that white abolitionists in general did not accept Blacks as full partners in the antislavery crusade and did not admit them fully to decision making. This circumstance contributed to the embitterment of some black abolitionists such as Frederick Douglass and Martin Delaney. Indeed a number of black reformers eventually founded their own associations and newspapers to carry on abolitionist activity independent from that of the Whites. But it was not the slights they may sometimes have suffered at the hands of white abolitionists that were chiefly responsible for their estrangement. Some Northern Blacks became impatient with the antislavery program as it was developed by white abolitionists. It was too abstract and too impractical in both goals and methods to offer immediate, positive benefits to an oppressed people. Despite its announced intent to help Northern Blacks and to battle prejudice, it could show few tangible accomplishments. Black abolitionists sought more effective tactics to reach more immediate goals than those offered by the moral and religious crusade of the white abolitionists.[38]

No doubt a significant number of white abolitionists possessed their share of the prejudice that afflicted most Americans of that day. Sarah Grimké in 1838 commented to the English abolitionist Elizabeth Pease on "the horrible prejudice which prevails against colored persons, and the equally awful prejudice against the poor."[39] Probably even the most enlightened of the abolitionists occasionally behaved as paternalistically toward Blacks as they sometimes did toward white persons who were poorer and less culturally advantaged than themselves. Some of them were unable to surmount the limitations of the culture to which they belonged and within which they worked. It would be difficult, however, to demonstrate any conspicuous degree of either paternalism or prejudice in such leading abolitionists as Lundy, Garrison, or Weld. They succeeded, so far as we can tell, in shedding their sense of racial pride and their desire for racial exclusiveness. Even those who failed in these respects were far ahead of the rest of their society in insisting that these things ought to be done. There should be no surprise to discover examples of abolitionists who retained notions of white superiority and sometimes behaved condescendingly toward the objects of their philanthropy. But it should be noted that such lapses on the part of certain abolitionists did nothing at all to endear them to the defenders of slavery or to the opponents of equality for Blacks. Whatever their personal failings may have been, the aim of the abolitionists was freedom and equality for black people. Their enemies at that time never misunderstood their purpose and generally enlightened point of view, even though some of their later critics may have done so.

So far as we can now tell, however, abolitionists had little appreciation for what a later age would call "black culture." They did not find anything precious or vital or especially worth cherishing in the black man's peculiar way of life—if indeed they thought it at all peculiar. They took for granted that Blacks would share the common American culture. Their observation led them to believe that Blacks held similar expectations. They expected them to be sober and thrifty, to work hard, to be law-abiding, to educate their children, to attend church faithfully.[40] The model they held up to Negroes was not fashioned for their exclusive use. They thought many poorer Whites as much in need of instructions in these respects as Blacks.

The great tragedy of the abolitionists was not that they themselves were blinded by prejudice but that however successfully they purged themselves of prejudice they could not overcome this flaw in the majority of their countrymen. Racial bias was not limited to poorer Whites, who understandably feared the eventual economic consequence to themselves of a rising black population. Persons of high standing in nearly every community likewise exhibited similar attitudes. Years of antislavery activity failed to do more than mitigate racial prejudice. Anti-Negro attitudes perhaps softened somewhat throughout the North as a consequence of the abolitionists' efforts, but those attitudes remained strong enough even during the Civil War to allow the Democratic party to capitalize on them in organizing opposition to Abraham Lincoln's war policies.[41]

This does not mean that Northerners were generally intent on debasing free Blacks and treating them cruelly. The contrary is true. Many persons in the North aided Negroes in their efforts to obtain education and extended help to them in other important ways. Quakers especially were noted for this kind of benevolent activity. Yet, while increasing numbers of Northerners were willing to aid Negroes and to cease being flagrantly oppressive toward them, few welcomed them into society as equals or believed that they might achieve as much as other men. Most Northerners still preferred that Blacks remain in the South and not attempt to settle in Northern white communities. In 1845—after more than a decade of intense abolitionist agitation—an Illinois state legislative committee asserted that "by nature, education, and association, it is believed that the negro is inferior to the white man, physically, morally, and intellectually; whether this be true to the fullest extent, matters not, when we take into consideration the fact that such is the opinion of the vast majority of our citizens."[42] Little evidence exists to prove that the Illinois committee was unjust in its charge.

Abolitionists of the 1830s thus discovered for themselves the same formidable obstacles that had stood in the way of all their predecessors' campaigns against slavery. Racial prejudice remained the strongest of these obstacles, but to it were added in still greater force other sources of opposition that had more recently become apparent: Increased Southern influence in the North exercised through the national political parties; strengthened economic ties between Northern business interests and the plantation South; and growing fears that antislavery agitation imperiled the Union and drove the sections toward civil war.

Southerners had long considered the Constitution of 1787, and the Union it created, as guarantors for their peculiar institution. Not long after the Constitution went into effect, Thomas Coke, an English clergyman visiting in the South, reported finding that "defenders of slavery began to link that defense to loyalty to the new federal constitution which recognized slavery. ... They now begin to take the position that attacks on slavery were attacks on the Constitution" and hence on the Union itself.[43] The threat of Southern secession, explicit at least as early as the debates over the admission of Missouri, became commonplace as abolitionist agitation grew during the 1830s. By that time leading Southerners, who regarded slavery as essential, repeatedly threatened to take their states out of a Union in which their fundamental institution was menaced.

Patriots—a term that encompassed the great majority of nineteenth-century Americans—who viewed the nation with pride and optimism and believed it had a mission to perform, could only deplore an agitation, however well intentioned it might be, which imperiled the Union. If the Union were destroyed, all else, they believed, would be lost. There could be no denying that sectional discord grew after 1830 and that abolitionist agitation contributed heavily to it. Some opposition to the antislavery movement derived from that fact.

Abolitionists were resented too on account of the religious zeal so many of them manifested and because of the uncompromising rigor of their ethic. Many a person of only ordinary virtue must have felt uncomfortable when in the presence of such awsomely intense spirits as Theodore Weld and his evangelical associates. The anticlericalism that became common in the Jacksonian era militated against the success of religious abolitionism. The abolitionists' critique of slavery could not be separated from their religious intensity or from the ecclesiastical organizations most of them represented. Westerners in particular resented the reform efforts of Easterners, whom they were likely to regard at best as pious meddlers and at worst as religious fanatics. Their ultimate aim, some suspected, was to extend New England's cultural and political hegemony throughout the land. It was no doubt easy for contemporaries to view them as hostilely as Judge Luke E. Lawless of St. Louis did in 1836, when he commented that abolitionists labored "under a sort of religious hallucination. They seem to consider themselves as special agents ... in fact, of Divine Providence. They seem to have their eyes fixed on some mystic vision—some Zion ... within whose holy walls they would impound us all, or condemn us to perish on the outside."[44]

For the many ordinary persons to whom such visions were not granted, who feared the impositions of organization, and who had no access to the evangelical spirit, abolitionists appeared to be mad. As purveyors of an impossibly austere ethic, they were sometimes thought objectionable on that account alone.

In view of all this, it was hardly surprising that opposition, frequently reaching to the pitch of mob violence, met the abolitionists' efforts to speak and to organize. When anti-abolitionist riots broke out in cities, they often shifted their focus from white abolitionists to the free black population, as in the New York City riots of July 1834, when a mob plundered Lewis Tappan's house and then moved on to destroy Negro churches, schools, businesses, and homes. A month after the outbreak in New York, mobs roamed the streets of Philadelphia destroying forty-five houses owned by Negroes.[45]

It was a rare abolitionist lecturer in the 1830s who did not repeatedly face harassment from mobs. Henry B. Stanton recalled that he was mobbed one hundred and fifty times before 1840. Popular fury reached its peak throughout the North on 21 October 1835. On that day a mob placed a rope around Garrison and led him through the streets of Boston; Stanton was attacked in Newport, Rhode Island; and at Utica, New York, a meeting of about six hundred delegates from all parts of the state convened to form the New York State Anti-Slavery Society, was disrupted by a mob that forced the delegates to leave the city.[46]

The violent reaction to abolitionists, so frequently expressed throughout the North in the mid-1830s, demonstrated deep-seated popular hostility toward them and their goals, but however general the hostility in a community may have been, some impulse always was needed to trigger the opposition into action. The anti-abolitionist mobs were generally made up of Negro-hating persons of very low social standing and by certain others who wished to be identified with the status quo and to win the favor of powerful men. With but few exceptions, however, mobs were either led or encouraged by "gentlemen of property and standing," who let it be known that they would do nothing to protect the rights and the persons of abolitionists.[47]

Abolitionists based their arguments on familiar religious teachings and on American principles as embodied in the Declaration of Independence; yet despite their association with those revered ideals, no special powers of discernment were needed to recognize them as disturbers of the existing order. They insisted on agitating issues that most persons preferred to ignore. In denouncing slavery as sin, they condemned a whole social system as illegitimate. In calling for the acceptance of Blacks as equals, they appeared to threaten the economic well-being of poorer Whites and to shake the foundations upon which the status and self-esteem of countless Americans were based. In working for abolition, they pledged themselves to the destruction of the plantation South and even of American society and government as it was then constituted. It would indeed have been strange had their activities not encountered violent resistance.

Slavery as an institution so patently contradicted the religious and political principles held by most Americans that it found few open defenders outside the South. Hence, part of the abolitionist argument gained general acceptance— slavery was wrong. Indeed, if everyone who agreed in theory with that statement had joined the organized antislavery movement, it could easily have overwhelmed the opposition. But it was one thing to condemn slavery as an evil; it was quite another to agree that slavery must be done away with at once. Such a policy, it was thought, would destroy the Union, lead to community discord, endanger property rights, and worst of all, require painful social adjustments. When abolitionists called for the acceptance of the Negro as an equal and for his elevation in America, great wrath fell upon them.

Abolitionists in the 1830s and afterward succeeded in persuading many Americans to agree with their assessment of the evils of slavery and of slaveholders, but they did not convince them that slavery should be ended immediately. Still less did they persuade them to discard their ingrained cultural notions of race.

Notes

1. Wendell Lloyd Garrison and Francis P. Garrison, *William Lloyd Garrison, 1805–1879; the Story of His Life Told by His Children* (New York: Century, 1885), I: 277–80; Oliver Johnson, *William Lloyd Garrison and His Times* (Boston, 1881), pp. 82–89; Samuel J. May, *Some Recollections of Our Anti-Slavery Conflict* (Boston: Fields, Osgood, 1869), pp. 30–32; Roman Zorn, "The New England Anti-Slavery Society: Pioneer Abolitionist Organization," *Journal of Negro History,* 43 (July 1957): 157–76.
2. Garrisons, *Garrison,* I, p. 282.
3. Lydia Maria Child to Anne Whitney, June 1879, *Letters of Lydia Maria Child* (Boston: Houghton, Mifflin, 1863), p. 255.
4. Lois Banner, "Religion and Reform in the Early Republic: The Role of Youth," *American Quarterly,* 23 (December 1971): 677–95; for a vivid case study see David C. French, "The Conversion of an American Radical: Elizur Wright, Jr. and the Abolitionist Commitment" (Ph.D. dissertation, Case Western Reserve University, 1970).
5. *Proceedings of the Anti-Slavery Convention, Assembled at Philadelphia, December 4, 5, and 6, 1833* (New York: Dorr and Butterfield, 1833); *Genius of Universal Emancipation,* 11 (July 1831): 35; *Liberator,* 14, 21 December 1833; Garrisons, *Garrison,* I, pp. 380–415; Joshua Leavitt, "Sketch of the American Anti-Slavery Society," *National Anti-Slavery Standard,* 24 October 1844; May, *Some Recollections,* pp. 84–88; May's account in *Proceedings of the American Anti-Slavery Society at Its Second Decade . . . 1853* (New York: the Society, 1854), pp. 7–10, 28–31; Bertram Wyatt-Brown, *Lewis Tappan and the Evangelical War Against Slavery* (Cleveland: Case Western Reserve University Press, 1969), pp. 89–90, 104, 108–9.

6. The "Declaration of Sentiments of the American Anti-Slavery Society" is most conveniently found in *The Abolitionists, a Collection of Their Writings*, ed. Louis Ruchames (New York: Putnam, 1963), pp. 78–83.

7. This abolitionist interest, ignored by most scholars, continued as long as slavery lasted. See Ruth Anna (Ketring) Nuermberger, *The Free Produce Movement, a Quaker Protest Against Slavery* (Durham, N.C.: Duke University Press, 1942).

8. For the New York reformers see Gilbert H. Barnes, *The Antislavery Impulse, 1830–1844* (New York: D. Appleton-Century, 1933), pp. 17–28.

9. *Anti-Slavery Record*, 1 (July 1835): 75; 2 (December 1837): 1–12; American Anti-Slavery Society, *Second Annual Report . . . 1834* (New York: the Society, 1834), p. 3. The New York State Anti-Slavery Society was nearly unique in its emphasis on political and economic matters. See *Proceedings of the First Annual Meeting of the New York State Anti-Slavery Society . . .* (Utica: the Society, 1836), pp. 9–12, 41–54; see also John Greenleaf Whittier, "Justice and Expediency . . .," *Anti-Slavery Reporter*, 1 (1833): 49–63.

10. Theodore Dwight Weld to Lewis Tappan, 18 March 1834, in *Letters of Theodore Dwight Weld, Angelina Grimké Weld and Sarah Grimké, 1822–1844*, ed. Gilbert H. Barnes and Dwight Lowell Dumond (New York: D. Appleton-Century, 1934), I: 132. Hereafter throughout referred to as *Weld-Grimké Letters*.

11. Benjamin Quarles, *Black Abolitionists* (New York: Oxford University Press, 1969), p. 248; Garrisons, *Garrison*, III, p. 320; Oliver Johnson paid tribute to abolitionism for having "delivered [abolitionists] from the fetters of superstition and witchcraft," enabling them to "'walk with God,' and in the fellowship of His Saints." *Proceedings of the American Anti-Slavery Society at Its Third Decade . . .* (New York: the Society, 1864), p. 79.

12. James G. Birney to Theodore Foster, 27 March 1847, in *Letters of James Gillespie Birney, 1831–1857*, ed. Dwight Lowell Dumond (New York: D. Appleton-Century, 1938), II: 1041. Hereafter throughout referred to as *Birney Letters*.

13. Quoted by permission. From James Dickey, "Snakebite," in *Poems 1957–1967* (Middletown, Conn.: Wesleyan University Press, 1967), p. 263.

14. C. Bruce Staiger, "Abolitionism and the Presbyterian Schism of 1837–1838," *Mississippi Valley Historical Review*, 26 (1949–1950): 395–409. For the relation of the churches to slavery see Dwight Lowell Dumond, *Antislavery: The Crusade for Freedom in America* (Ann Arbor: University of Michigan Press, 1961), pp. 343–49.

15. Leonard L. Richards, *"Gentlemen of Property and Standing:" Anti-Abolition Mobs in Jacksonian America* (New York: Oxford University Press, 1970), pp. 30–31.
16. Garrisons, *Garrison,* I, pp. 290–314; William Lloyd Garrison, *Thoughts on African Colonization ...* (Boston: Garrison and Knapp, 1832).
17. Massachusetts Anti-Slavery Society, *Twenty-first Annual Report ... 1853* (New York: the Society, 1854), pp. 47–53.
18. Dumond, *Antislavery,* pp. 159–65.
19. Theodore Weld to Lewis Tappan, 18 March 1834, *Weld-Grimké Letters,* I: 132–35.
20. Richard C. Wade, "The Negro in Cincinnati, 1800–1830," *Journal of Negro History,* 39 (January 1957): 43–57.
21. [James Hall], "Education and Slavery," *Western Monthly Magazine,* 2 (May 1834): 266.
22. Birney to Gerrit Smith, 13 September 1835, *Birney Letters,* I, p. 243.
23. The process may be followed in Clement Eaton, *Freedom of Thought in the Old South* (Durham, N.C.: Duke University Press, 1951).
24. Benjamin Lundy to Elizabeth M. Chandler, 6 September 1832, Elizabeth M. Chandler Papers (Michigan Historical Collections, University of Michigan, Ann Arbor); Gerda Lerner, *The Grimké Sisters from South Carolina, Rebels Against Slavery* (Boston: Houghton Mifflin, 1967), p. 147; W. T. Allan to T. D. Weld, 15 December 1834, *Weld-Grimké Letters,* I, p. 182; Birney to Gerrit Smith, 11 November 1835, *Birney Letters,* I, p. 262.
25. See Amos Dresser, *The Narrative of Amos Dresser, with Stone's Letters from Vicksburg ...* (New York: American Anti-Slavery Society, 1836).
26. Richards, *"Gentlemen of Property and Standing,"* pp. 32–34; for this and other sources of opposition, see also Lorman Ratner, *Powder Keg: Northern Opposition to the Antislavery Movement, 1831–1840* (New York: Basic Books, 1968).
27. Weld to Lewis Tappan, 22 February 1836, *Weld-Grimké Letters,* I, p. 263.
28. An abolitionist agent found that persons in Peoria County, Illinois could not believe his reports that segregated schools had been abolished in Massachusetts and that racial prejudice had declined there. See *Liberator,* 25 March 1859.
29. *Anti-Slavery Record,* 1 (April 1835): 32.
30. American Anti-Slavery Society, *Second Annual Report ... 1834,* p. 23; *Quarterly Anti-Slavery Magazine,* 2 (July 1837): 348.

31. A full account of the Crandall episode is in Edmund Fuller, *Prudence Crandall; an Incident of Racism in Nineteenth-Century Connecticut* (Middletown: Wesleyan University Press, 1971).

32. Birney to Gerrit Smith, 14 July 1835, *Birney Letters,* I, p. 202; American Anti-Slavery Society, *Sixth Annual Report ... 1839* (New York: the Society, 1839), p. 103.

33. An influential essay urging such policy was Lydia Maria Child, *An Appeal in Favor of That Class of Americans Called Africans* (Boston: Allen and Ticknor, 1833).

34. Garrisons, *Garrison,* I, p. 282; New England Anti-Slavery Society, *First Annual Report ... 1833* (Boston: the Society, 1833), p. 22; see also *Anti-Slavery Record,* 1 (June 1835): 68.

35. Weld to Lewis Tappan, 22 February 1836, *Weld-Grimké Letters,* I, p. 263.

36. John L. Myers, "American Anti-Slavery Society Agents and the Free Negro, 1833–1838," *Journal of Negro History,* 52 (July 1967): 200–219; *Quarterly Anti-Slavery Magazine,* 2 (July 1837): 348; Ralph Volney Harlow, *Gerrit Smith, Philanthropist and Reformer* (New York: Henry Holt, 1939), pp. 237, 243–46.

37. The most effective presentation of the view that abolitionists were themselves racially prejudiced is William H. Pease and Jane H. Pease, "Antislavery Ambivalence: Immediatism, Expediency, Race," *American Quarterly,* 17 (Winter 1965): 682–95.

38. Leon F. Litwack, "The Emancipation of the Negro Abolitionist," in *The Antislavery Vanguard: New Essays on the Abolitionists,* ed. Martin Duberman (Princeton: Princeton University Press, 1965), pp. 137–55; August Meier and Elliot N. Rudwick, *From Plantation to Ghetto, An Interpretive History of American Negroes* (New York: Hill and Wang, 1966), pp. 101–12.

39. Grimké to Pease, 20 May 1838, *Weld-Grimké Letters,* II, p. 679.

40. See American Anti-Slavery Society, *Address to the People of Color, in the City of New York ...* (New York: S. W. Benedict, 1834), pp. 4–7; black antislavery leaders gave much the same advice to others of their race. See, for example, *Freedom's Journal,* 16 March 1827.

41. For details see V. Jacque Voegeli, *Free But Not Equal; the Midwest and the Negro During the Civil War* (Chicago: University of Chicago Press, 1967).

42. Illinois, House of Representatives, *Reports,* 14th General Assembly, 1st sess., II, pp. 247–48. For a similar earlier official statement in Ohio, see *Liberator,* 4 February 1832.

43. Samuel Drew, *Life of the Rev. Thomas Coke* (New York: T. Mason and G. Lane, 1837), pp. 110, 185.
44. *Missouri Republican,* 26 May 1836.
45. Linda Kerber, "Abolitionists and Amalgamators: The New York Race Riots of 1834," *New York History,* 48 (January 1967): 28–39.
46. Wyatt-Brown, *Lewis Tappan,* p. 161.
47. Richards, *"Gentlemen of Property and Standing,"* pp. 131–50; Dumond, *Antislavery,* p. 205.

CHAPTER FIVE

The "Slave Power" Strikes Back

The antislavery movement progressed with amazing speed, despite resistance from planters and their allies and despite its own admitted failure to destroy racial prejudice. It might have been predicted that the creation of an antislavery constituency in the face of such obstacles would be the work of many generations, if it could ever be accomplished at all. Yet within ten years after the founding of the American Anti-Slavery Society, a political coalition against slavery was organized. Within another twenty years Abraham Lincoln issued the Emancipation Proclamation, and in 1865, with the ratification of the Thirteenth Amendment, the death of slavery was assured. Such spectacular achievement is not easily explained.

Had they been forced to rely solely on their own resources, it does not seem likely that the abolitionists could have accomplished so great a revolution in public opinion and policy as these events imply. Among their leaders were men and women of great energy and determination and a few of first-rate talent. Yet the powers of such persons, impressive though they were, probably would have proved inadequate to persuade a Northern majority to oppose slavery. Something beyond moral commitment and skill was necessary to assure·abolitionist success.

Not even the most powerful argument and propaganda proved adequate by themselves to marshall decisive support for the antislavery cause. Even in that conspicuously religious age the number of persons who could be influenced by either evangelical or moral appeal was far from being coextensive with the population.

A good many Northerners who recognized slavery as an evil, even as a sin, nevertheless considered it a problem so remote from their own lives that it did not require their active interference. The vast emotional gulf that separated the slave in the South from the potential abolitionist in the North in some way had to be bridged if the antislavery crusade were to succeed. The frequently quoted Biblical admonition, "Remember them that are in chains as bound with them" [Hebrews 13:3], was the simplest and most direct effort to establish the connection.[1]

Moving beyond simple admonition, abolitionists tried to create emotional involvement by presenting Northerners with poignant and moving accounts of the sufferings of slaves. Harriet Beecher Stowe's immensely successful novel, *Uncle Tom's Cabin,* published in 1853, was perhaps the most effectual of all such efforts, but it was only one of many. Antislavery orations and printed tracts by the hundreds had earlier employed similar themes. Abolitionists addressed countless appeals to parents depicting the agonies of separation and forced parting that were the lot of slaves. Dramatizations of the plight of the tragic octoroon —the nearly white slave—cleverly played on both the empathy and the racial bias of white audiences.[2]

Southern-born abolitionists and converted slaveholders held Northern audiences spellbound as they recounted first-hand observations of the abuses that accompanied slavery. In the 1840s and 1850s, fugitive slaves often appeared on abolitionist lecture platforms as testimony both to the cruelties of slavery and to the capacity of Blacks. Numerous books revealed the atrocities slavery could give rise to. The most graphic and encyclopedic of these was *American Slavery as It is, the Testimony of a Thousand Witnesses,* compiled by Theodore Weld with the help of Sarah Grimké and her sister Angelina, who became Weld's

"Persecution of Amos Dresser"

wife in 1838.³ After reading the Welds' book, no one with good conscience could ever again defend slavery as a benevolent institution, nor was a reader likely to avoid resenting a section and a social system that allowed human beings to be subjected to the harrowing treatment so thoroughly documented by the Welds.

Yet the persuasive power of such works had obvious limits. Revulsion and pity, sharp though those emotions might be, probably would not in themselves have provoked many Northern Whites to antislavery action, for sooner or later the normal reader would remind himself that, after all, it was not *his* child who was about to be sold to the Louisiana sugar planter; *his* wife had not fallen into the clutches of the slavetrader. Some force more powerful than analysis, rhetoric, and moral appeal was needed to convince Northerners that their own fate was tied with the fate of slaves, that freedom was indivisible. Abolitionists needed allies. They found such allies in the persons of their opponents.

The enemies of abolition unwittingly promoted the anti-slavery cause by demonstrating to Northerners, far more convincingly than abolitionists themselves ever were able to do, that the continuance of slavery in the South threatened the interests of free men everywhere in the country.

The actions of their opponents joined with the abolitionists' moral and religious arguments to convince Northerners that slavery directly concerned them and that its continued existence imperiled their own liberties and well-being. Efforts by Northern foes of abolitionism to silence antislavery speakers, to destroy antislavery newspapers, and to break up antislavery meetings reflected the same tyrannical spirit that was thought to sustain slavery. Southern intellectual defenses of slavery and assertions of Southern political power within the United States government were construed as assaults on the rights and interests of Northern white men.[4]

By their ill-chosen defensive tactics, the South and its partisans advanced the abolitionist cause more rapidly than abolitionists, alone and unaided, ever could have done. The offending gestures of slaveholders were often a response to abolitionist policy. By maneuvering their opponents into taking ever more extreme and outrageous action in defense of slavery, abolitionists provoked the South into self-destruction.

Northerners who may have felt little sympathy for Blacks and little moral revulsion at slavery nevertheless came to believe that Northern interests and republican values were menaced by slavery and the political combination that abolitionists called "the slave power." Slavery, it appeared, threatened to destroy the rights of white men just as it destroyed the rights of black men. Abolitionists were responsible for the development of this awareness. But the insight was only in part the product of the moral and religious arguments they so tirelessly presented. The abolitionists' crucial accomplishment was to demonstrate that in order to preserve and to spread slavery slaveholders and their Northern friends were willing to deny civil rights to white Americans. By attacking slavery, abolitionists caused

Southerners to defend their interests in ways that menaced free institutions. It appeared that Southerners aimed at nothing less than the suppression of free discussion and the absolute domination of the Union.

In every sectional crisis during the years from 1830 to 1860, Southern politicians responded to abolitionist initiative in a manner admirably suited to promote the antislavery cause. Advances made in this fashion, however, were achieved at high cost to reformers. A momentous but subtle change occurred in the antislavery movement as Northern public opinion became increasingly anti-Southern after 1835. Northern men who joined the antislavery movement in response to events which they regarded as Southern aggression were likely to be more concerned for the welfare of white men than they were for the rights of free black men and slaves.[5]

While abolitionists by their continued propaganda attempted to crystalize the North's vague antislavery sentiments, Southerners helped them by pushing Northerners into anti-Southern attitudes. The two processes took place simultaneously. They were interrelated and dependent upon each other. Together they resulted in a momentous revolution in Northern sentiment with respect to slavery and the South and, to a much lesser degree, with respect to the Negro.

Northern antipathy to slaveholding society had been expressed long before 1830 and became more evident as sectional self-awareness developed. Many persons did not believe slavery "right," and needed little encouragement to condemn it as a curious and exotic institution having no legitimate place within America's emergent bourgeois society. In particular, they resented the sexual license for both Blacks and Whites that was implicit in slavery. To such diffuse moral objections was added the belief that slavery contributed to the growth of aristocracy in the nation and therefore menaced republican institutions.[6]

The prevalent Northern antagonism to the South, based in part on opposition to aristocracy, was also related to popular sentiments of nationalism and love for the Union. The conservatives' charge that abolitionist agitation imperiled the Union was double-edged. On several occasions during the years when abolitionists were organizing their campaign, Southern politicians followed policies that also undeniably threatened to destroy national unity.

During the Missouri Controversy in 1819–1820, Southerners put forth bold assertions of state sovereignty and issued lightly veiled threats of secession. A later and more dramatic incident was the nullification crisis precipitated by South Carolina in 1832. South Carolina's opposition to the growth of federal power focused upon the protective tariff, but it went deeper than that. Some South Carolina politicians saw in the majority's adherence to a tariff policy that ignored Southern economic interest a forecast of what might happen to slavery should an antislavery majority someday gain control of the national government. The doctrine of states' rights, and nullification then proclaimed by South Carolina was designed not only to solve the tariff problem but, more importantly, to provide the means to safeguard slavery from attack by the federal government.[7]

In opposing the tariff, South Carolina defied national authority and threatened even to secede from the Union. To a highly nationalistic and patriotic people capable of responding emotionally to Daniel Webster's ringing periods glorifying the Union, such sentiment and action seemed little short of treason. There is no reason to suppose that the nullification experiment brought new adherents to the abolitionist cause; yet it stimulated anti-Southern feeling. A generalized hostility to the South grew in the 1830s, and within that context antislavery sentiment developed. While some Northern patriots were beginning to suspect that a coterie of Southern slaveholders schemed to break up the Union, the South responded to a new abolitionist tactic in a manner so despotic as to suggest that its leaders had little respect for civil rights.

In early 1835, the executive committee of the American Anti-Slavery Society decided to expand its efforts at "moral suasion"—the program of using argument to win converts to abolitionism. The society's Declaration of Sentiments, adopted at the Philadelphia convention less than two years earlier, had set forth its intention to rely on "the potency of truth . . . the power of love and . . . the spirit of repentance" in winning new members. In practice, this meant that the Society would rely on antislavery agents and on tracts and periodicals to spread the abolitionist gospel. By 1835, a number of lecturing agents already were in the field, and the society was publishing the weekly *Emancipator*. (Garrison's *Liberator,* although supported by the Massachusetts Anti-Slavery Society, was Garrison's own responsibility and the official organ of no society.) But no spectacular results had come from these propaganda efforts. Lewis Tappan, a leading member of the executive committee of the American Anti-Slavery Society, proposed a more ambitious campaign. Abolitionism spread too slowly to suit him. In particular, he was concerned that it did not penetrate the South.

An expanded publication program might change that situation.[8] At Tappan's suggestion the second annual meeting of the American Anti-Slavery Society agreed to budget $30,000 to finance the greatest pamphlet campaign in evangelical history. It would publish four different monthly journals, one to appear each week. These would be sent free to prominent persons in all parts of the country.

The South was made the particular target of the avalanche of journalism, for antislavery print could go where antislavery lecturers dared not venture. Perhaps the reading of such literature would bring a few slaveholders to repentance, abolitionists still being optimistic enough to believe this possible; but the chief purpose of the pamphlet campaign was to convince Southerners, by the sheer mass of antislavery argument, that public opinion outside the South deplored slavery. It was supposed that the antislavery men in the South—and abolitionists were sure that these existed in substantial numbers—would then be willing to reveal themselves and join the antislavery movement. The social pressure thus exerted against slavehold-

ers would become irresistible. Finding their moral burden
intolerable, they would repent and voluntarily free their
slaves.[9] If by chance this did not happen, then the newly
aroused Southern antislavery majority would abolish slavery by law. Such were the expectations of the American
Anti-Slavery Society's publication board as it launched its
great pamphlet campaign of 1835.

During the summer, writers and editors busied themselves at their desks in New York, and by fall the printing
presses were turning out a flood of their products. Before
the society's next anniversary meeting in May 1836, the
publication board issued over one million copies of antislavery items.

The results of the campaign were different from what its
organizers expected, for slaveholders were not without
means for exerting counter pressures. When the abolition
material reached Charleston, South Carolina, a mob broke
into the United States Post Office and seized the mail sacks
and burned them. It then hanged Tappan and Garrison in
effigy. A vigilance committee was formed to search the mail
as it arrived on later ships and to confiscate "incendiary"
literature. With the concurrence of President Jackson, Post-
master General Amos Kendall gave his unofficial approval
to South Carolina's censorship of the mails. In his message
to Congress in December 1835, Jackson declared the antislavery tracts "unconstitutional and wicked." He joined
South Carolinians in calling on the Northern states to out-
law abolitionist activity, and he urged Congress to pass legislation that would prevent "incendiary" publications from
being sent into the South, where, he claimed, they would
incite a slave rebellion.[10]

In retaliation for the journalistic attack against slavery,
Southerners planned an economic boycott of Tappan's mer-
cantile business and even of all New York firms until the
abolitionists ceased their operations. A county grand jury in
Virginia demanded the extradition of the executive committee of the American Anti-Slavery Society to stand trial.
Some South Carolinians petitioned the state's attorney gen-

eral to bring Tappan and other abolitionists to Charleston for the same purpose.

Threats of assassination against the New York abolitionists seemed real enough to cause near panic among them and their friends. Lydia Maria Child, herself an active abolitionist, writing from Brooklyn, New York, on 15 August 1835, described the excitement:

I have not ventured into the city, nor does one of us dare go to church to-day, so great is the excitement here. You can form no conception of it. 'Tis like the times of the French Revolution, when no man dared trust his neighbors. Private assassins from New Orleans are lurking at the corners of the streets to stab Arthur Tappan; and very large sums are offered for anyone who will convey Mr. [George] Thompson [an abolitionist visiting from England] into the Slave States . . .; five thousand dollars were offered on the Exchange in New York for the head of Arthur Tappan on Friday last. Mr. [Elizur] Wright [secretary of the American Anti-Slavery Society] was yesterday barricading his doors and windows with strong bars and planks an inch thick.[11]

In the winter of 1835–1836, the legislatures of Alabama, Georgia, South Carolina, North Carolina, and Virginia took official action to resist the abolitionists' postal campaign. They sent resolutions to the Northern state governments calling for legislation to suppress antislavery societies and to prevent the printing and circulation of antislavery material. Some Northern legislatures appointed special committees to consider the Southern requests. Generally, the committee reports condemned abolitionist activity. Publicity given to the Southern legislative resolutions and to the Northern legislative reports probably encouraged mob activity against abolitionist lecturers and agents. But no Northern legislature passed the repressive laws the Southern leaders demanded.

Southern reaction to the pamphlet campaign stimulated rather than checked antislavery sentiment in the North. The number of antislavery societies grew from 200 in May 1835 to 527 a year later. Southern demands that abolitionists be silenced and that prominent abolitionists be extradited to stand trial in Southern courts struck some Northerners as the very height of arrogance. "I do not choose to surrender the power of executing justice into the hands of slaveowners of South Carolina," wrote Philip Hone, a conservative New Yorker, when he learned of the Southern demands.[12] By exercising rights guaranteed them by both state and nation, abolitionists provoked a reaction that could be turned to their advantage. Southerners, it appeared, were attempting to extend to white Americans the despotic authority they customarily exercised over their slaves. Slavery bred an arrogance in Whites that menaced civil rights and republican institutions. Instead of silencing the abolitionists and discrediting their principles, Southern opposition only publicized them further. As a result of the postal campaign of 1835 and the unrestrained opposition it provoked, far more Northerners than before were made aware of abolition doctrine. By their efforts to silence their critics, Southerners created the important issue of free speech that in the 1830s became inseparable from the campaign against slavery.

Probably the innumerable mobs that assailed abolitionist agents and lecturers across the North in 1835 and 1836 were encouraged in their acts by the Southern reaction to abolitionism. But mob violence, like other efforts at repression, had an effect on the fortunes of the antislavery movement quite different from the one intended. Every mob that attempted to destroy an antislavery newspaper or to silence an antislavery speaker brought sharply into public view the issue of civil rights. Evidence of widespread popular hostility to abolitionism may have convinced the timid to shy away from so hazardous a cause, but attempts at repression brought other more resolute persons into active affiliation with it.

Efforts in Connecticut in 1833 to close Prudence Crandall's school after she admitted black girls persuaded a number of persons that the issues of slavery, race, and civil rights were inseparable, and that so long as slavery and racial prejudice persisted, civil rights were secure for no one. Gerrit Smith actively committed himself to abolitionism only after mobs at Utica, New York, dispersed the state antislavery convention.[13] The incident that most clearly linked civil rights with abolitionism involved the Reverend Elijah P. Lovejoy, a newspaper editor murdered by a mob while defending his press at Alton, Illinois.[14]

Lovejoy, a pious, college-trained native of Maine, established a Presbyterian reform newspaper, the *Observer,* at Alton after mobs drove him from St. Louis because of his antislavery and anti-Catholic editorial policy. He found fellow abolitionists in Illinois; yet a free state proved not much more receptive to the antislavery argument than Missouri was. In January 1837, a state legislative committee issued a pro-slavery, anti-abolitionist report in response to Southern demands that such publications as Lovejoy's be suppressed. The legislators called upon public opinion "firmly and powerfully" to rebuke antislavery activity in the state. This, of course, might be construed as an invitation issued by state authority for mob action against abolitionists.[15]

Violence did not occur until several months later, after Lovejoy had published a call for the formation of a state antislavery society. As soon as plans to organize abolitionist activity became known, a group of Alton's civic leaders requested Lovejoy to cease his "unwise agitation." Lovejoy made no move whatever to placate his opponents. To yield to popular opinion would be to abandon the freedoms of speech and press, and in his opinion would signify his surrender to pro-slavery forces.

St. Louis newspapers joined in the campaign against Lovejoy, assuring the people of Alton that he had "forfeited all claims to the protection of that or any other community." Spokesmen for the slave states alluded to the lucrative economic ties Illinois had with the South. If Alton acquired a reputation as an abolitionist center, Southerners might shift their trade elsewhere. A St. Louis editor reminded the citizens of Alton that "every consideration for their own and their *neighbor's* prosperity [required them] to stop the course of the *Observer.* "[16]

Violence still might have been averted had not local politicians—both Whigs and Democrats—let it be known that they would not defend Lovejoy's right to publish his newspaper in defiance of local sentiment. A few days later when a mob wrecked his press, no law enforcement official ventured to intervene. Instead of using his powers to protect Lovejoy's constitutional rights, the state attorney general agreed that the mob's action had been justified.

Hoping to draw off support from Lovejoy's abolitionist program, conservatives in the city revived the defunct local branch of the American Colonization Society. They seized on its proposal to send Blacks to Africa as a solution to the racial issue and as a means of evading the painful moral decisions Lovejoy and other abolitionists asked them to make. Even some of Lovejoy's friends wavered as they realized the strength of popular antipathy against him. They decided that civil rights would have to be yielded in the interest of social tranquillity. But Lovejoy refused to yield.

The lack of support from prominent citizens freed Lovejoy's enemies to act against him, confident that authority would not stand in their way. Those persons who counseled moderation and respect for law called upon both sides to compromise. They urged Lovejoy to moderate his stand against slavery in exchange for a decline in popular hostility. He could continue to publish his newspaper, they promised, if he would stop printing abolitionist articles. Lovejoy refused to pay so high a price for survival. The new press he had ordered to replace the one recently destroyed was wrecked by a mob before it could be put into operation. Alton's mayor watched the mob—which he described as "quiet and gentlemanly"—as it took the press apart and threw the pieces into the river. Efforts of the Reverend Edward Beecher, who was president of Illinois College and a brother of Harriet Beecher Stowe, to organize public sentiment in support of Lovejoy's constitutional rights failed. The colonizationists, led by local preachers, continued to condemn the abolitionists, and prominent businessmen and politicians continued to insist that Lovejoy must give up his newspaper. The result was the gathering of another mob. On 7 November 1837, it surrounded the warehouse where Lovejoy and others were guarding still another new printing press. The building was set afire. When Lovejoy emerged from the burning warehouse, he was shot and killed. The mob then destroyed his press.

Lovejoy's murder brought converts to the antislavery societies and persuaded men to join them who perhaps would not have done so had they not seen civil liberties endangered. Knowledge that this probably would happen helped Lovejoy's associates interpret his death as more than a meaningless sacrifice. Edward Beecher, for a time overwhelmed by the events at Alton, at last found consolation for the death of his friend in the conviction that "his enemies have failed in their purpose & he has triumphed in his fall." Owen Lovejoy, too, was confident that his brother had accomplished more by dying than "living and unopposed he could have done in a century."[17]

Throughout the North, the death of Lovejoy created enormous resentment. The Alton riots supplied persuasive evidence to illustrate the "bloodthirstiness" of the "slave power." Numerous sermons were preached and public meetings held to protest the event. The American Anti-Slavery Society, officially adopting Lovejoy as a martyr, issued writing paper bearing a crest with the caption, "LOVEJOY the first MARTYR to American LIBERTY. MURDERED for asserting the FREEDOM of the PRESS. Alton Nov. 7, 1837." But he did not receive the title of martyr without protest from the nonresistants within the antislavery movement. Back in the East, Benjamin Lundy criticized Lovejoy's physical defense of his press, and Sarah Grimké mourned that any abolitionist would resort to "physical force, to the weapons of death to defend the cause of God."[18]

"The Fugitive's Song"
Composed for and dedicated to Frederick Douglass

Theirs, however, was a minority voice. Most abolitionists decided to capitalize on Lovejoy's murder to further their cause, and this they did effectively.

A few months after the shocking events at Alton, a mob in Philadelphia burned Pennsylvania Hall, a building only recently constructed by popular subscription and dedicated to free discussion of public issues. City authorities did little to try to save the structure. The special offense that inspired popular wrath was the close association of the building with abolitionism; it housed the local antislavery office, and at the Anti-Slavery Convention of American Women held in the building following the dedicatory ceremonies, white and black delegates freely associated with each other in disregard of local prejudice. An official investigating committee found that abolitionists rather than the mob should be held responsible for the fire. The committee reported that the mob "was occasioned by the determination of the owners of the building, and their friends to persevere in openly promulgating in it doctrines repulsive to the moral sense of a large majority of our community ... reckless of its consequences to the peace and order of the city."[19]

The destruction of Pennsylvania Hall and the murder of Lovejoy were only the two most flagrant incidents in a wave of violence that swept the North in the mid–1830s. The mob action against abolitionists, like Southern opposition to the American Anti-Slavery Society's pamphlet campaign, encouraged certain persons to support the abolitionist cause. Theodore Weld understood the dynamics of the situation perfectly. He explained how Lovejoy's murder led Wendell Phillips, an aristocratic Boston lawyer who had long held antislavery sympathies, finally to join the abolitionists.

Phillips, said Weld, had early "learned the folly of gradualism, the inadequacy and falseness of colonization, and the duty and safety of immediate emancipation." Yet despite his long-held antislavery convictions, Phillips had never actually participated in the antislavery movement until he learned of the riots at Alton. Opinions and sentiment alone do not galvanize a man into action, Weld observed. "They may lie dormant a lifetime. Half dormant Phillip's anti-slavery opinions were till he saw slaveholding horror ablaze in the frenzy of pro-slavery mobs."[20] From 1837, in the wake of Lovejoy's murder, Phillips devoted his life to abolitionism and other radical causes.

As Catherine Beecher—another of Lyman Beecher's famous children—observed at the time, a great many persons either declared or implied that in joining the abolitionists in the 1830s "they were influenced, not by their arguments . . . but because the violence of opposers had identified that cause with the question of freedom of speech, freedom of the press, and civil liberty."[21] But for some persons it was only a short step from defending the abolitionists' right to advocate their principles to actively sharing those same principles.

Abolitionists made the most of the association of despotism with slavery. So long as slavery existed, they contended, civil rights for all Americans had only a frail and uncertain existence. James G. Birney, one of the most prominent of the Southern-born abolitionists, accounted for his own anti-slavery commitment in related terms. "Long and patient observation of the influence of Slavery on the principles of our government, and on our happiness as a people," he wrote on 14 November 1835, "convinced me, some time since, that its relinquishment was essential to the preservation of both." Birney's record of devotion to the welfare of the Negro already was a long one; yet he admitted that his antislavery convictions were confirmed and strengthened by events in the 1830s that more directly concerned the welfare of Whites than of Blacks.[22] Birney was by no means unique in this experience. Lydia Maria Child reported from Northampton, Massachusetts, in 1838 that "many in this region have 'their dander up' (as some express it) about their own rights . . . , but," she added, "few really sympathize with the slave."[23]

For some antislavery advocates the welfare of black people became only part of a more general concern for liberty.

William Jay expressed that circumstance explicitly when, in 1836, he resigned as president of the New York Anti-Slavery Society. "We commenced the present struggle to obtain the freedom of the slave," said Jay on that occasion; "we are compelled to continue it to preserve our own. We are now contending, not so much with the slaveholders of the South about human rights, as with the political and commercial aristocracy of the North, for the liberty of speech, of the press, and of conscience."[24]

Jay himself remained a life-long champion of abolition and the rights of black men; yet it is easy to see how in some minds those issues might be made secondary to a concern for the welfare of white Americans. Abolitionists were often apprised of the danger. Charles Fitch, a Boston clergyman, warned members of the Massachusetts Anti-Slavery Society in 1837 "that while we look well to the dangers which threaten ourselves, as the advocates of free discussion, we ought also to keep full in mind the wrongs and sufferings of the slave."[25] It was a warning that would demand frequent repetition.

Although anti-abolitionist mobs were by no means unknown after 1840, they became less common after that date. Opponents of abolition learned that the discussion of slavery could not be stifled by violence and that, in any event, their worst apprehensions as to its results would not soon be realized. The slaves were not going to be incited to rebellion by antislavery propaganda, and the abolitionists were not likely to achieve their goals in the immediate future. But neither slaveholders nor their Northern friends had any reason to become complacent.

Even though abolitionists remained a small minority in the population, anti-Southern and antislavery sentiment continued to grow in the North during the 1830s and 1840s. Slavery became a major political issue and thus a matter of pressing concern to Northerners who had been insensitive to its moral aspects. For this result Southern politicians were responsible. Those men, who thought of themselves as the chief defenders of Southern interests, proved instead to

be in this instance even more effective allies of the abolitionists than were Northern mobs. "How remarkably the
cause gains strength," commented an Ohio abolitionist in
1838. "The course of the Slave party in Congress is precisely
the needful, to help on the work."

The event that elicited such satisfaction was a controversy in Congress produced by an avalanche of abolitionist-
sponsored antislavery petitions.[26] Just as the American
Anti-Slavery Society's pamphlet campaign of 1835 provoked a Southern reaction beneficial to the antislavery
cause and just as mob reaction to abolitionist agitation revealed new antislavery sympathizers, so Southern resistance to antislavery petitions contributed to the further
growth of the movement.

Legislative petitions had long been used by abolitionists
as a means of placing their sentiments and programs before state legislatures and Congress. Great numbers of
them had been sent in earlier years to protest the slave
trade, and a small but steady flow had continued throughout the 1820s.[27] With antipathy to slavery and to the South
growing in the 1830s, increasing numbers of antislavery
memorials, resolutions, and petitions reached Congress. By
the congressional session of 1835–1836, the numbers of such
documents had become so great as to constitute an annoy-
ance not only to Southern congressmen, who felt insulted
by them, but to all legislators who wished to get on with
business they regarded as more pressing than slavery.

Some congressmen decided that the time had come to bar
the issue of slavery from Congress altogether. Their decision, reached while anti-abolitionist mobs raged across the
North and while slaveholders attempted to repulse the
American Anti-Slavery Society's pamphlet campaign, was
part of a coordinated effort to safeguard slavery by making
it a forbidden topic for public discussion anywhere. Discussion of slavery, Southerners believed, threatened the
institution. Moreover, intersectional discord produced dis-
sensions within the political parties and perhaps even
menaced the Union itself.

On 18 December 1835, James Hammond, a representative from South Carolina, moved that the House refuse to receive antislavery petitions. This would seriously infringe an historic right, but Hammond presented strong arguments for its necessity in the current emergency. Passage of his motion, Hammond urged, would set the House of Representatives' "decided seal of reprobation" on abolitionist activities and thus help to end them. Just as abolitionists assailed the South with antislavery literature in the belief that slaveholders would yield to moral pressure exerted by Northern public opinion, so Hammond assured his colleagues that abolitionists would wither before the judgment of Congress.

For six weeks the House debated Hammond's motion, while John C. Calhoun led a similar fight in the Senate. If discussion of slavery in Congress could be prevented, the abolitionists would be severely handicapped by losing their national forum. If abolitionist publications could be kept out of the South, abolitionists silenced in the North, and Congress barred to their petitions, they would be neutralized and slavery would be made secure. But despite the utility of these measures, it was extremely rash to propose them. Hammond's and Calhoun's motions would restrict a fundamental right and thus almost certainly create a new grievance throughout the North.

Martin Van Buren, the political wizard of New York whom President Jackson was about to designate as his heir-apparent to the presidency, arranged an alternative to the Southern strategy that he hoped would not altogether alienate the North. He worked through Henry L. Pinckney, a prominent Southern Democrat, to secure a less stringent measure by which antislavery petitions would be received but immediately tabled. This eventually became the famous "gag rule," which by provoking prolonged and bitter congressional debate in the end strengthened rather than weakened the abolitionist cause. The "gag rule" stimulated the abolitionists' determination to address petitions to Congress. In May 1837, the executive committee of the American Anti-Slavery Society voted to launch a campaign to flood the House with these petitions. It reported a year later that 414,471 petitions had been sent between May 1837 and May 1838.

The society's petition campaign was tightly organized and effectively waged. The directors of the campaign—Henry B. Stanton, John Greenleaf Whittier, and Theodore Weld—intended to miss no one in the effort to gather signatures. "Let petitions be circulated wherever signers can be got," ran their instructions. "Neglect no one. Follow the farmer to his field, the wood-chopper to the forest. Hail the shop-keeper behind his counter; call the clerk from his desk; stop the waggoner with his team; forget not the matron, ask for her daughter. Let no frown deter, no repulses baffle. Explain, discuss, argue, persuade." Women were especially active in circulating petitions as well as in signing them, and in that way took an important step toward full involvement in public affairs.

The petition campaign significantly expanded the numbers of antislavery adherents. The mere act of signing one's name to an antislavery petition meant personal commitment and identification with the movement. Thus the petition campaign created a network of loyal workers who had actually taken part in the movement against slavery.

The dogged effort of Southern congressmen to dam the flood of petitions failed. The passage of the "gag rule" had broadened the antislavery agitation into still another fight for civil rights. The continuing struggle in Congress to introduce petitions made the connection between slavery and the denial of free speech clear to citizens who were otherwise indifferent to abolition. The slaveholding South apparently was intent on preserving its basic institution, even at the cost of denying constitutional rights to free men. The concept of a despotic slave power bent on dominating the nation took clear form in Northern minds. This development more than anything else was responsible for widening the base of the antislavery movement.

Congress renewed the "gag rule" each year until 1840. From then until its repeal on 2 December 1844, the proce-

dure of receiving and immediately tabling antislavery petitions remained a standing rule in the House. But this did
not mean that slavery was not discussed there. Former
president John Quincy Adams, then a representative from
Massachusetts, led the effort to interject the subject into
congressional debate on every conceivable occasion. By
1840, he had been joined in his fight by a little group of
antislavery Whig congressmen as eager as he was to defend
the right of petition and to make political use of it. These
men—Seth M. Gates of New York, William Slade of Vermont, and Joshua Giddings of Ohio—resolved not to bow to
the order for silence. They delivered antislavery speeches
in the House even though this defied the will of party leaders. Their speeches were widely reported in the press and
distributed throughout the country under the franking
privilege.

Anti-Southern feeling—and hence antislavery feeling—
received a further stimulus in the mid-1830s by the Texas
Revolution and consequent efforts to annex Texas to the
United States. Proposals to acquire new Western territory
renewed the apprehensions that had surrounded the
admission of Missouri as a slave state some fifteen years
earlier.[28] Certain Northern politicians and reformers, especially those in New England, vowed to resist any move to
add territory that would aggrandize the South and
strengthen slavery. It was an old issue, but one with an
undiminished capacity to enflame.

In the 1820s, the Mexican government welcomed settlers
from the United States into Texas, granting them land, full
rights of citizenship, and, in an exception to the country's
abolition law, allowing them to own slaves. But by 1830, as
Texas filled with emigrants from the United States, Mexican authorities began to have second thoughts. They closed
the borders to further settlement from the United States
and at the same time instituted a program to centralize
political authority.

Anglo-Americans in Texas interpreted the new policy as
a threat to the near autonomy they had enjoyed and, what
was probably even more distressing to them, as a threat to

slavery. While South Carolinians in the same years took alarm at the growing power of the United States government with its potential threat to slavery and raised the standard of states' rights and nullification in order to resist it, the Texans launched a resistance movement to maintain their "rights" against the Mexican government.

When remonstrance proved unavailing, the Texans turned to war. Success on the battlefield assured their political independence and their power to maintain slavery. All these events were observed with great interest in the United States. The Jackson administration, while only partially concealing its sympathy for the rebels, proclaimed a policy of official neutrality, but Americans nonetheless were heavily involved in the affair. Volunteers from the United States, including such heroes as David Crockett and the Bowie brothers, flocked to Texas to fight in the rebellion; and agents from Texas collected large sums of money, especially in Boston, New York, and Philadelphia, to finance the military operations.

In less tense, more settled times, it might have been possible for Americans in general to view the uprising in Texas with complete sympathy; after all, oppressed subjects of Mexico were following the example set by American colonists fifty years earlier in rebelling to safeguard their freedoms. But in the 1830s, no such event taking place in the path of the westward expansion of slavery could escape the closest scrutiny. Examination of the Texas Revolution blasted the idea that the Texans' devotion to unalloyed principles of liberty had precipitated the rebellion. But even had such doubts not been raised, certain Northern political and class interests were sure to be alarmed at the prospect that Southern influence was about to be augmented by acquisition of a vast territory on the southwestern frontier. The annexation of Texas would mean more Southern congressmen to vote against tariffs, against internal improvements, against national banks, against the discussion of slavery. Texas would mean more Democrats, more despotic planters, more slaves.

It happened that Benjamin Lundy, in a futile effort to establish a colony of free Blacks, had made three trips to Texas in the early 1830s and had lived in that remote place during the first stages of the revolution. With good reason Lundy could claim to be an authority on the little-known region. The frustrations and unpleasant experiences he encountered there at the hands of members of Stephen F. Austin's settlement turned him against the Texans and convinced him that their chief purpose in rebelling was to preserve slavery. The entire revolutionary movement, he concluded, was part of a conspiracy developed in the South to add slave territory to the United States.[29]

Upon returning to Philadelphia in 1835, Lundy wrote an account of the revolution setting forth his view of its origin and purpose. The circumstantial evidence presented in his pamphlet, *The War in Texas,* was highly persuasive in support of the conspiracy theory.[30] Lundy sent copies of his work to John Quincy Adams, whom he recognized as the most strategically placed public official having an antislavery, anti-Southern point of view. Adams, about to begin his speeches opposing the annexation of Texas, found material in Lundy's writings that helped him justify his position. Soon the two men were engaged in regular correspondence. Lundy supplied Adams with information showing the Texas Revolution to have been inspired not by an impartial love of liberty but by a slaveholders' plot to dominate the nation.[31] Lundy's view harmonized so admirably with suspicions and antipathies then spreading in the North that it soon became standard, particularly among abolitionists. His account of the Texas Revolution made an important contribution to the belief in the existence of a malevolent and aggressive "slave power" whose aim was control of the country.[32]

Petitions opposing the annexation of Texas soon reached Congress in large numbers and became part of the great petition campaign that so vexed Southerners in 1837. Even Adams grew somewhat impatient with the deluge and counseled abolitionists to call a halt to their campaign, which he thought had become over-enthusiastic. Abolitionist efforts to change the opinions of congressmen with respect to slavery were useless, Adams declared.[33]

The advice was wasted, for as Lewis Tappan reminded Adams, the abolitionists by their petition efforts did "not expect so much to convert members of congress, as their constituents."[34] The purpose of the petition campaign was propagandistic: to engage large numbers of Northerners in antislavery activity and to convince them that Southern policy endangered their rights and influence within the Union. In carrying out these purposes, the abolitionists succeeded magnificently. No other issue in the sectional contest up to that time aroused such widespread concern in the North; none proved so effective in obtaining support from persons who did not consider themselves to be abolitionists. It helped persuade Northerners that slavery imperiled their own interests and that political organization to combat the "slave power" was essential.

Theodore Weld remarked in 1839 that the abolitionist cause grew only as fast as racial prejudice died.[35] Evidence of the death of prejudice was not very substantial. Yet the antislavery cause still grew. This apparent contradiction did not prove Weld wrong. It suggested instead that the emerging hostility to slavery was something different from the abolitionism Weld and other antislavery reformers envisaged. It was an antislavery sentiment mingled with hostility to Southern culture and to Southern power. The resultant antislavery, anti-Southern amalgam possessed great strength and potential for accomplishment. But it was not quite the equivalent of a commitment to the cause of universal human rights. And in that fact lay danger for the success of abolitionism and for the future of Blacks in America. This was the warning conveyed to members of the Massachusetts Anti-Slavery Society in 1837 by the Reverend Joshua Easton, a black abolitionist: "Abolitionists may attack slaveholding," he said, "but there is danger still that the spirit of slavery will survive, in the form of prejudice, after the system is overturned. Our warfare ought not to be against slavery alone, but against the spirit which makes color a mark of degradation."[36]

Easton had raised once again the issue that was central to the success of the abolitionist cause. His reminder was especially appropriate at a time when anti-Southern sentiment swept much of the North, bringing with its heightened resentment toward slaveholders a corresponding antagonism toward slavery, while leaving racial attitudes only slightly changed.

The situation clearly offered abolitionists opportunity for significant gains. They found, however, that even in that propitious atmosphere their program still encountered stubborn resistance. The emergent resentment toward "the slave power" was not strong enough to dispel the aura of radicalism that still surrounded the abolitionists and their program. A part of the abolitionist brotherhood now attempted to alter the movement's radical image on the ground that no truly radical program stood much chance of winning acceptance by nineteenth-century Americans.

Notes

1. Aileen S. Kraditor, *Means and Ends in American Abolitionism; Garrison and His Critics on Strategy and Tactics, 1834–1850* (New York: Pantheon Books, 1969), p. 237.
2. Jules Zanger, "The 'Tragic Octoroon' in Pre-Civil War Fiction," *American Quarterly,* 18 (Spring 1966): 63–70.
3. (New York, 1839).
4. Russell B. Nye, *Fettered Freedom: Civil Liberties and the Slavery Controversy, 1830–1860* (East Lansing: Michigan State University Press, 1949), esp. pp. 41–85.
5. See Larry Gara, "Slavery and the Slave Power: A Crucial Distinction," *Civil War History,* 15 (March 1969): 5–18. The problem persisted: "I think you have erred, in encouraging 'Liberty conventions' to prate, in their resolutions of 'the equal rights' of men, when you knew that not one in ten, voting for such resolutions, was aware of their significance, or would so vote if he were." George Bradburn to Salmon P. Chase, 25 June 1848, Salmon P. Chase Papers (Manuscript Division, Library of Congress); see also Josiah Quincy, *Address . . .* (Boston, 1856), p. 4: "My heart has always been much more affected by the slavery to which the free states have been subjected than with that of the negroes."
6. Theodore Dwight, *An Oration Spoken Before the Connecticut Society, for the Promotion of Freedom . . .* (Hartford: Hudson and Goodwin, 1794), pp. 14–16; *American Museum,* 1 (March 1787): 245–48; 2 (November 1788): 416; R. G. Walters, "The Erotic South: Civilization and Sexuality in American Abolitionism," *American Quarterly,* 25 (May 1973): 177–201.
7. William W. Freehling, *Prelude to Civil War; the Nullification Controversy in South Carolina, 1816–1836* (New York: Harper and Row, 1966), pp. xii, 115–16, 118.

8. The following account of the postal campaign is based chiefly on Bertram Wyatt-Brown, *Lewis Tappan and the Evangelical War Against Slavery* (Cleveland: Case Western Reserve University Press, 1969), pp. 149–63.

9. Early abolitionists frequently expressed the belief that Southerners could be moved to free their slaves by appeals to their "higher natures." Kraditor, *Means and Ends,* pp. 270–71. For an example see the *Speech of James A. Thome of Kentucky, Delivered at the Annual Meeting of the American Anti-Slavery Society . . .* (Boston: the Society, 1834), pp. 7–11.

10. James D. Richardson, ed., *A Compilation of the Messages and Papers of the Presidents* (Washington, D.C.: Government Printing Office, 1896), II: 1394–95.

11. Lydia Maria Child to Mrs. Ellis Gray Loring, 15 August 1835, *Letters of Lydia Maria Child* (Boston: Houghton, Mifflin, 1863), p. 15.

12. Allan Nevins, ed., *The Diary of Philip Hone, 1828–1851* (New York: Dodd, Mead, 1927), I: 171–72.

13. Ralph Volney Harlow, *Gerrit Smith, Philanthropist and Reformer* (New York: Henry Holt, 1939), pp. 122–25.

14. The following account of the Alton riots is based chiefly on Merton L. Dillon, *Elijah P. Lovejoy, Abolitionist Editor* (Urbana: University of Illinois Press, 1961), pp. 94–174.

15. Illinois, Senate, *Senate Journal,* 10th General Assembly, 1st sess., pp. 195–98, 297.

16. *Missouri Republican,* 28 August 1837.

17. Edward Beecher to Owen Lovejoy, 14 November 1837, Owen Lovejoy Papers (William L. Clements Library); Owen Lovejoy to Henry G. Chapman, 9 December 1837, Chapman Papers (Boston Public Library).

18. S. W. Benedict to Owen Lovejoy, 2 July 1838, Owen Lovejoy Papers; *Philadelphia National Enquirer,* 16 and 23 November 1837; Sarah Grimké to Sarah Douglass, 23 November 1837, *Weld-Grimké Letters,* I, pp. 480–81.

19. For a full account see *History of Pennsylvania Hall, Which Was Destroyed by a Mob on the 17th of May* (Philadelphia: Merrihew and Gunn, 1838). According to Elliott Cresson, foreman of the grand jury, abolitionists were responsible for the riot because under their encouragement, "associations were formed which naturally tend to offend the nicer feelings of the public." "Minutes," 24 October 1838, Minute Book of the Board of Managers of the Pennsylvania Hall Association (Manuscript Division, Library of Congress).

20. *Memorial Services Upon the Seventy-Fourth Birthday of Wendell Phillips, Held at the Residence of William Sumner Crosby . . .* (Boston, 1886), pp. 24–26.

21. Catherine E. Beecher, *An Essay on Slavery and Abolitionism, with Reference to the Duty of American Females* (Philadelphia: Perkins, 1837), p. 36.
22. Birney to Charles Hammond, 14 November 1835, *Birney Letters,* I, p. 263.
23. Child to Theodore Weld, 29 December 1838, *Weld-Grimké Letters,* II, 735.
24. William Jay to "Rev. Sir," 26 September 1836, *Proceedings of the First Annual Meeting of the New-York State Anti-Slavery Society,* p. 55.
25. Massachusetts Anti-Slavery Society, *Fifth Annual Report ... 1837* (Boston: the Society, 1837), pp. xxv–xxvi.
26. The petition drive and ensuing controversy may be followed in Gilbert H. Barnes, *The Antislavery Impulse, 1830–1844* (New York: D. Appleton-Century, 1933), pp. 121–45; Dwight Lowell Dumond, *Antislavery: The Crusade for Freedom* in *America* (Ann Arbor: University of Michigan Press, 1961), pp. 209–11; and James M. McPherson, "The Fight Against the Gag Rule: Joshua Leavitt and Antislavery Insurgency in the Whig Party, 1839–1842," *Journal of Negro History,* 48 (July 1963): 177–95.
27. Betty L. Fladeland, *Men and Brothers: Anglo-American Anti-Slavery Cooperation* (Urbana: University of Illinois Press, 1972), pp. 63–64.
28. "My spirit is sorely tried concerning Texas. ... If this territory be acquired, I shall think it is the mysterious will of Providence to throw back abolition half a century." Lydia M. Child to Ellis Gray Loring, 30 May 1836, Lydia Maria Child Papers (William L. Clements Library, Ann Arbor); for still earlier apprehensions, see *Genius of Universal Emancipation,* 11 (March 1831): 185, and 12 (August 1831): 51.
29. Merton L. Dillon, "Benjamin Lundy in Texas," *Southwestern Historical Quarterly,* 63 (July 1959): pp. 46–62.
30. Benjamin Lundy, *The War in Texas; a Review of Facts and Circumstances, Showing That This Contest Is the Result of a Long Premeditated Crusade Against the Government ...* (Philadelphia: Merrihew and Gunn, 1836).
31. See the series of letters in May and June 1836, The Adams Family Papers (microfilm edition).
32. William Ellery Channing (*A Letter to the Hon. Henry Clay, on the Annexation of Texas to the United States* [Boston: J. Munroe, 1837]) developed a similar thesis.
33. Samuel Flagg Bemis, *John Quincy Adams and the Union* (New York: Alfred A. Knopf, 1956), p. 351.
34. Lewis Tappan to John Quincy Adams, 3 May 1837, Adams Papers.

35. Theodore Weld to Gerrit Smith, 23 October 1839, *Weld-Grimké Letters,* II, p. 811.
36. Massachusetts Anti-Slavery Society, *Fifth Annual Report ... 1837,* (Boston: the Society, 1837), p. xxxix.

CHAPTER SIX

The Attempted Purge of the Garrisonian Heretics

A great many abolitionists were dismayed to find their cause so freely labeled "radical," "dangerous," "fanatical," and themselves tagged as "incendiaries," "madmen," and worse. Such words did not fit their own self-image, for they generally pictured themselves as respectable citizens and as staunch defenders of orthodox religion and traditional values. In their own eyes they were neither revolutionary nor irresponsible. The only points at which many of them diverged from the majority were in their extraordinary devotion to religion and in their adherence to the antislavery cause. Their style of life and their attitudes were in other respects wholly conventional.

The nation, although in great need of reform, was fundamentally sound, these moderate abolitionists believed. Their only purpose was to restore it to its proper course by removing the evil that had been allowed to corrupt an otherwise admirable system. However radical abolitionism might be in its implications, men and women who belonged to the majority wing of the antislavery movement did not envision themselves as carrying out changes that extended much beyond the ending of slavery. They had no further ultimate aim.

But such moderates knew that among their comrades in the antislavery cause were men and women whose view of America was by no means so benign as theirs and whose goals were less limited than their own. The ranks of abolitionism included partisans of fundamental and far-reaching change who did not shrink from advocating causes, ideas, and even tactics that for their day were extreme indeed.[1]

Some of them proclaimed their other-mindedness by defying convention even in personal appearance and conduct. The free spirited Grimké sisters, for instance, abandoned the style of clothing uniformly worn by other women of their time in favor of the outlandish Turkish-style costume originated by Amelia Bloomer. Some abolitionists affected shaggy, unkempt beards in a day when beards were not in style. Some neglected to cut their hair. New Englanders seemed especially prone to such eccentricities. Charles Calistus Burleigh, an antislavery agent from Connecticut, was subjected to ridicule on account of his flowing sandy beard and long ringlets. Parker Pillsbury and Stephen Symonds Foster, whose wife, Abby Kelley, wore the Bloomer costume, shocked the staid wherever they lectured—and their lecturing commitments took them from Maine to Michigan.[2] These men sometimes accompanied the extremism of their message with irritating, disruptive behavior as a means of protest, and occasionally couched their condemnation of slavery and slaveholders in pungent language heavily laced with sexual allusions that some understandably found offensive. One of Garrison's closest associates, Henry C. Wright, not himself notably eccentric in either appearance or conduct, nonetheless espoused social views that marked him as radical indeed with respect to such basic concerns as marriage, child-rearing, and education.

Garrison, the most conventional of men in dress and behavior, seemed, however, to attract and inspire extremists of that sort; in fact and by conviction, he was one of them himself. The object of the movement, Garrison came to believe, was not to reform America but to radically change it. This could be accomplished only by producing profound alteration in the value system of the American people, a

"The Condition of American Slaves"

change to be effected by unremitting agitation. Unlike more moderate abolitionists, whose goal was to make anti-slavery views prevail by making them popular, Garrison and those who thought as he did, aimed to plant the seeds of revolution. These radical ideas then would grow and take whatever form they would. Men who held such expectations were hardly surprised to find that their ideas ran against the prevailing currents of popular thought and practice.

A movement for change such as Garrison and his close associates envisioned focused on no limited aim; it knew no dimensions; it could not be contained within the ordinary bounds of institutional reform; it carried its advocates into realms of speculation scarcely dreamed of by more culture-bound reformers. The public mind must be freed from its ideological shackles before any significant change in government or in human relationships could be realized. Relentless moral suasion must be undertaken in order to bring about deep popular commitment to all human rights. Only in that way could the authoritarian philosophy and the coercion that lay behind slavery as well as behind most other institutions be destroyed. Abolition was central to that radical concept, but it was not the whole of it.

The 1830s in America was a time of marked social restlessness and intellectual ferment. No institution, practice, belief, or relationship was considered too venerable or too sacred to escape questioning. Private property, marriage, the churches, schools, subordination of women, war, capital punishment, even government itself—all these and more found their reformers, their skeptics, and their opponents.[3]

Iconoclasm could take root almost anywhere, but it flourished best in western New York and New England, areas that also fostered abolitionism. Garrison, a devout champion and practitioner of free discussion, opened the columns of the *Liberator* to advocates of numerous advanced causes and philosophies, and he himself began to speculate on women's rights, nonresistance, perfectionism, and anarchy. For a time he considered becoming a universal reformer and giving the antislavery cause no greater prominence in his newspaper than he accorded other reforms. He found kindred spirits among some other prominent abolitionists who would willingly have followed him on such a course. "What woulds't thou think of the *Liberator* abandoning abolitionism as a *primary* object," asked Angelina Grimké in August 1837, "and becoming the vehicle of all these grand principles?"[4]

Such abolitionists as Arthur and Lewis Tappan, James G. Birney, and William Jay could only shudder at Miss Grimké's eclectic proposal. That abolitionism was about to become submerged in a headlong movement for universal radical reform was the grim apprehension of moderate abolitionists as they watched Garrison and his followers unfold ever more advanced ideas. Garrison would not bar from the antislavery brotherhood persons who advocated eccentric causes in addition to abolition. Jay, the Tappans, and others of the New York group feared that in their zeal for creating a new heaven and new earth some abolitionists were being led astray from what should be their primary concern—the freeing of the slaves. Beyond that they worried that good, solid men and women—the conservative majority whom they hoped to recruit for the antislavery movement—would be repulsed by abolitionist association with bizarre and radical theories. Garrison's flirtation with universal reform, they believed, threatened to wreck the abolitionist cause at the very time when it began to show some promise of winning popular support. They feared too that the churches, whose support they still eagerly sought, would never endorse abolitionism so long as it was closely identified with Garrison, who was well on the way to becoming notorious as a free-thinker.[5]

Garrison's name soon became a byword for extremism and crazy causes. A special reason for this was the little war he fought with the orthodox New England clergy in the late 1830s. A number of influential Congregational preachers had become staunch abolitionists, but still more of them had as yet established only a tenuous connection with the movement, and some opposed it altogether. Garrison regularly denounced clergymen who refused to cooperate with abolitionist lecturers (some of whom happened to be women) when they appeared within their parishes. He went still further. He called into question clerical authority to govern congregations; he repudiated the institution of the Sabbath; and he went on to expound the heretical theory of perfectionism. Finally he demoted the Bible itself. Not everything in it was divinely inspired, he declared: "Truth is older than any parchment."[6]

All this seemed scandalous indeed. It was too much for some of the orthodox clergy to tolerate. In March 1837, the General Association of Connecticut adopted the Norfolk Resolutions, which excluded revivalists and abolitionists from Congregationalist pulpits in Connecticut. Three months later five Massachusetts clergymen prepared a "Pastoral Letter" deploring Garrison's anti-clericalism and his endorsement of women's rights. In particular they took issue with the New England Anti-Slavery Society's practice (which Garrison condoned) of sending lecturers—especially women lecturers—"within the parochial limits of settled pastors without their consent." Ministers, they insisted, must retain absolute control over the topics discussed in their churches. "Deference and subordination are essential to the happiness of society," declared the preachers, "and peculiarly so in the relation of a people to their pastor." The employment of women as public antislavery lecturers—Sarah and Angelina Grimké were the first and by far the most famous of these—defied custom and the laws of nature. It threatened to destroy the family and thus to topple society itself.

When a woman appears publicly in the role the Grimké sisters had undertaken, "her character becomes unnatural," the clergymen declared. "If the vine, whose strength and beauty is to lean upon the trellis-work and half conceal its clusters, thinks to assume the independence and the overshading nature of the elm, it will not only cease to bear fruit, but will fall in shame and dishonor into the dust."[7]

Garrison summoned his usual pungent rhetoric to castigate the authors of these documents. He responded by characterizing the clergy as "blind leaders of the blind, dumb dogs that cannot bark, spiritual popes—that ... love the fleece better than the flock." In what must have been an unthinking, certainly an uninformed moment, he appealed to the conservative, evangelically-oriented New York executive committee of the American Anti-Slavery Society for support in his quarrel with the New England preachers. Of course he was rebuffed.[8]

Lewis Tappan and the rest of the Society's executive committee worried that Garrison's heresies would hamper the spread of abolitionism. Already they were preparing to ally with his clerical opponents in New England, whose support they anxiously sought. Garrison had received no inkling of this development; but even had he known the extent to which he had already fallen into disfavor with the moderate New Yorkers, it is not likely that he would have changed his anti-clerical course. He continued to answer each of the ministers' attacks in a temper at least as sharp as theirs, and with even more agitated language. Theodore Weld, who was working in the West to build the church-based movement that Garrison appeared to be tearing down, followed the controversy in the columns of the *Liberator*. He was unapproving. Hoping to find in Garrison's newspaper "the heart of Jesus," he was offered instead (as he said) only "the vibrations of serpents tongues and the darting of envenomed stings."[9]

Garrison refused to accept the clerics' authoritarian presumptions as valid. He denied their right—or the right of any authority whatever—to proscribe discussion. Abolitionists must be free, he insisted, to concern themselves with any cause they found interesting and believed important, however unpopular or unconventional it might be. For a time in the 1830s, women's rights, anti-Sabbatarianism, and nonresistance seemed to him as worthy of consideration as did abolition. And he believed especially that women should be as welcome as men to take part in every aspect of the movement.

In contrast to Garrison, the majority of abolitionists were intent only on abolishing slavery. They had no large vision of otherwise renovating American society. They were not ready to follow Garrison in his heady quest toward perfectionism. They feared they understood his extravagances only too well—he had become a Christian anarchist. Less adventuresome men did not believe that so visionary a program and so impractical a philosophy could ever lead to the end of slavery.

It was not only that Garrison's energies were being wasted. Some of his friends and associates became deeply concerned also that his course would have a destructive effect on the antislavery movement. The abolitionist leadership had expected to make the Protestant churches the agencies through which slavery would be ended. This

meant that the churches should be courted, not antagonized. Thus Garrison's jousts with the New England clergy
were seen as serious matters indeed.

Not only were the clergy formidable opponents in themselves, but many other persons were likely to resent attacks
on men whom they admired as community leaders and
whose office they respected. How could the majority of
Americans ever be brought to join a movement which had
an extremist such as Garrison at its very forefront? How
could the churches be won to abolitionism if Garrison remained closely associated with the cause? The New York
executive committee of the American Anti-Slavery Society
issued a statement urging the public not to confuse its familiar (if still unpopular) doctrines with the eccentric programs put forward by certain individual abolitionists, and
it prepared to struggle with Garrison and his circle for control of the movement.[10]

Garrison came under attack even from some persons who
once had been his closest associates. Lundy, now back in
Philadelphia from his Texas enterprises, did not hesitate to
criticize the conduct of his former partner. Like members
of the New York group, he berated Garrison for "arrogance" and for injecting "wild and absurd theories" and
"vagaries" into the slavery controversy.[11]

Garrison retorted that his critic's pique merely reflected
envy of Garrison's greater fame and influence within the
antislavery movement.[12] In this there may well have been
a kernel of truth, just as it is tempting to suspect that an
important ingredient in the Tappan brothers' opposition to
Garrison was their personal ambition to dominate abolitionism. Theodore Weld was to write with customary
shrewdness in 1843 "that all hope of fusing into one the
various divisions of the Anti Slavery host seemed to me
utterly vain. Deep, irreconcilable, *personal* animosities
and repulsions ... make such a cooperation impossible."[13]
There was much wisdom in Weld's comment, yet the dispute that wracked the unity of the antislavery movement

went deeper than mere personal rivalry. As we have seen, it involved both ideology and strategy.

An underlying issue that helped precipitate the crisis between Garrisonians and more moderate abolitionists was the proper relation that should exist between abolitionists and party politics. By the late 1830s, antipathy to slavery and to the South had become sufficiently widespread to make some leading members of the American Anti-Slavery Society believe the time had come to redefine the Society's political role. The abolitionists' original hope of converting the nation solely by moral suasion was near collapse. The younger, more secularly oriented men who entered the movement in the late 1830s were inclined to look to political action as a better means of furthering the antislavery cause. Politics seemed to them the most effective way to take advantage of the antislavery, anti-Southern sentiment that had been created by such episodes as the petition campaign and Lovejoy's murder.

Nothing abolitionists had yet tried accomplished as much as they had hoped. The means by which antislavery sentiment could be translated into antislavery action remained a matter of dispute. There was an abundance of sentiment, but action was rare, partly because no one could say what that action ought to be. "Too many seem to think that all our objects are to be effected by resolutions," complained William Jay in 1838.[14] A feeling grew that more should be attempted, that some new tactic must be devised if success ever were to be attained.

If limited political pressure exerted through petitions and the questioning of candidates for office had thus far accomplished little in changing governmental policy, antislavery work within the churches had proved equally frustrating. The abolitionists had failed to persuade a single large religious denomination to adopt an unequivocal abolitionist policy. Although the New York leaders of the American Anti-Slavery Society still professed hope that this eventually could be done, some of them were now willing to shift an increasingly large part of their efforts from the church to the state. A few even believed the time had come to organize a third party based exclusively on abolitionist principles.

It was at this point that Garrison's reputation as an irresponsible radical became a matter for concern. His "infidelity" alone would be sufficient to repulse churchgoers, while his extremism on secular matters would antagonize others. If abolitionists were to act as an effectual political force, they must attract support from conservative antislavery voters who were not affiliated with any abolitionist society, and the American Anti-Slavery Society must itself become a political pressure group. These goals were not likely to be attained so long as the Garrisonians remained within the Society.

Few of Garrison's followers favored organizing an antislavery political party, and some of them opposed voting at all. Garrison himself did not go so far. He did not reject political action in the antislavery cause. Indeed, as the historians Aileen Kraditor and James B. Stewart have recently shown, he thought politics useful as a means of agitating the issue in public forums and thus of spreading antislavery views more widely than might otherwise be done.[15] Yet he feared the result of the abolitionists' entering politics, for he favored the ending of slavery through a change of heart rather than by the compulsion that must be the ultimate recourse of political power.

Thus Garrison opposed founding a third party on the ground that an insufficient number of voters were morally prepared for political antislavery action. They had not yet undergone that spiritual reformation without which their use of power in the antislavery cause could not be trusted. Antislavery, anti-Southern politicians would cut and trim their principles in the interest of party success and harmony just as other politicians did. They would compromise for the sake of favor and office at the expense of the abolitionist cause. They would be more intent upon winning office and building a political party than with defending human rights. And if in some unexpected manner they should succeed in ending slavery, the result would not be the establishment of a reign of justice. If the end of slavery were brought by compulsion and not by moral regeneration, its results would be unsatisfactory. The institution of slavery would disappear, but the racial prejudice associated with it would remain in the unregenerate heart to make freedom for Blacks an ambiguous gain.

In many respects, Theodore Weld was one of Garrison's severest critics; yet Weld admitted to similar misgivings about the wisdom of the rapid movement of abolitionists toward party politics in the late 1830s. He too believed that the antislavery movement had recently attracted an inordinate number of half-hearted crusaders whose antislavery convictions proceeded from some other source than repentance. "Our Abolition Army needs a Gideonite expurgation," wrote Weld in 1839, using a Biblical allusion [Judges 7:1–25] that all his fellow workers would have understood. "We shall have to come yet to the pitchers and trumpets. The Lord speed the day."[16]

Garrison's no-human government position, if widely adhered to, obviously would block the transformation of the American Anti-Slavery Society from an agency for moral reform into a political organization. At the same time, his unorthodox religious views alienated potential support for antislavery politics. Therefore the New York leaders of the Society at last resolved to expel its Garrisonian element and officially to repudiate his doctrines. "It is in vain to think of succeeding in emancipation without the co-operation of the great mass of the intelligent mind of the nation," wrote James G. Birney. "This can be attracted, only by the reasonableness, the *religion,* of our enterprise."

Birney, who recently had been brought from Cincinnati to assume a position in the New York antislavery headquarters, and Henry B. Stanton were delegated to lead the effort to rid the movement of its radical element. "The 'no-Government' doctrines . . . seem to strike at the root of the social structure; and tend . . . to throw society into entire confusion," explained Birney as he prepared to carry the war against Garrison into his home territory.[17] Birney and Stanton attended antislavery meetings in various parts of New England for the purpose of arousing support for their position. To their dismay, they repeatedly found their moderate resolutions voted down. Garrison's followers were more numerous than they had supposed.

At the 1839 national meeting of the American Anti-Slavery Society the delegates defied the New York leadership by granting women the right to vote in the proceedings and by defeating Birney's motion to condemn "no-government" and "nonresistance," those twin Garrisonian heresies that so offended moderates. The final break between the factions came at the Society's anniversary meeting in May 1840. By that time the New York committee had already accepted its defeat as inevitable and had begun to liquidate the Society's property in anticipation of Garrison's victory.

The immediate issues before the delegates in 1840 were the duty of abolitionists to vote and the right of women to participate fully in the Society's affairs, but behind these matters stood a more fundamental question. Should abolitionism be a reform movement appealing to a wide constituency and using conventional religious and political means to attain its limited ends, or should it be an agitational movement relying largely on moral suasion to produce moral renovation and a fundamental restructuring of values?

When the convention assembled, it became clear that the Garrisonian faction, having exerted more energy than its opponents in packing the convention with delegates, could control the proceedings. The test issue came when Abby Kelley, an adherent of Garrison, was nominated to the Society's executive committee and was elected by a vote of 557 to 451. The defeated faction then withdrew and under the leadership of the Tappan brothers founded a rival organization, the American and Foreign Anti-Slavery Society.[18]

The schism the moderates sought had come, though not in the manner they desired. The victory proved hollow for

"I Am Going There" (or "The Death of little Eva")
A song written and inscribed to the readers of *Uncle Tom's Cabin*

both groups, for converts to abolitionism were no more easily won after the Society's split than before. The churches for the most part still refused to endorse the doctrine of the sinfulness of slavery and the program of immediate emancipation, whether preached by a representative of the new American and Foreign Anti-Slavery Society or by Garrison. It was the doctrine and program that proved unacceptable. The rhetoric in which the doctrine was couched and the other views held by its advocates were irrelevant.

In reality, both the new society dominated by the Tappans and the old one that Garrison now controlled were nearly powerless. The societies had lost control of the movement. Events in the mid–1830s had created enough popular opposition to the South and its institutions to place the antislavery movement beyond the confines of a reform organization. Further, a decentralizing process had already transferred some activities from central headquarters to the state societies at the same time that the depression of the later 1830s had handicapped nearly all reform efforts.[19]

Both national Societies continued their activities, though on a diminished scale—the American and Foreign Anti-Slavery Society until 1855, the American Anti-Slavery Society through the Civil War. But neither henceforth could dominate the antislavery movement or claim to speak for it. It was clear by 1840 that the majority of abolitionists would now engage in some form of conventional, organized political activity. Abolitionism had inescapably become a force that would make itself felt in party politics. "This *moral* and not *political* abolitionism will very soon be as stale as bread a month old." was the prediction in 1840 of S. B. Treadwell, editor of the *Freeman.* Gerrit Smith, one of the most erratic of the New York abolitionists, took to speaking on party politics at Sunday church services and in 1842 ran successfully for a seat in Congress. Zebina Eastman, who had been an editorial assistant of Benjamin Lundy during the last months of Lundy's life, composed what may be taken as the epitaph of the old antislavery societies: "The Societies have done a good work in their day," Eastman wrote in 1843, "and we can cherish them still, for the love of old associations, if we choose, without any detriment to the work they have so successfully built up. —But the advanced state of the cause, the political aspect which it has taken, require a different organization, as one which has not the stiffness and sluggishness of age upon it."[20]

Eastman's appraisal reflected commonly held opinion, for the old state and local antislavery societies practically expired in the early 1840s. The few that remained were Garrisonian organizations. Henceforth individual abolitionist spokesmen became far more important than the societies they nominally represented. Garrison and his circle never dropped from sight. They continued the agitation which they hoped would create a revolution in popular sentiment with respect to slavery and human rights, but in the eyes of persons who sought immediate, tangible results, the most effective antislavery workers were those who joined the work of political party organization. Such Western politicians as Owen Lovejoy in Illinois and Joshua Giddings and Salmon P. Chase in Ohio replaced Theodore Weld and Henry B. Stanton as leaders of the antislavery movement.

Interest in party politics was not a new departure for abolitionists. Early opponents of slavery had looked to Congress and the state legislatures as agencies that could deal with certain aspects of slavery, and even abolish it. If slavery were maintained by law, they reasoned, it could be destroyed by law. While some had believed that an all-encompassing religious revival would in itself be sufficient to end slavery, the aim of others from the first had been to awaken the nation's conscience only as a prerequisite to antislavery political action.[21]

Whatever the intent and wish of abolitionists, the growth of antislavery sentiment among Northern voters was certain to be reflected in politics. But during much of the 1830s, the religiously patterned campaigns of abolitionists as waged by such leaders as Weld had obscured the earlier view promulgated most consistently by Lundy that the ultimate antislavery weapon must be the ballot.

The appearance of the slavery issue in Congress in 1836, in the form of the petition controversy and in proposals for the annexation of Texas, revealed its political aspect to persons who until then had remained unaware of it. As a consequence of events in Washington, abolitionists, whether committed to political action or not, could hardly avoid the conclusion that to refrain from political antislavery action was to surrender control of the nation to slave-holding interests.

In 1836, while their opponents mobbed antislavery meetings, censored the mails, and talked of enacting laws to repress abolitionists, the American Anti-Slavery Society's executive committee advised its members to vote only for candidates who would not sacrifice their "rights." The practice soon developed of questioning candidates for office in order to determine their position on slavery and on such related topics as the right of petition and the annexation of Texas. The purpose of such tactics was to demonstrate that abolitionists held the balance of power between the two parties and would cast their vote for the candidate who most nearly agreed with their antislavery position. But the questioning of candidates, it soon appeared, had serious limitations. Too often all candidates took wholly unacceptable stands, and then as always some made bright promises during campaigns but after election failed to deliver. Furthermore, it seemed unrealistic to suppose that either of the two national parties could be transformed into genuine antislavery institutions so long as each party's leadership believed it essential to retain its Southern members.

When antislavery Whigs or Democrats were elected, as happened on a few occasions, they could accomplish little for the antislavery cause. If they made the attempt, they soon were confronted with party discipline and the demand for party regularity. The constraint of party was somewhat weakened in 1842 when Representative Joshua Giddings was reelected to Congress after his Whig colleagues had censured him for presenting certain antislavery resolutions in defiance of party edict.[22] But it would be too much to say that this success for political insurgency moved either the Whig or Democratic party toward abolitionism. In theory, abolitionists could continue to work within the old parties and try to move them toward abolitionist positions. In practice, it appeared that reformation accomplished by boring from within would take an incalculably long time, if it ever could succeed at all.

Some abolitionists finally concluded that it was senseless to continue participation in empty ceremonies of choice—the ritual on election day of attempting to select between two more-or-less similar pro-slavery candidates. A few began to insist on the necessity of making independent nominations so that voters could have the opportunity of a genuine antislavery choice. As religiously inspired reformers they reminded fellow workers that God does not allow men to select the lesser of two moral evils. He demands rigid adherence to the right. Since God, by their calculation, would not sanction voting for either Martin Van Buren or William Henry Harrison for the presidency in 1840, abolitionists felt duty bound to provide themselves with a morally acceptable alternative.

In 1838 and 1839, antislavery societies, especially those in the West, began to pass resolutions calling for independent political action. But such a course was seldom adopted without much soul-searching and controversy. Religiously oriented abolitionists typically viewed political activity with suspicion and distaste. Their observation of what they regarded as the unsavory aspects of Jacksonian Democracy led them to believe that if the antislavery movement entered party politics moral principle inevitably would be sacrificed to expediency, and abolitionists would be dragged through the sullying mire of political intrigue. "I have little confidence in the abiding and true-hearted abolitionism of any devotee to politics," Lewis Tappan told his brother Benjamin in 1839. "Party, party, party!—is the watchword, and moral questions are lost sight of too frequently."[23]

Other, more sanguine churchmen marched in the vanguard of the abolitionists' movement toward independent political action. Preaching, prayer, and talk would free no slaves, they pointed out, so long as voters continued to elect slaveholders and their friends to office. Failure to vote would not end slavery in the District of Columbia and would not repeal state laws discriminating against free Blacks. Only independent political action could accomplish these things.

The proposal that abolitionists should organize their own political party apparently was first advanced by Myron Holley, a former New York state legislator. He and a few supporters held a series of conventions during 1839 to try to persuade their fellow abolitionists to make nominations for the 1840 elections. But Holley's proposal set no bandwagons in motion. The lack of enthusiasm can be explained in part by the abolitionists' optimistic appraisal of Whig prospects for victory after the lackluster Democratic administration of Van Buren. Probably a majority of voting abolitionists in 1840 were Whigs, and 1840 looked to them like a Whig year —the first ever. Why sacrifice Whig prospects for victory by draining away votes into an abolitionist party that had no chance of success? Even the abolitionist candidates, James G. Birney and Francis J. LeMoyne, who were nominated by a convention held at Warsaw, New York, in March 1839, declined the honor.[24]

But the advocates of independent political action persisted, and as it appeared increasingly likely that the Democrats would renominate the unfortunate Van Buren and that the Whigs would run Harrison—both unacceptable to avid opponents of slavery—more abolitionists came to agree on the wisdom of naming a third-party ticket. In April 1840, at Albany, New York, a "National Convention of Friends of Immediate Emancipation" again nominated Birney, this time with Thomas Earle of Pennsylvania as his running mate. The two men accepted and thus became candidates for the new Liberty Party, as Gerrit Smith named it.[25]

Their platform called for abolition of slavery in the District of Columbia and for the ending of the interstate slave trade. While they condemned slavery wherever it existed, the party still adhered to the states' rights view that Congress had no authority over slavery in the states, an interpretation that had been set forth by Congress in 1790 and adopted by the American Anti-Slavery Society at its formation in 1833. But that restrictive view did not go unchallenged.

According to Ellis Gray Loring writing in 1838, only a few persons in Boston then believed that Congress's power extended over slavery in the states. These advocates included the ever radical Angelina and Sarah Grimké, the Unitarian preacher Alanson St. Clair, and perhaps his colleague Samuel J. May, and the aristocratic Garrisonian Maria Weston Chapman.[26] To an increasing extent, however, abolitionists, especially those outside New England, were taking the position that the Constitution was not a pro-slavery document, but rather that it gave the national government ample power to destroy slavery everywhere in the country. All that was lacking to accomplish abolition was a political majority dedicated to use that national emancipating power.

As early as 1838, Alvan Stewart, a lawyer of Utica, New York, called for the removal of the clause, from the American Anti-Slavery Society constitution, which asserted that slavery within the states was immune from congressional legislation. His proposal was of course rejected at that time as being far too radical and inciting. The abolitionist William Jay expressed the majority's conviction when he declared that a congressional law abolishing slavery would be "a most wicked and detestable act of usurpation—an act that would inevitably and properly sever the Union and necessarily result in bloodshed and national calamity."[27]

The view embodied in Stewart's proposal was not abandoned, however. The next year the American Anti-Slavery

Society heard Henry B. Stanton pledge that if congressional power were found to be in fact inadequate to destroy slavery, "we will alter the constitution and bring slavery in the States within the range of federal legislation and then annihilate it at one blow." As the years passed, antislavery politicians found this direct approach increasingly attractive. At Macedon Lock, New York, in 1847, an antislavery political convention pronounced slavery "illegal and unconstitutional" and declared that Congress had the power and responsibility to abolish it. The delegates held out no hope to slaveholders that they would ever compromise on the issue. "If the South demurs," they said, "let her, peacefully, withdraw from the Union." Stanton and others of similar mind served notice that an important group of abolitionists had become so intent on ending slavery that they would allow neither public opinion, nor precedent, nor institutions to stand permanently in their way.[28]

Debate over the nature of the Constitution and the power of Congress with respect to slavery continued for twenty years. Not until the victories of the Union armies during the Civil War rendered further discussion of the point altogether academic did the controversy cease. Throughout all the wearisome debate, most advocates of political abolition (of whom Birney was perhaps the most able) held that the Constitution, as an antislavery document, empowered Congress to end slavery in the District of Columbia and to bar it from the territories, but not directly to interfere with it in the states. These men accepted existing political institutions and the federal system and sought to gain control of them in order to facilitate abolition. This was the position finally incorporated in the Republican party's platform in 1856 and 1860. Garrison, in contrast, condemned both the Constitution and the government it had established as being so influenced by the spirit of slavery and so dominated by slaveholders as to be altogether useless in accomplishing abolition.

Garrison's and Birney's positions seem contradictory, yet in a sense both men were correct—Garrison when he made the self-evident observation that government as it then functioned served to protect slavery; Birney when he pointed out that government had the potential power to limit slavery. Perhaps the shrewdest evaluation of the controversy was offered by Samuel May, Jr., in his common-sense observation that whatever the Constitution's makers may originally have intended, the document in practice could be either pro-slavery or antislavery, "whichever the people pleased to make it." In short, it was the responsibility of the generation then living to end slavery or to preserve it—they need not be governed by strict construction from the grave.[29]

All abolitionists operated from a premise like May's, whether they acknowledged doing so or not; for the goal of all of them was to change public opinion with respect to slavery and the Negro and to mobilize the power of the people to destroy the institution and to change race relations.

In the 1830s and 1840s, "the people" evidently chose to make the Constitution a pro-slavery document. If this situation led one important group of abolitionists to organize a political party, it led others to take the extreme stand of either advocating separation from the South or of rejecting the authority of government altogether. Some, whether willing to use antislavery political action or not, were ready to defy a government that seemed to them totally subservient to slaveholders. Increasing numbers of abolitionists in the 1840s took their stand on the "higher law," the customary refuge of men who find earthly power ranged against them. They recognized the incontrovertible fact that American governments generally were controlled by persons unfriendly to abolition and that laws and judicial decisions supported both slavery and the debasement of Blacks. But, they declared, despite the preponderance of pro-slavery law, there is a higher authority than human government, and there is a law paramount to that made by man; and with these slavery is in total permanent conflict.[30]

For Garrison, this meant that the United States Constitution and the government that operated under it lacked legitimacy. The Constitution, as the Massachusetts Anti-Slavery

Society proclaimed in 1843, was "a covenant with death, and an agreement with hell." [Isaiah 28:28].[31] In effect Garrison accepted Southern claims that the Constitution recognized and protected slavery. The North, he insisted, must break with the Union in order to avoid responsibility for maintaining slavery.

Garrison's antipathy to the Constitution and to the Union certainly was not generally shared by other abolitionists. In particular, it was not shared by those who had decided to use the ballot box as the instrument to free the slaves. Yet alienation from government as it then operated and from the Union as it then was constituted was by no means peculiar to him and his small circle. Such alienation became widely evident in the 1840s.

The operation of the Fugitive Slave Law of 1793 brought significant numbers of Northerners to the point of openly defying the authority and legitimacy of the United States government. Beginning in the early 1840s, a larger number of slaves than ever before made their way into the North. They were aided in their flight by members of their own race and by sympathetic white persons willing to defy a law they rejected as unjust.[32] Inevitably some of the fugitives were captured, and some of their benefactors were tried and convicted of violating federal law. The result, again, was a further growth of abolitionist sentiment. Perhaps more noteworthy is the fact that enforcement of the Fugitive Slave Law contributed to abolitionist militancy.

The reaction in Illinois, following several such incidents in that state in 1842 and 1843, may be taken as typical. Observing the enforcement of the Fugitive Slave Law, the Reverend Owen Lovejoy, younger brother of the murdered abolitionist editor, Elijah P. Lovejoy, denied that the Constitution and the laws made under its authority must in all circumstances be obeyed. "Is the individual swallowed up in the citizen?" he asked. "Is there, must there not be, an ultimate appeal to conscience and the Supreme Court, not of the nation, but of the Universe?" Lovejoy answered the latter question in the affirmative and demonstrated the correctness of his answer, at least for himself, by aiding runaway slaves in defiance of federal law.[33]

Members of a session of the First Presbyterian Church in Chicago in 1843 pledged themselves to "obey God rather than men, when human and divine legislation come into conflict." An abolitionist meeting in Adams County, Illinois, in 1842, resolved that laws and constitutions contrary to the higher law are not morally binding. Persons who feel aggrieved by unjust laws ought to endure them rather than resort to revolution, said the Illinois abolitionists—but only so long as remonstrance and petition may be expected to be effective. Their own patience, they implied, was about to end.[34]

In 1842, the Supreme Court ruled in *Prigg v. Pennsylvania* that the power to legislate with respect to fugitive slaves lay exclusively with Congress, and that all state legislation touching the subject was unconstitutional. Following that decision several Northern states passed "personal liberty laws" denying to the federal government the aid of state authorities and the use of state facilities in enforcing the Fugitive Slave Law. Between 1842 and 1848, Vermont, New Hampshire, Massachusetts, Connecticut, Rhode Island, and Pennsylvania enacted such legislation.[35] To that limited extent those states separated themselves from the national enterprise of maintaining slavery. Limited in effect though they were, the personal liberty laws may be taken as one of the few evidences of tangible abolitionist accomplishment during the decades immediately prior to the Civil War. Abolitionists had succeeded in transforming the indignation produced by slavery and Southern policy into antislavery political action. Yet that victory decreased Southern influence in the national government not at all, and so far as one then could tell did nothing whatever to bring closer the day of emancipation.

Despite plentiful evidence of Northern antagonism toward the slaveholding South, the politically oriented abolitionists, now organized as the Liberty party, attracted only scant support. A Liberty convention once declared that the party's origin lay in "the ordinance of heaven,"[36] but for an organization claiming celestial sanction, earthly accomplishment seemed disproportionately modest.

Notes

1. See Aileen S. Kraditor (*Means and Ends in American Abolitionism; Garrison and His Critics on Strategy and Tactics, 1834–1850* [New York: Pantheon Books, 1969]) for a persuasive exposition of ideological factionalism within the antislavery movement. Lewis Perry, *Radical Abolitionism: Anarchy and the Government of God in Antislavery Thought* (Ithaca: Cornell University Press, 1973), argues that all abolitionist factions were, in essence, exponents of a species of anarchism.
2. Henry B. Stanton, *Random Recollections* (New York: Harper and Brothers, 1887), p. 71; Thomas Wentworth Higginson, *Contemporaries* (Boston: Houghton, Mifflin, 1899), p. 331.
3. For a general survey see Alice Felt Tyler, *Freedom's Ferment* (Minneapolis: University of Minnesota Press, 1944).
4. Angelina Grimké to Henry C. Wright, 27 August 1837, *Weld-Grimké Letters*, I, p. 440.
5. Bertram Wyatt-Brown, *Lewis Tappan and the Evangelical War Against Slavery* (Cleveland: Case Western Reserve University Press, 1969), pp. 185–200.
6. The course of Garrison's radicalization may be followed in Wendell Lloyd Garrison and Francis P. Garrison, *William Lloyd Garrison, 1805–1879; the Story of His Life Told by His Children* (New York: Century, 1885), II, pp. 106–20, and Walter M. Merrill, *Against Wind and Tide; A Biography of Wm. Lloyd Garrison* (Cambridge, Mass: Harvard University Press, 1963), pp. 140, 145–46.
7. *Liberator,* 11 August 1837, Merrill, *Against Wind and Tide,* p. 135.

138   *The Abolitionists*

8. Garrison to Lewis Tappan, 13 September 1837, *The Letters of William Lloyd Garrison,* ed. Louis Ruchames (Cambridge, Mass.: Harvard University Press, 1971), II: 298–300.
9. Theodore Weld to Gerrit Smith, 23 October 1839, *Weld-Grimké Letters,* II, p. 810.
10. Wyatt-Brown, *Lewis Tappan,* pp. 185–200; Merrill, *Against Wind and Tide,* pp. 153–57.
11. *Genius of Universal Emancipation,* 16 (28 June 1839): 19.
12. Garrisons, *Garrison,* II, pp. 321–22.
13. Weld to Lewis Tappan, 3 February 1843, *Weld-Grimké Letters,* II, p. 974.
14. Bayard Tuckerman, *William Jay and the Constitutional Movement for the Abolition of Slavery* (New York: Dodd, Mead, 1893), p. 85.
15. Kraditor, *Means and Ends,* pp. 121–36, 158–61; James B. Stewart, "Aims and Impact of Garrisonian Abolitionism," *Civil War History,* 15 (September 1969), pp. 197–209.
16. Weld to Gerrit Smith, 5 November 1839, *Weld-Grimké Letters,* II, p. 812.
17. *Liberator,* 28 June 1839.
18. Wyatt-Brown, *Lewis Tappan,* pp. 197–99; Garrisons, *Garrison,* II, pp. 120–98, 258–365.
19. *Birney Letters,* I, pp. viii–ix; Gilbert H. Barnes, *The Antislavery Impulse, 1830–1844* (New York: D. Appleton-Century, 1933), pp. 161–67.
20. *Western Citizen,* 30 March 1843; for an account of the movement toward political organization see Dwight Lowell Dumond, *Antislavery: The Crusade for Freedom in America* (Ann Arbor: University of Michigan Press, 1961), pp. 290–97.
21. Early examples may be found in the *Genius of Universal Emancipation,* 3 (November 1823): 70; (March 1824): 131; and Amos A. Phelps, *Lectures on Slavery and Its Remedy* (Boston: New England Anti-Slavery Society, 1834), pp. 192, 195.
22. James B. Stewart, *Joshua R. Giddings and the Tactics of Radical Politics* (Cleveland: Case Western Reserve University Press, 1970), pp. 73–76.
23. Lewis Tappan to Benjamin Tappan, 13 February 1839, Benjamin Tappan Papers (Manuscript Division, Library of Congress).
24. Dumond, *Antislavery,* pp. 290–304.
25. Ralph Volney Harlow, *Gerrit Smith, Philanthropist and Reformer* (New York: Henry Holt, 1939), p. 148; William Goodell, *Slavery and Anti-Slavery; a History of the Great Struggle in Both Hemispheres; With a View of the Slavery Question in the United States* (New York: W. Goodell, 1852), pp. 468–71.

26. Tuckerman, *William Jay,* p. 91.
27. Dumond, *Antislavery,* p. 294; see also James G. Birney to George Benson, 13 June 1838, *Birney Letters,* I, pp. 458–59.
28. Dumond, *Antislavery,* p. 303. For the founding of the Liberty League at Macedon, N.Y., see *National Era,* 24 June 1847. An account of the development of the abolitionists' interpretation of the Constitution is in William Goodell to Gamaliel Bailey, 7 March 1847, ibid., 1 April 1847.
29. For a similar view attributed to John Quincy Adams, see *National Era,* 25 November 1847.
30. "Supremacy of the Divine Law," *Liberty Tree,* 1 (1843): 81–87. An exponent of the Higher Law argued his case thus: "Wicked laws not only may be broken, but absolutely must be broken; there is no other way to escape the wrath of God. It is not optional with men whether they keep such laws or not; to keep them is death, and not to keep them is the way to life." William Hosmer, *The Higher Law in Its Relations to Civil Government: with Particular Reference to Slavery and the Fugitive Slave Law* (Auburn: Derby and Miller, 1852), p. 176.
31. *Liberator,* 3 February 1843; Massachusetts Anti-Slavery Society, *Eleventh Report . . . 1843* (Boston: the Society, 1843), p. 95.
32. Larry Gara, *The Liberty Line: The Legend of the Underground Railroad* (Lexington, Ky.: University of Kentucky Press, 1961), *passim.*
33. *Western Citizen,* 9 December 1842; 3 August and 26 October 1843; *Peoria Register and North-Western Gazetteer,* 13 May 1842.
34. *Western Citizen,* 1 November 1842.
35. Norman L. Rosenberg, "Personal Liberty Laws and the Sectional Crisis: 1850–1861," *Journal of Negro History,* 57 (1971): 25–44.
36. "Minutes," Illinois State Anti-Slavery Society, pp. 156–157.

CHAPTER SEVEN

"No Union with Slaveholders": Radicals Challenge the Status Quo

THE 1840s

The sole plank in the Liberty party's platform in 1840 was opposition to slavery. This single-minded concern no doubt constituted a point of strength in the eyes of moralists; yet a party so austere had slight chance of winning elections because however devoted antislavery voters might be to the abolitionist cause, most of them also were interested in such mundane issues as the tariff, the banking system, and public land policy. A party that took no stand on topics of such pressing concern obviously restricted its vote-getting appeal.

Liberty party spokesmen soon recognized this weakness in their platform and began to make up the deficiency. Allusions to economic issues and to the conflict between what Liberty men called "free labor" and "slave labor" soon began to appear in party orations that previously had digressed little from the single theme of slavery as a moral issue. As abolitionist voters and abolitionist candidates began to explore the effects of slavery on the economic welfare of the North, a subtle change took place in the character of the Liberty party and of the antislavery movement itself.

The severe economic troubles that followed the Panic of 1837 probably encouraged antislavery voters to demand commitments from party candidates on matters other than slavery. Political abolitionists blamed the long depression on slavery. They began to speak of the damaging political encroachments of the "slave power" and of the economic burden slavery placed on free Northern labor. "The immense drains which slavery makes upon us, through the federal government and the credit system, constitute our chief source of pecuniary distress," ran a typical antislavery analysis. In a letter addressed to a Western Liberty party convention in 1842, the New York abolitionist Alvan Stewart was specific in depicting North-South conflict in terms of economic interest. "Slave Labor is the antagonist interest of Free," he explained, "and the *horrible Compromise* [Tariff] *Act* of 1833 made by Calhoun and Clay, under the threats of dissolving the Union, virtually ruined us. . . . [W]e are a ruined and an undone people, by Slavery crushing the Northern Laborer. . . . We lose more than ten millions a year on our wool, and all the public works stand still."[1]

Explanations of the sort put forward by Stewart were persuasive, for they placed the blame for Northern distress on a section and an institution that many persons already condemned as malevolent. Southerners who disregarded the civil rights of both Blacks and Northern Whites naturally would have no regard for the economic welfare of either. Slaveholding aristocrats who garnered wealth from the labor of slaves might be expected also to use their sinister powers to drain away the products of free workers. It was easy to add exploitation of Northern free labor to the long list of the South's crimes. Soon Liberty men across the North were repeating Stewart's analysis and elaborating upon it.

Stewart, Joshua Leavitt, William Goodell—all of New York—and Salmon P. Chase of Ohio were in the forefront of the movement that in the early 1840s united abolitionism with broad economic and political issues. Leavitt, an evangelical abolitionist who had helped found the American Anti-Slavery Society, served on its executive committee, and edited its publications, now turned his enthusiasm toward exposing the economic influence of slavery. In pamphlets and speeches he developed his favorite themes of the

"William Peterson—The Heroic Colored Boy"

"financial power of slavery" and the "political power of slavery" to prove that the South dominated the nation and exploited the North. While slavery through economic processes drained Northern capital into the South, so Leavitt's argument ran, the "Slavocracy" employed its vast political power to stifle the growth of the North's manufactures and agriculture.[2]

It is clear from the prevalence of such economic appeals that the moral crusade against slavery was fusing with new, secular issues, as anti-Southern sentiment in the North found expression in a political movement. Albert G. Riddle, a Northern Ohio politician, observed in 1842 that "a wide and deep" anti-Southern feeling was "silently stealing upon the hearts of our people. . . . Agitate the question of Southern dictation and you see their eyes flash and their faces burn."[3]

The rising political fortunes of such antislavery politicians as Joshua Giddings, Whig representative from Ohio's Western Reserve, were linked with the development of a sense of oppression at the hands of the South. In 1843, Giddings noted the remarkable growth of anti-Southern sentiment in his district. "The truth is," he wrote, "our Northern men are beginning to think of Northern rights and the South must come under."[4] Efforts to suppress civil rights had stimulated that attitude in the 1830s. In the 1840s, economic issues powerfully contributed to it. When in 1846 Congress struck from a river and harbors bill a provision to appropriate money to improve the harbor of Charleston, South Carolina, Giddings was jubilant because, he explained, that act demonstrated "the progress of northern feeling" against the South.[5]

Giddings gained a large reputation among abolitionists for his congressional work in the antislavery cause, but with Giddings, as with many others in those years, it became increasingly difficult to tell whether antislavery conviction reflected a genuine belief that all men should be free or only a hatred and fear of the South for what was conceived to be its threat to Northern interests.

Hostility to slavery on such grounds certainly did not preclude sympathy for the individual slave and for the free Blacks, but neither did it require such sympathy; nor did it bear much relation to a determination to aid them in their struggle for freedom and equality. Liberty party conventions customarily passed resolutions calling for repeal of state laws discriminating against free Negroes, and many individual party members worked devotedly in that cause; yet as antislavery politics gained in favor in the 1840s and 1850s, the issues of slavery and the welfare of Blacks were given less emphasis in party deliberations and campaign oratory than the issue of the encroachments of the "slave power," which was not exactly the same thing.[6]

The extent to which those who followed the new political tack diverged from the method and rationale of the evangelical abolitionists may be gauged by comparing the economically oriented antislavery arguments employed by Stewart and other Liberty men in the early 1840s with Theodore Weld's description of his own techniques of persuasion in the 1830s.

In discussing the subject of slavery, I have always presented it as pre-eminently a *moral* question, arresting the conscience of the nation. . . . As a question of politics and national economy, I have passed it with scarce a look or a word, believing that the business of abolitionists is with the heart of the nation, rather than with its purse strings.[7]

But other arguments than those based on religion and morality had always been available to opponents of slavery, and abolitionists once had used them freely. Especially in the 1820s, before the movement became specifically tied to evangelicalism, they had emphasized the harmful economic effects of slave labor and the dangerous social and political implications of the development of a class of slaveholding aristocrats.[8] Now in the 1840s, as the political influence of slavery became more apparent, that kind of secular appeal again assumed prominence.

As the Liberty party's presidential candidate in 1840 and 1844, James G. Birney inevitably was identified with the secularization of the abolitionist argument and did not hesitate to disclose his own views on all sorts of topics besides slavery. Yet Birney remained a devout morally-directed abolitionist. As such he did not altogether approve the preoccupation of the new party with economic and political issues, for he feared that the moral focus of abolitionism would thereby be lost and the party debased. After the Ohio Liberty Convention of December 1841, Birney noted with evident regret that never before had opposition to slavery been "considered so much a matter of money-policy—so little as a matter of religious duty."[9]

Leaders of the Liberty party and—to an even greater degree—leaders of its successor, the Free Soil party, constantly were tempted to view slavery chiefly as it affected the interests of white men. This obviously was a natural extension of the discovery made in the 1830s that slavery endangered the civil rights of free Northerners. Few antislavery politicians could resist capitalizing on the growing anti-Southernism of Northern voters. However firm their own antislavery convictions may have been, politicians in the 1840s, intent on building a party and securing votes, were tempted to put forward a more moderate and less demanding antislavery doctrine than had been associated with abolitionists of the preceding decade. At the same time the old-line abolitionists in the churches, and the Garrisonians—some of whom supported the Liberty party and some of whom did not—continued their moral agitation unabated and undiluted with secular issues.

The moral reformers and the antislavery politicians constantly quarreled with each other and exchanged vituperative comments. The moralists berated politicians for having descended from the lofty pinnacle of principle and for neglecting the interests of Blacks. The politicians accused moralists of ignoring social realities and of antagonizing potential antislavery voters with their disruptive tactics and radical theories.

But in actuality theirs was only a lovers' quarrel. Discordant as reformers and politicians sometimes seemed to be, the activities of each in practice supported the other. The reformers cherished the antislavery politicians for carrying the slavery issue into arenas to which reformers had no access, and the politicians recognized that without the moralists' relentless agitation, they would have had no constituency. In 1844, Wendell Phillips, the Boston Garrisonian, complained that "as fast as *we* ... make abolitionists, the new converts run right into the Liberty Party, and become almost or wholly hostile to us"—a result, he added, of "the strong leaning of our national character to politics."[10] With understandable pleasure, Giddings noted the same process taking place in Ohio. "You beat the bush," he advised an abolitionist lecturer, "and I will catch the birds."

There was no necessary antagonism between political and nonpolitical abolitionists. Giddings, Charles Sumner, and other antislavery Whig politicians often were invited to attend and take part in abolitionist meetings (even those organized by Garrisonians) in such widely separated places as New England, Ohio, and Michigan. They received the generous congratulations and encouragement of abolitionists—sometimes of Garrison himself—on those occasions when their actions were thought to serve the abolitionist cause.

In August 1848, Garrison explained his own policy toward antislavery politicians in these words: "I feel that great care is demanded of us . . . in giving credit to whom credit is due, and yet in no case ever seeming to be satisfied with it."[11] The Garrisonians welcomed every evidence of the advance of antislavery political power but remained at the same time ever critical of antislavery politicians, insisting always on the most elevated abolitionist standard of performance as the ideal. And since in practical politics this ideal seldom was attained, antislavery politicians repeatedly fell under abolitionist reproach. Abolitionists remained merciless critics of antislavery politicians, never allowing concession or compromise or inconsistency to pass unreproved.

The unacknowledged alliance between political and nonpolitical abolitionists produced only small results in the presidential election of 1840, when Birney polled only a few more than 7,000 votes. But that scanty return was by no means indicative of abolitionist strength. Most abolitionists in 1840 voted according to their accustomed party loyalties, which meant that the majority cast Whig ballots. For most antislavery voters, abolitionism was not the whole of life. In their minds the sphere of morality and the sphere of politics were not precisely coexistent. Such secular matters as the tariff and banking could not be altogether ignored even in the interest of antislavery politics.

Despite the overwhelming defeat of the Liberty party's national ticket, some of its candidates made better showings in local contests. The outstanding example occurred in Massachusetts in 1842, when Samuel Sewall, the Liberty candidate for governor, received 5.4 percent of the votes, enough to throw the election into the state legislature. The Liberty party held the balance of power in the Massachusetts gubernatorial elections of 1843 and 1844, and several times held the balance in various county elections. Henceforth the antislavery, anti-Southern issue played a major role in Massachusetts politics.[12]

Whatever advantages abolitionists may justifiably have expected from William Henry Harrison's election in 1840, they were lost when the new Whig president died after serving only a month in office. He was succeeded by John Tyler from whom not even the most sanguine abolitionist could anticipate anything good. Tyler was a Virginia slaveholder who surrounded himself with Southern advisors. Moreover he was an exponent of narrow, states' rights principles, and he favored annexing Texas. Intent on salvaging something from the Liberty party's defeat in 1840, advocates of independent antislavery political action did not delay in using the unhappy outcome of the election as an object lesson for reluctant antislavery voters: continued bondage to the South was the price of persisting to vote for the old parties or of following the counsel of certain adherents of Garrison and not voting at all.

Shortly after Harrison's death, the Liberty party started preparations for the presidential election of 1844. Antislavery, anti-Southern sentiment continued to grow, causing abolitionist politicians to feel more hopeful of victory than was warranted. The persisting depression, the widespread sympathy aroused for the increasing numbers of fugitive slaves who sought refuge in the North, and the popular outrage when they were captured; the skilled propaganda use abolitionists made of the *Amistad* and *Creole* cases concerning the legal status of mutinous slaves on the high seas; the prolonged controversy over the right of petition— all these contributed to Northern hostility toward slavery and to support for anti-Southern political policies. But such sentiment furnished only 63,200 votes in 1844 for Birney, who again ran on the Liberty Ticket as an avowed abolitionist. The Liberty party campaign had more than ordinary significance, however, for Birney managed to take enough votes in New York from Henry Clay, the Whig candidate, to give that state's thirty-six electoral votes—and the presidency—to the Democrat, James Knox Polk.

Polk's election meant that the Republic of Texas, so long in contention, would at last be annexed to the United States. Polk's election also meant that efforts would be made to expand American territory even farther westward at Mexico's expense. Expansionist spirit in the 1840s was by no means confined to the South. Considerable support for acquiring Texas and California could be found in the North, and some Northerners also aspired to acquire Oregon, a region the United States then occupied jointly with Great Britain.

Robert J. Walker of Mississippi cleverly argued, for the benefit of Northern voters, that the acquisition of Texas would help solve the vexing problems of both slavery and race. Unless slavery could expand, he wrote in a widely circulated pamphlet,[13] it was doomed to early extinction in the states where it then existed. Failure to take Texas would require Southerners to abolish slavery, Walker predicted. Huge numbers of Blacks then would be free to move North, a prospect few Northerners could face without dread. But with Texas in the Union, slavery—and even the black population of the North—would be drawn toward the southwest. Eventually slavery would move south of the Rio Grande (and thus safely out of the United States). Walker had exploited Northern racial anxieties as well as a contorted antislavery sentiment to help create Northern support for the annexation of Texas.

Even though the acquisition of Texas was not altogether a sectional measure, its annexation obviously served the immediate interests of the South and added to Southern political power. Thus abolitionists easily concluded that passage of the congressional resolution to annex Texas in February 1845 was the consequence of pro-slavery influence and that it had been engineered solely from a Southern design.

Opposition to annexing Texas was a stand against slavery, but as in the 1830s when the issue first was prominently raised, it remained also a means of resisting the "slave power's" continued dominance of the Union. Joshua Gid-

dings saw the matter as a question of "*slavery* or *liberty.*"
But since he recognized that those words were abstractions,
he then proceeded to define them in terms of concrete issues. To annex Texas, Giddings explained, would be "to
give the South the preponderance of political power," and
thus "would be itself a surrender of our Tariff, our harbor
improvements, our distribution of the proceeds of the public lands."[14] Southwestward expansion could easily be
viewed as an issue of sectional political power entirely di-
vorced from the morality of slavery and the welfare of
black people.

For more than a decade, abolitionists had campaigned to
prevent the annexation of Texas and with near unanimity
had predicted dire results to follow. Now that the calamity
at last had happened, they understandably regarded it as
the gravest of defeats and as further evidence that slaveholders controlled governmental policy. But the most striking effect of annexation on abolitionists was to foster
disunionist sentiment of the sort Garrison already had
begun to advocate. Repeated abolitionist defeats and frustrations invited extremism in doctrine, rhetoric, and action.[15] It was tempting to believe that institutions were so
thoroughly corrupt as to be beyond the possibility of reformation. The annexation of Texas strengthened certain abolitionists in their conviction that government was utterly
immoral and immune to their influence. Their only recourse was to separate from the slaveholding Union.

Just as "immediate abolition" was the radical slogan of
the 1830s, so "no union with slaveholders" became the abolitionists' slogan in the 1840s. Perhaps few of its proponents
intended it as a political program to be put into effect, but
rather advanced it as another means of forcing citizens to
consider the corrupt state of the nation and to recognize the
chasm that separated American libertarian pretension
from American practice. Disunionism and come-outerism
(the companion policy of separating from anti-abolitionist
churches) resulted from the abolitionists' awareness of
their minority position. The major American institutions

had remained unresponsive to their argument. Since there seemed to be no possibility that the institutions could be reformed, some abolitionists concluded that good men must leave them.

John Greenleaf Whittier, though by 1845 no longer closely associated with Garrison, momentarily shared the disunionist sentiment and the bitterness that Garrison, along with many others, experienced when Texas entered the Union. A stanza from Whittier's poem "Texas" as published in the *Liberator* at that time expressed belligerent disunionism:

Make our Union-bond a chain,
We will snap its links in twain,
We will stand erect again.[16]

But Whittier soon retreated from his radical position, and when the verse appeared in book form a few years later, the lines and sentiment had been altered to become syntactically and poetically ambiguous and thus politically neutral:

Make our Union-bond a chain,
Weak as tow in Freedom's strain
Link by link shall snap in twain.

If Southern dominance continued, the Union would dissolve, Whittier seemed to say, but not from abolitionist initiative.

Only a minority, even of Garrison's loyal followers, espoused disunionism, and whenever its proponents raised the issue in the Garrisonian societies, serious discord almost always resulted. Nonetheless, the slogan was as well publicized in the 1840s and 1850s as "immediatism" had been in the 1830s and with much the same public response. An advocate of disunion invited opposition, even riot, whenever he ventured to speak.[17]

Proponents of the doctrine were generally condemned as dangerous to society. Like many other legislative bodies, the Ohio senate received abolitionist petitions calling for a legislative resolution that would declare the Federal Union dissolved. The select committee to which the petitions were referred issued a report in February 1847 branding the proposal "traitorous and disloyal." As a means of preventing such sedition from taking root in the rising generation, the committee recommended the distribution of a copy of George Washington's Farewell Address to every school district in the state.[18]

The slogan "No union with slaveholders" was on the face of it an expression of nonresistant, pacifistic conviction—one would not fight with evil, but rather would turn away from it. But the slogan had another, bloodier aspect that has frequently been overlooked, although its proponents at the time were fully aware of it. Abolitionists believed that slavery was sustained by the coercive power of the federal government. Remove that power by dissolving the Union and slavery would collapse in a great slave rebellion.[19] The result was expected to be the same whether the Union ended at the insistence of an antislavery North or by Southern initiative. On that account disunionism was regarded as a radical and dangerous proposal quite apart from its blatant conflict with patriotism and nationalism.

The Constitution and the Union, according to the Garrisonians, served as shields for slavery; indeed, slavery was inextricably intertwined with them. The Union had come to assume a value in itself, despite the evil practices that flourished under its aegis. "My country, right or wrong" was a sentiment that evidently found an abundance of defenders in the pre-Civil War era. Thus as a necessary preliminary to the ending of slavery, abolitionists aimed to destroy the near reverence in which both the Constitution and the Union were held.

Southerners looked to the Union and specifically to the Constitution as their main line of defense against abolition and had themselves often threatened to secede if the national government ever should cease to protect slavery. Garrison met the issue head-on. If the Union served to perpetuate slavery, if Southerners found in it a defense for their institutions, then the Union was not worth preserving. Let it be destroyed for the iniquity it was.

Repetition of the slogan "No union with slaveholders" was a means of dramatizing the point John Quincy Adams had made—the national government was thoroughly implicated in the preservation of slavery; or, to use Adams's more pungent words, the Constitution suffered from "the saturation of the parchment with the infection of slavery, which no fumigation could purify, no quarantine could extinguish."[20] If Adams's view of the desperate condition of the nation was accurate, if slavery really was inseparably a part of the United States Constitution, how could reform come, an abolitionist might ask, short of revolution? Despair for the success of the antislavery cause was already being expressed by some persons most closely associated with it. "What the end is to be of our A[nti]-S[lavery] movement it is hard to tell," said Birney in a letter to Lewis Tappan in 1842. "There is no reason for believing that the virtue of our own people would ever throw off Slavery. Slavery has corrupted the whole nation."[21]

The disunionist sentiment of the 1840s, which was scorned as eccentric and irresponsible when voiced by Garrison and his followers, found adherents in men whose repute was of a quite different order. On 3 March 1843, John Quincy Adams and twelve congressmen, including Giddings of Ohio, Seth M. Gates of New York, and William Slade of Vermont, signed a resolution asserting that the annexation of Texas would so violate the national compact as "fully to justify" a dissolution of the Union. Thus informed of Slade's views, Lewis Tappan, an evangelical abolitionist whose sentiments generally placed him far from Garrison's camp, urged Slade to "blow the trumpet" for disunionism in Vermont if Texas should join the Union. Later in the year William Jay, among the most cautious and conservative of the abolitionists and, like Tappan, no sympathizer of Garrison, pledged that if Texas were annexed, then "my voice, my efforts, will be for dissolution."[22]

The Miscegenation Ball

"at the Headquarters of the Lincoln Central Campaign Club, Corner of Broadway and Twenty Third Street New York Sept. 22*d*. 1864 being a perfect fac simile of the room &c. &c (From the New York World Sept. 23*d*. 1864) No sooner were the formal proceedings and speeches hurried through with, than the room was cleared for a 'negro ball,' which then and there took place! Some members of the 'Central Lincoln Club' left the room before the mystical and circling rites of languishing glance and mazy dance

commenced. But that MANY remained is also true. This fact WE CERTIFY, *that on the floor during the progress of the ball were many of the accredited leaders of the Black Republican party,* thus testifying their faith by their works in the hall and headquarters of their political gathering. There were Republican OFFICE-HOLDERS, and prominent men of various degrees, and at least one PRESIDENTIAL ELECTOR ON THE REPUBLICAN TICKET" [This was an attack on the Republican party and assumed race prejudice on the part of the readers.]

Jay remained true to his word. In 1845, when Congress annexed Texas, he declared that the event had changed all the rules of the antislavery contest. Henceforth in the struggle against slavery, Jay asserted that "every possible means not forbidden by the law of God" might be employed, adding that "dissolution must take place, and the sooner the better." Giddings, whose primary realm of action was politics and not agitation, similarly did not repudiate the disunionist resolution he signed in 1843. With the annexation of Texas, he declared, "our Union of 1787 has been entirely dissolved."[23]

The critical difference between the views of such men and those of Garrison was that while Giddings, Jay, and Tappan held that the specific act of adding slave territory had destroyed the Union, Garrison considered the very existence of slavery and the compromises included in the Constitution to be adequate grounds for disunion. Thus Garrison's position was in a sense more extreme than theirs, and he adhered to it more consistently than they did; yet, it would be rash to insist that the difference in their views was fundamental. In effect, all of them held that Southern action had destroyed the comity of the sections. An important group of Americans had become so alienated from prevailing institutions and policies that they advocated the destruction of the Union which made such institutions and policies possible.

A parallel development took place in the churches during the 1840s, as abolitionists began to call upon members to secede from denominational organizations that they deemed pro-slavery. The trend was by no means a new one, nor did it originate with Garrison. Since ancient times, Christians of a certain persuasion had been enjoined to separate from associations they deemed evil rather than attempt to purify them. "Come out from among them, and be ye separate, and touch not the unclean thing," was the Biblical requirement.[24]

Separation from the churches as a remedy for contamination inevitably suggested itself to abolitionists, particularly in the many instances where it was obvious that their minority position allowed them to do nothing to control church policy. In the first years of the nineteenth century, tiny groups of antislavery Baptists in Kentucky broke with their slaveholding brethren to form independent congregations calling themselves "Friends of Humanity." The pattern later was also followed by a few Baptists in Missouri and Illinois. When those obscure antislavery churches came to Benjamin Lundy's attention in the 1820s, he hailed them as an example of purity others should follow. "Come out from among them, come out from among them," he urged in the *Genius of Universal Emancipation.*[25] But there is no record that many church members at that time followed his advice, and probably few abolitionists ever knew of the secessionist experiments of the frontier antislavery Baptists.

In the 1840s the call for *Come-Outerism, the Duty of Secession from a Corrupt Church* (as William Goodell, an organizer of the Liberty party, entitled a pamphlet he wrote on the subject in 1845) began to be heard throughout the North and aroused favorable response from some abolitionists. A number of antislavery leaders, including Beriah Green, Gerrit Smith, and James G. Birney, withdrew from the Presbyterian church and helped organize independent, antislavery congregations. In western New York, a group seceded from the Methodist church, which they considered polluted on account of its Southern membership and its reluctance to condemn slavery, and formed the Wesleyan Methodist Connection under the leadership of Orange Scott, LaRoy Sunderland, and Luther Lee.[26]

In New England the duty of "come-outerism" was promulgated most conspicuously by two eccentrics, Parker Pillsbury and Stephen S. Foster, whose special mode of agitation was to enter churches while regular services were under way and then to interrupt the sermon by delivering their own antislavery lectures from the congregation. They seldom completed their message, for generally either members of the congregation or town authorities closed in to enforce decorum. Since both Foster and Pillsbury were nonresistants, they unprotestingly let themselves be carried or dragged outside and thus silenced.[27]

Most church-oriented communities considered such disruptive conduct scandalous, yet the outrageous actions of these men helped dramatize their indignation over the fact that a respected church filled with respected people failed to concern itself in any effective way with what they regarded as the nation's overriding sin. According to Garrison, the come-outers were led to resort to crude, disruptive methods—to use "a lamb's horn instead of a silver trumpet," as he described it, "because thus only could the walls of our slaveholding Jericho be shaken to their overthrow." Only in some such striking manner as the one they employed could complacency be moved, abolitionists believed, and the hypocrisy of the majority's conventional values and behavior be exposed.

Come-outerism sometimes was mistakenly thought to be a peculiarly New England phenomenon, perhaps because of the notoriety of such New Englanders as Foster and Pillsbury. But in fact it moved across the Hudson and spread far into the West. At a large regional meeting of antislavery churchmen at Cincinnati, Ohio, in 1850, the delegates passed a resolution submitted by the Reverend John G. Fee, a Lane Seminary graduate whose uncomfortable assignment was to head the American Missionary Association's agency in slaveholding Kentucky, advising abolitionists to separate from churches that admitted slaveholders. One of the strongest endorsements for Fee's motion came from southern-born John Rankin of Ripley, Ohio, whose abolitionist and underground railroad activities dated from the 1820s. Rankin had already put his own secessionist principles into effect. By 1850 he was pastor of a congregation of the antislavery Free Presbyterian church, a schismatic denomination he had helped organize a few years earlier.[28]

The intersectional schisms that occurred in the Presbyterian, Methodist, and Baptist churches beginning in 1837 were precipitated in large part by issues growing out of slavery and reflected the institutional tensions produced by abolitionist agitation. But even though these several divisions in the churches rid their Northern branches of slaveholding members, they did not transform them into abolitionist agencies, a goal of reformers since 1830. Abolitionists had intended to use the churches as the institutions for regenerating or—as a later generation might have said—revolutionizing American society. But the churches for the most part remained unresponsive, and the effort failed. Abolitionists might have agreed by 1850 that trying to change society through the church was, as Barrington Moore, Jr., has written in another connection, "like trying to pry up a stump with a bamboo crowbar."[29]

The despair certain abolitionists came to feel for the churches therefore was understandable. All rational and religious appeals had been inadequate to persuade them, as institutions, to take abolitionist positions. Indeed, abolitionists still sometimes encountered overt clerical opposition. In the 1840s especially, a number of prominent and influential churchmen wrote books and delivered sermons specifically designed to counter the abolitionist argument that Christians were personally responsible for the existence of slavery, and these same men used their influence to prevent their churches from endorsing abolitionism.

Some non-Garrisonian abolitionists found it as difficult to accept the implications of ecclesiastical opposition as they did to accept what Garrison conceived to be the pro-slavery character of political institutions. Conservative social pressures made it difficult to proclaim oneself either a disunionist or a come-outer. Yet the Garrisonian critique of clergymen and churches was echoed by persons whose abolitionism bordered on the respectable: by the non-Garrisonian Reverend Albert Barnes, a Presbyterian who had been tried by his church for heresy, and by James G. Birney, whose exposé of organized religion appeared in 1840 in his pamphlet *The American Churches, the Bulwarks of American Slavery.*

Dissatisfaction with orthodox religion and conventional forms of worship became common even among abolitionists who did not dramatically break with their churches. A number of leading figures in the antislavery movement simply drifted away from the churches in the 1840s and 1850s. Besides Garrison, Henry C. Wright, and others of their circle whose "infidelity" became scandalous, the company of abolitionist apostates from orthodoxy included Birney, Gerrit Smith, and Theodore Weld and his wife, Angelina. These abolitionists moved from the traditional religious position of their youth towards the acceptance of a diffuse and non-institutional religion of humanity. Orthodox religious ideas and conventional forms of worship seemed to them sterile and inadequate to meet their spiritual needs. Perhaps the experience of Daniel Howell Hise, an obscure abolitionist of Salem, Ohio, may be taken as typical. Hise recorded in his diary in the 1850s the fact that he had attended the Methodist church only twice in seventeen years. The second—and last—time that he went, he left the service after only ten minutes, finding the spiritual fare, as he said, "rather thin feed for Souls as hungry as mine."[30]

All those persons, like Hise, who for years watched the churches and the national government resist abolitionist influence had little cause for surprise when President James K. Polk in May 1846 sent Congress his request for a declaration of war against Mexico. Accustomed as they were to expect the worst from a government they pictured as a corrupt instrument of slaveholding power, their reaction was predictable. The war with Mexico contributed further to abolitionist alienation and to their questioning of American motives and pretensions to rectitude. Perhaps Whittier most vividly captured the hypocrisy abolitionists discerned in the Mexican adventure: "Christian America," he wrote, "thanking God that she is not like other nations, ... goes out, Bible in hand, to enslave the world."[31]

Whatever degree of nationalistic fervor the war spirit momentarily generated, it did nothing to allay the disunionist sentiment proclaimed by the Garrisonians. Frederick Douglass, the black abolitionist, depicted the war as a natural consequence of slavery and as further proof that the Union must be dissolved. "This is but another link around your necks of the galling chain which your fathers placed about the heels of my race," he told New Englanders. "It is the legitimate fruit of compromise—of attempting a union of freedom with slavery. All was lost in that sad moment." The Union must end, he added, else New England would be "lost and swallowed up by the slave-power of the country."[32]

Abolitionists saw the war as the means chosen by the Polk administration to protect and extend slavery. A Southern-dominated government, they believed, had committed all Americans against their will and interest to a war of aggression that could benefit only the South. At the same time, Polk accepted a settlement of the northwestern border dispute with Great Britain that placed the United States boundary with Canada far to the south of the original claim.[33] Once again, it could reasonably be charged, the welfare of the North and of free labor had been sacrificed to the interests of an aggressive "Slavocracy."

It was circumstances such as these that allowed Charles Francis Adams, an antislavery or "conscience" Whig, to write easily in 1847 of the "slave domination of the last twenty years," that is, of the period since his father left the presidency.[34] Events other than the admission of Texas and the war with Mexico made Adams's view of the nation's recent past seem plausible. The Tariff of 1842, which had modestly raised rates for the benefit of certain Northern interests, was supplanted in 1846 by the Walker tariff, which lowered them. At the same time, on grounds of economy, Polk vetoed a river and harbor bill that had been designed to placate portions of the North by its generous allocations of money for improvements in certain strategic areas. The President found money lacking for Northern domestic improvements; yet he did not hesitate to request war funds in abundance for the purpose, abolitionists charged, of extending the limits of slavery. A great river and harbor convention attended by some ten thousand persons met at Chicago in the summer of 1847 to protest these events.[35]

As the war with Mexico raged on, the conviction grew among political abolitionists that no antislavery measures and no measures beneficial to the North could be anticipated from any political party which felt itself dependent on Southern votes. Northern Democrats, in particular, suffered from being associated with what was widely regarded as a slaveholders' war. It was largely to demonstrate to the growing numbers of anti-Southern, antislavery voters that their party was not waging war to expand slavery that a group of Northern Democratic congressmen in 1846 sponsored David Wilmot's Proviso.[36] Wilmot's amendment to a military appropriation bill specified that no territory acquired as a result of the Mexican War should be open to slavery. If the measure had been adopted, the war probably would have lost much of its support in the South and would, to some extent, have been redeemed in the eyes of antislavery Northerners. But the much-debated proviso, although approved a number of times in the House, could never pass the Senate. And abolitionists remained convinced that the war formed part of a slaveholders' conspiracy to spread slavery and to increase Southern power.

A number of important Northern literary figures, most of them Whiggish in sentiment, echoed the abolitionist charge. Henry David Thoreau, moved by both antislavery and peace principles, protested the war by refusing to pay his state poll tax; he spent a night in jail in consequence. Ralph Waldo Emerson spoke against the war, yet he eventually relinquished the role of advocate for that of philosopher. As though from an Olympian height, he concluded that Anglo-Saxons were destined to overrun both Mexico and the Oregon country, "and it will be of small import by what particular occasions and methods it was done." Some questions, he observed, "look very differently to the centuries and to the years."[37] James Russell Lowell had no such second thoughts. Throughout the war he worked in the interests of its opponents through his "Biglow Papers," a series of antislavery writings that allied him solidly with the abolitionists in their hostility to the war with Mexico.[38]

Garrisonians characteristically took advanced anti-war stands. By so doing they encountered the Administration's extreme displeasure. A few of Polk's supporters followed the President's lead in charging critics of United States foreign policy with prolonging the war and giving "aid and comfort to the enemy."[39] Perhaps a few abolitionists were intimidated by the implied threat that they might be indicted for treason, but others demonstrably were not. Stephen S. Foster, speaking before the New Hampshire Anti-Slavery Society in 1846, explained that "there was a wide difference between treason to the country, and treason to the government. Treason to the government may be a duty. Such is the case now." Then he added a characteristically outrageous afterthought. "Every true friend of his country," said Foster, " . . . will be found fighting in defense of freedom—under the banners of Mexico."[40] Senator Thomas Corwin, former governor of Ohio, did not go quite so far as Foster, yet to the consternation of the conventionally patriotic, he too expressed sympathy for the beleagured Mexicans, remarking in the Senate on 11 February 1847, that if he were a citizen of Mexico, he would greet the invading Americans "with bloody hands" and welcome them "to hospitable graves."[41]

Abolitionist opposition may have reached its peak at the anniversary meeting of the Massachusetts Anti-Slavery Society in 1846. There Garrison introduced a resolution "that all who participate in this war, or who give it any countenance, are the enemies of the country, and traitors to liberty and . . . that the American troops, now occupying Mexican soil, ought immediately to be withdrawn, and full reparation made to Mexico." The Reverend William H. Channing offered a resolution "denying the existence of any lawful government of the United States, of any Union, of any obligation of allegiance or countenance, to either, and pledging ourselves to give no aid or support to the Mexican war."

Supporting speeches were made by the black orator, Charles L. Remond, and by Theodore Parker, the controversial Boston Unitarian.[42]

"This war has given additional excitement to the fanaticism of Abolition," wrote Fitzwilliam Byrdsall of New York to John C. Calhoun in 1847. Byrdsall was not mistaken in believing that the war stimulated antislavery sentiment. The Iowa Anti-Slavery Society resolved in November 1846 that it could "never expect our government will be well administered, and the highest good of the whole nation sought by those in power, while slavery exists." That sentiment seemed mild indeed when compared with statements voiced in regions where abolitionism was more highly developed than in Iowa. An antislavery convention in Ashtabula County, Ohio, on 7 May 1847, resolved that those who started the war "for the purpose of subjecting us to the slave power" were "traitors to the free States and enemies to the inalienable rights of man."[43]

"Is it not the great business of this country to take care of slavery,—to pay its bills, to fight its battles, and generally to do its scavenger work?" was Owen Lovejoy's scathing question as he observed Polk's conduct of the war with Mexico. It was a war "legitimately growing out of the twenty years' plottings of our southern masters," asserted the (Chicago) *Western Citizen,* Zebina Eastman's politically oriented newspaper.[44]

But while even humble and obscure men and women in the North came to scorn the military expedition against Mexico as "Mr. Polk's War," they did not generally repudiate its results, anymore than Emerson had done, nor did they reject the politicians who supported it. In their morally inspired opposition to the war as in nearly all other respects, abolitionists remained a minority. Indeed, among an important segment of the voters opposition to the war on the part of politicians was never quite forgotten nor forgiven. In their eyes, unpatriotic refusal to support martial enterprises could not be altogether excused. If the war with Mexico came to be unpopular in the North, its severest critics were unpopular too. Stephen A. Douglas, for instance, during the Illinois senatorial campaign of 1858, more than a decade after the war ended, thought it useful to remind voters that his opponent, Abraham Lincoln, had criticized the war and had questioned Polk's explanation of its origins. The charge probably cost Lincoln votes, especially in southern Illinois, where the war had been generally favored.[45]

With slavery and the North-South conflict receiving expanded attention because of the Mexican War, Lewis Tappan decided the time had come to establish an antislavery newspaper in Washington, where it could help coordinate antislavery sentiment and action among government officials. Gamaliel Bailey, whom Tappan regarded as "discreet," was brought from Cincinnati, where he had edited the antislavery *Philanthropist,* to take charge of the new publication.[46] The first issue of the *National Era* appeared on 7 January 1847.

Some abolitionists distrusted Bailey, believing him much too moderate for so strategic a post. The antislavery movement had become so widespread and in the process so fragmented that it was unlikely there would be general agreement on the wisdom of Bailey's editorial policy. The *National Era* especially served the interest of the political wing of the movement. It opposed legal discriminations against Blacks and advocated the end of prejudice. Although a close search of the newspaper reveals statements suggesting a certain ambivalence on Bailey's part toward Negroes, the general tone of the publication was abolitionist rather than merely anti-Southern.[47]

Bailey's political antislavery demands were modest and restrained: The ending of slavery in the District of Columbia and adoption of the Wilmot Proviso. A number of politically oriented abolitionists by that time had advanced much further. They no longer were calling merely for the containment of slavery but for its destruction by constitutional means. That doctrine was encouraged by *The Unconstitutionality of Slavery,* a pamphlet published by

Lysander Spooner, a Massachusetts lawyer, in 1845. Spooner claimed that in order to be valid, manmade laws must coincide with the higher law and must embody natural rights. His argument imposed on Congress the duty to abolish slavery even within the slave states. By 1845, Birney also had progressed beyond his earlier states' rights view of slavery. He now reasoned that slavery could not lawfully exist in any state added to the Union since the Constitution was ratified.[48]

While the eastern Liberty party leadership persisted in its one-plank idea and seemed to become less resolute as to how even that idea was to be implemented, the party splintered. Its feeble numbers led it to seek to be a balance-of-power pressure group, rather than a permanent party. A New York faction, dissatisfied with that tactic, formed the Liberty League at Macedon Lock, New York, under the leadership of William Goodell and Gerrit Smith, and nominated Smith and Elihu Burritt, the peace advocate, as candidates for the presidential election of 1848. Its planks calling for extremely strict limits on governmental functions proved more attractive to Democrats than to Whigs. To an increasing extent, antislavery politics were becoming a concern of men in both parties.[49]

Victory in the war with Mexico created new political opportunities for antislavery forces. The success of American arms brought with it the near certainty of heightened intersectional strife. In a relatively short and easy war, the nation acquired the west coast with its coveted harbors as well as a vast extent of new territory directly in the path of Southern expansion. Mexican claims north of the Rio Grande and the threat of British influence were swept away. The United States now reached from sea to sea; its mastery of the continent henceforth would be unchallenged. But in that imperial achievement lay the likelihood of national destruction; for there now seemed no way to evade direct confrontation with the highly divisive issue of the status of slavery in the new territory.

Did Congress have authority to determine whether or not slavery might exist in the territory acquired from Mexico? On the answer to this question hinged the future of the West as well as the relative strength of North and South within the Union. The stakes were so high that each faction was willing to risk everything for victory. Yet the explosive force of the issue led leaders of both political parties to evade it in the presidential campaign of 1848. The Democrats nominated Lewis Cass, who ran on a platform that ignored slavery altogether. The Whigs hoped to rise above partisanship by nominating the popular war hero General Zachary Taylor.

But party harmony, like national tranquility, was too trivial a goal to satisfy antislavery Democrats (known in New York and New England as Barnburners) and antislavery Whigs (known as Conscience Whigs, in contrast with Cotton Whigs). At a convention held at Buffalo in August 1848, these two groups joined with various antislavery leaders to form the Free Soil party with the slogan "Free Soil, Free Speech, Free Labor, and Free Men." They named as their presidential candidate Martin Van Buren, once an object of antislavery scorn but now restored to favor because of his stand against the annexation of Texas.[50]

The new party was not an abolitionist organization and resisted being identified as one; yet it received support from a number of leading figures in the antislavery movement. Joshua Leavitt and Henry B. Stanton, both of whom possessed unassailable credentials as full-fledged abolitionists gave the movement full backing. Even Garrison, who had renounced participation in party politics, welcomed the Free Soil movement "as the beginning of the end of slavery." All but ignored in the ensuing campaign were the Liberty League and its radical candidate, Gerrit Smith.

The Free Soil party aimed to separate the national government from slavery, to keep slavery solely a state institution, and to confine it to the limits it then occupied. To that extent, the party's goal was similar to that of many abolitionists. The abolitionist principle most conspicuously lacking in the Free Soil party was any strong commitment to equal rights for Negroes.

In general, the new party emphasized the needs and interests of free, white labor. The Barnburner element in the party, true to its Democratic origins, insisted on omitting any call for equal rights for Negroes from the platform in 1848. The party platform was constructed so as to endorse the lowest common denominator of antislavery sentiment —the containment of slavery. In some states the party went much further, however, and certain individual Free Soilers, such as Charles Francis Adams, John G. Palfrey, and Henry Wilson—all of Massachusetts—were noted as champions of equal rights. In Ohio Free Soilers secured the balance of power in the legislature and as the price of cooperation, required the repeal of some of the state's restrictive Black Laws. The party even advocated Negro suffrage in Ohio, although this was not achieved. But the Ohio branch of the party also contained persons who favored rigid separation of the races and advocated "internal colonization," a project to set aside a portion of the public lands exclusively for Blacks. Free Soilers in Illinois favoring a similar project suggested that Illinois Negroes would be well advised to move far to the North into sparsely settled Osceola County, Michigan. Black leaders such as Frederick Douglass were as quick to oppose such suggestions as were white abolitionists.[51]

In Massachusetts, to a greater extent than elsewhere, the party was dominated by an abolitionist, equalitarian spirit. Some of its leaders there had long worked to eradicate racial prejudice and discriminatory practices. Charles Francis Adams (the party's candidate for vice-president in 1848), John G. Palfrey, and Henry Wilson had earlier demonstrated their egalitarianism by opposing Massachusetts' laws banning racial intermarriage and helping secure their repeal in 1843. Adams had led a campaign against segregation on railway cars. All three opposed the exclusion of Blacks from the militia and worked against segregated schools in Boston. Such schools were outlawed in 1855.

The issues of slavery and race, as presented by the Free Soil party, attracted only a minority of voters, however. The political antislavery forces were shattered by their sharp defeat in 1848 at the hands of the Whigs, and might have succumbed had it not been for the Compromise of 1850.

Rivalry for control of the territory won from Mexico enflamed passions in both sections. As a consequence, all outstanding issues between North and South were exacerbated. Southern politicians seemed about to lead their states out of the Union. The nation stood at the brink of dissolution, a fate some abolitionists could not regret. The necessity for adjusting sectional disputes if the Union were to be held together led Senator Stephen A. Douglas to exercise all his political skills and aroused the "Great Compromiser," Henry Clay, to the last important legislative effort of his long career. After long debate and intricate political maneuver, Congress admitted California as a free state and fixed the western boundary of Texas at the 103rd meridian. Texas received ten million dollars for giving up her claims to part of New Mexico. Two new territories, Utah and New Mexico, were created, with the provision that the question of slavery be left for the people of those territories to decide at the time they made state constitutions. Slave trading was prohibited in the District of Columbia, and the Fugitive Slave Law of 1793 was amended to include a number of new, more stringent provisions.

Once more, as in 1820 and 1833, the Union had been saved. In the Compromise of 1850, presumably, the politicians had resolved all outstanding issues between the sections and enabled the nation to continue its development undisturbed by turmoil over the slavery question. But politicians had been wrong before in assessing their capacity to allay the inflammatory passions produced by slavery. They might be wrong again. This time it was slaves themselves who destroyed the politicians' hopes for serenity.

Notes

1. *Western Citizen,* 26 July 1842.
2. Julian P. Bretz, "The Economic Background of the Liberty Party," *American Historical Review,* 34 (January 1929): 250–64.
3. Albert G. Riddle to Joshua Giddings, 7 June 1842, Papers of Joshua Giddings (Ohio Historical Society, Columbus); see Larry Gara, "Slavery and the Slave Power: A Crucial Distinction," *Civil War History,* 15 (March 1969): 4–18.
4. Joshua Giddings to Comfort Giddings, 25 December 1843, Giddings Papers.
5. Giddings to Joseph A. Giddings, 21 March 1846, ibid.
6. "There is no real question now before the country, except as to the Slave Power." Charles Sumner to Salmon P. Chase, 12 December 1846, Chase Papers (Library of Congress).
7. Theodore Weld to J. F. Robinson, 1 May 1836, *Weld-Grimké Papers,* I, p. 297.
8. *Genius of Universal Emancipation,* 1 (January 1822): 102–3; 2 (July 1822): 11–13; *Edwardsville Spectator,* 6 September 1823; Morris Birkbeck, *An Appeal to the People of Illinois on the Question of a Convention* (Shawneetown, Ill.: C. Jones, 1823), p. 10.
9. Birney to Salmon P. Chase, 2 February 1842, *Birney Letters,* II, p. 670.
10. Phillips to Elizabeth Pease, April 1844, Wendell Lloyd Garrison and Francis P. Garrison, *William Lloyd Garrison, 1805–1879; the Story of His Life Told by His Children* (New York: Century, 1885), III, p. 233n. The abolitionist-politician alliance is a chief theme of James B. Stewart, *Joshua R. Giddings and the Tactics of Radical Politics* (Cleveland: Case Western Reserve University Press, 1970). But sometimes the reverse process occurred.

See the complaint that under the influence of Garrisonian lecturers in northern Ohio "the whole Liberty force has gone over to Disunionism." Russell Errett to Salmon P. Chase, 9 May 1846, Chase Papers (Library of Congress). For a similar report from western New York see Aaron Powell to Samuel May, Jr., *Liberator,* 25 January 1856.

11. Garrison to Edmund Quincy, Garrisons, *Garrison,* III, p. 235.
12. Kinley J. Brauer, *Cotton Versus Conscience: Massachusetts Whig Politics and Southwestern Expansion, 1843–1848* (Lexington, Ky.: University of Kentucky Press, 1967), p. 22.
13. Robert J. Walker, *Letter of Mr. Walker of Mississippi Relative to the Re-annexation of Texas* (St. Louis: Missourian office, 1844).
14. Giddings to Joseph A. Giddings, 28 April 1844, Giddings Papers.
15. James B. Stewart, "Peaceful Hopes and Violent Experiences; the Evolution of Reforming and Radical Abolitionism, 1831–1837," *Civil War History,* 17 (December 1971): 293–309.
16. *Liberator,* 19 April 1844; Whittier regarded the Liberty party as the result of political come-outerism and defended it on that ground. *National Era,* 20 May 1847.
17. "I don't think we shall have a mob, unless the dissolution of the Union is broached; if it is, we unquestionably shall." Lydia Maria Child to Ellis Gray Loring, 6 May 1842, Lydia Maria Child Papers (William L. Clements Library, Ann Arbor). Apparently some abolitionists were urging northern secession as early as the mid-1830s. See Catherine Beecher, *An Essay on Slavery and Abolitionism, with Reference to the Duty of American Females* (Philadelphia: Perkins, 1837), pp. 140–41.
18. Massachusetts Anti-Slavery Society, *Sixteenth Annual Report ... 1848* (Boston: the Society, 1848), pp. 21–22; Ohio, Senate, *Senate Journal,* 54th General Assembly, 1st sess., 1846–1847, Appendix, pp. 307–8.
19. Robert H. Abzug, "The Influence of Garrisonian Abolitionists' Fears of Slave Violence on the Antislavery Argument, 1829–1840," *Journal of Negro History,* 55 (January 1970): 14–28; see also John Quincy Adams's prediction of 29 November 1820, *Memoirs of John Quincy Adams* (Philadelphia: J. B. Lippincott, 1874–1877), V: 210; Garrison to editor of *Boston Courier,* 11 August 1828, in *Letters of William Lloyd Garrison,* ed. Walter Merrill (Cambridge, Mass.: Harvard University Press, 1971), I: 65; Carleton Mabee, *Black Freedom; the Nonviolent Abolitionists from 1830 through the Civil War* (New York: Macmillan, 1970), p. 249.
20. Quoted in George W. Julian, *Speeches on Political Questions, 1850–1871* (New York: Hurd and Houghton, 1872), p. 157.

172 *The Abolitionists*

21. Birney to Lewis Tappan, 14 January 1842, *Birney Letters,* II, p. 658.
22. *National Intelligencer,* 3 March 1843; William Jay to *Liberty Press,* 21 October 1843, *British and Foreign Anti-Slavery Reporter,* 27 December 1843, p. 240.
23. Giddings to "Gentlemen," 3 June 1846, *Liberator,* 31 July 1846.
24. For an account of come-outerism see Thomas, *Liberator,* pp. 318–23.
25. *Genius of Universal Emancipation,* 2 (February 1823): 114.
26. William Goodell, *Slavery and Anti-Slavery; a History of the Great Struggle in Both Hemispheres; With a View of the Slavery Question in the United States* (New York: W. Goodell, 1852), pp. 489–90; Donald G. Mathews, "Orange Scott: The Methodist Evangelist as Revolutionary," in *The Antislavery Vanguard: New Essays on the Abolitionists,* ed. Martin Duberman (Princeton: Princeton University Press, 1965): 71–101. William Jay argued forcefully against efforts to break up the churches. Jay to S. P. Chase, 30 May 1846, Salmon P. Chase Papers (Philadelphia: Historical Society of Pennsylvania).
27. Mabee, *Black Freedom,* pp. 205–43.
28. *Minutes of the Christian Anti-Slavery Convention Assembled April 17th–20th, 1850, Cincinnati, Ohio* (Cincinnati: B. Franklin, 1850), pp. 15–16, 19, 84.
29. "On Rational Inquiry in Universities Today," *New York Review of Books,* 14 (23 April 1970): 33.
30. Lewis E. Atherton, "Daniel Hise, Abolitionist and Reformer," *Mississippi Valley Historical Review,* 26 (1939): 356.
31. John Greenleaf Whittier to "Dear Friend," 13 June 1846, *Western Citizen,* 7 July 1846.
32. Frederick Douglass to the Lynn Anti-Slavery Sewing Circle, 18 August 1846, in *Life and Writings of Frederick Douglass,* ed. Philip S. Foner (New York: International Publishers, 1950), I: 188.
33. A comprehensive account of the diplomacy of the period may be found in David M. Pletcher, *The Diplomacy of Annexation; Texas, Oregon, and the Mexican War* (Columbia: University of Missouri Press, 1973).
34. Adams to Joshua Giddings, 27 January 1847, Giddings Papers.
35. *Western Citizen,* 13 July 1847; Mentor L. Williams, "The Chicago River and Harbor Convention, 1847," *Mississippi Valley Historical Review,* 35 (March 1949): 607–26. The convention's purpose, according to one partisan, was "to deliberate on the interests of this young Empire; interests which have been wantonly sacrificed, by the hair-splitting abstractions, of the Southern politicians." S. Lisle Smith and others to Daniel Web-

ster, 12 May 1847, The Papers of Daniel Webster (microfilm edition).

36. Eric Foner, "The Wilmot Proviso Revisited," *Journal of American History,* 56 (September 1969): 262–79.

37. *Journals of Ralph Waldo Emerson, 1841–1849,* ed. Edward Waldo Emerson and Waldo Emerson Forbes (Boston: Houghton Mifflin, 1909–1914), VI: 494–95.

38. James Russell Lowell, *The Biglow Papers* (Boston: Houghton, Mifflin, 1885). The verses appeared periodically during the war in the *Boston Courier.*

39. James D. Richardson, ed., *A Compilation of the Messages and Papers of the Presidents* (Washington, D.C.: Government Printing Office, 1896), IV: 473; see also U.S., Congress, *Congressional Globe,* 29th Cong., 1st sess., pp. 837, 879, 880.

40. *Liberator,* 12 June 1846.

41. U.S., Congress, *Congressional Globe,* 29th Cong., 2d sess., Appendix, pp. 237–46.

42. Massachusetts Anti-Slavery Society, *Fifteenth Annual Report . . . 1847* (Boston: the Society, 1847), p. 93.

43. Byrdsall to John C. Calhoun, 19 July 1847, in *Correspondence of John C. Calhoun, Annual Report of the American Historical Association for 1899,* ed. J. Franklin Jameson (Washington D.C.: Government Printing Office, 1900), II: 1121; *Western Citizen,* 22 December 1846; *National Era,* 10 June 1847.

44. *Western Citizen,* 23 June 1846.

45. Benjamin Thomas, *Abraham Lincoln, a Biography* (New York: Alfred A. Knopf, 1952), p. 189.

46. Bertram Wyatt-Brown, *Lewis Tappan and the Evangelical War Against Slavery* (Cleveland: Case Western Reserve University Press, 1969), p. 279; see also Tappan to Salmon P. Chase, 9 March 1846, Chase Papers (Historical Society of Pennsylvania).

47. Louis Filler, *The Crusade Against Slavery, 1830–1860* (New York: Harper Brothers, 1960), p. 194.

48. On Birney's constitutional ideas see Betty Fladeland, *James G. Birney, from Slaveholder to Abolitionist* (Ithaca: Cornell University Press, 1955), p. 288.

49. Goodell, *Slavery and Anti-Slavery,* p. 475.

50. Eric Foner, *Free Soil, Free Labor, Free Men: The Ideology of the Republican Party Before the Civil War* (New York: Oxford University Press, 1970), pp. 124–25; Frederick J. Blue, *The Free Soilers: Third Party Politics, 1848–1854* (Urbana: University of Illinois Press, 1973), pp. 44–48.

51. Eric Foner, "Politics and Prejudice: The Free Soil Party and the Negro, 1849–1852," *Journal of Negro History,* 50 (October 1965): 232–56; *Western Citizen,* 27 October 1846.

CHAPTER EIGHT

Fugitive Slaves Force The Issue

THE 1850s

Politicians who arranged the Compromise of 1850 promised that the new measures would restore intersectional harmony and assure lasting peace. Time proved them poor prophets, for although the compromise may have lessened discord for a little while, the calm was short-lived. The complex political arrangement settled no fundamental issue, and signs were abundant that the nation teetered on the brink of dissolution after its passage, just as it had done before.

For abolitionists, as for advocates of Southern rights, the tactic of compromise itself had become reprehensible. Abolitionists condemned the new legislation as being the latest and most shameful in a line of pro-slavery concessions that reached back to the original compromises made by the Founding Fathers in the Constitutional Convention of 1787.

They reserved their special reprobation for the new Fugitive Slave Law, passed as an amendment to the Fugitive Slave Act of 1793. Its primary purpose was to placate a South outraged by the growing Northern reluctance to allow the recovery of runaway slaves. Abolitionists had always opposed the constitutional requirement to return fugitives, and there always had been some men in the North —Whites and free Blacks alike—willing to violate the law in the interest of humanity. In the 1840s, as sectional antipathies mounted, it became apparent that increasing numbers of Northerners flouted their constitutional duty with respect to fugitive slaves. The personal liberty laws, enacted by several Northern states during that decade, institutionalized popular hostility to the activities of slave catchers and, in effect, proclaimed the common belief that slaves had every right to flee from their masters. Nothing could have been more offensive to slaveowners. To their distress, larger numbers of slaves did flee in the 1840s and did receive aid in the North. While much of the aid was surreptitiously given, a few escapes were accompanied by widespread publicity. On such occasions, the antislavery press acclaimed both the fugitives and their abettors as heroes. Southern pride, as well as Southern material interest, suffered in consequence. Something must be done, Southern politicians insisted, to force the North to abide by its constitutional responsibilities. The new Fugitive Slave Law was thus as much an assertion of Southern power and dominance within the nation as it was an effort to facilitate the recovery of valuable property. Northerners would find it particularly offensive for that reason.[1]

In carrying out its purposes, the law of 1850 used means more objectionable to abolitionists than the law of 1793. Citizens now were required to help apprehend fugitives, and severe penalties were imposed on persons who aided slaves to escape. Still unavailable to the alleged fugitive were the legal devices that traditionally protect the accused from false arrest, among them the right to call witnesses in one's own behalf, trial by jury, and writs of habeas corpus. Thus, under the law of 1850, even a free person might find himself defenseless against attempts to enslave him. In such circumstances it was not surprising that a considerable number of Negroes who had been living in Northern states fled to Canada as soon as they became aware of the peril in which the new law placed them.

For some time, many abolitionists had recognized a moral and humanitarian obligation to aid fugitives, irre-

The Destruction of Abolitionist Presses

spective of legal provisions, and, as we have seen, had risked imprisonment in order to carry out a responsibility they believed paramount to the demands of legislation. Passage of the new Fugitive Slave Law added to their numbers. So flagrant was its disregard for accepted standards of justice and legal procedure that even some Northerners who had never protested the existence of slavery were inclined to join abolitionists in denouncing it.

The new law also aroused longstanding states' rights sentiment among Northerners, especially in the Old Northwest. Fears of centralized authority were not peculiar to the South. Northerners, too, dreaded the consequence of a strong national authority that might transgress state prerogatives and trample the rights of individuals. The new law did both. Its grant of power to the national government was the more objectionable because it appeared to be exercised at the behest of the South. By achieving their demands for legislation to secure their economic interests and to assert their authority, Southerners had created still more anti-Southern feeling in the North.

The law at once provided a new rallying point for abolitionists of every persuasion. The Garrisonians, who had long made a cult of the demands of individual conscience, were quick to denounce the law and defy it, but other antislavery men also joined the clamor. The differences that had nearly estranged them momentarily disappeared as political antislavery men, evangelicals, nonresistants, members of the American Anti-Slavery Society and of its rival, the American and Foreign Anti-Slavery Society, all agreed on the law's iniquity and the necessity to resist it.

In its report for 1851, the American and Foreign Anti-Slavery Society observed that "the power of sympathy is an essential element in every moral enterprise."[2] Fugitive slaves at an early date had demonstrated their usefulness in arousing sympathetic concern. The appearance of one fugitive in a community could contribute more to arousing opposition to slavery than dozens of lectures on the abstract evils of the institution. Those abolitionist leaders whose special function was to develop antislavery strategy and who were adept at manipulating public opinion grasped this fact at once. The new law had obvious value as propaganda. "It will, not withstanding the alarm and distress it occasions, do great good in opening the eyes of the people," predicted Lewis Tappan. Tappan had already had such a useful prospect brought to his attention. As early as 1846, Theodore Weld counseled him on the wisdom of harboring fugitives within the Northern states rather than encouraging them to continue their flight to Canada. So long as they remained in the United States, they would of course be subject to recapture. Thus their presence in the North, explained Weld, would "make home the battle ground . . . and do more to abolitionize the free states than all other instrumentalities afoot."[3] The legislation of 1850 had great potential for that accomplishment.

A number of prominent Northerners publicly vowed to defy a measure they regarded as monstrously evil, and here and there a political body recorded its indignation. The Common Council of Chicago, by a vote of ten to three, condemned the new law as "revolting to our moral sense, and an outrage upon our feelings of justice and humanity" and pledged not "to aid or assist in the arrest of Fugitives from oppression." The fact that the Democratic Senator Stephen A. Douglas soon was able to sway the Council to rescind its action by a vote of twelve to one did nothing to temper abolitionist assessment of the extent of Southern influence over Northern affairs.[4]

In the wake of the Fugitive Slave Act, abolitionists in several Northern cities formed vigilance committees to aid runaway slaves and to protect free Negroes from kidnappers. In some places such organizations had developed many years earlier as free Blacks joined together for their own protection and self-help. The New York Committee of Vigilance, for instance, was founded by Negroes in 1835 with David Ruggles as its secretary. In 1845, New England Negroes formed the Freedom Association. During the 1850s, some white abolitionists were welcomed into the old organizations; others formed parallel vigilance committees.[5]

The higher law doctrine, for many years the buttress to the abolitionists' claim that slavery was illegal, received additional support, as abolitionists found in it justification for their decision not to obey the new legislation. Among the most vocal advocates of lawbreaking after 1850 were an array of able clergymen who before that time had not been especially noted for their commitment to the antislavery cause. Both Charles Beecher and his more famous brother, Henry Ward Beecher, now emerged as strong proponents of the higher law and of resistance to the Fugitive Slave Act. In New England in 1850, Gilbert Haven, a young Methodist preacher, started his notable ecclesiastical career of which the first phase centered on outspoken opposition to the rendition of fugitives. George Barrell Cheever of New York, an early clerical abolitionist whose fervor had waned during the 1840s, now reentered the movement and soon established himself as one of the North's strongest antislavery voices.[6]

Defiant views such as abolitionist preachers set forth were hotly contested by conservative elements within the churches. Abolitionists who claimed to find sanction for their lawless course in Biblical precedents faced rebuke from the pulpit. "The agitators of the present day, who would break the Constitution and resist the laws of our country, can have no such defense as had Daniel and his companions, and Paul and Peter," warned the Reverend John O. Fiske of Maine.[7]

The Reverend D. D. Whedon, a Methodist preacher who also held appointment as professor at the University of Michigan, was dismissed by the Board of Regents in December 1851 on the ground that he "publicly preached" and "openly advocated" the higher law doctrine. Accordingly, he was guilty, the regents charged, "of a species of moral treason against the government."[8]

For every clergyman who, like Whedon, appealed to the higher law and urged resistance to the Fugitive Slave Act, another more conservative one came forward to preach the duty of obedience to government. A familiar sermon text of the decade, not often used since the American Revolution, was "Let every soul be subject to the higher powers." If Cheever and the Beechers boldly denounced governmental policy, several older and even more prominent Northern clergymen declared their support for the Compromise of 1850 in all its parts and asserted the citizen's moral duty to abide by the Constitution and every law made under its authority. Among the most prominent of these elderly Northern defenders of Southern rights were the prestigious Nathaniel W. Taylor, Dwight Professor of Didactic Theology at Yale Divinity School (born 1786); Orville Dewey, famed Unitarian preacher in Boston (born 1794);

Moses Stuart, Professor of Sacred Theology at Andover Theological Seminary (born 1780); and Gardiner Spring, a prominent Old School Presbyterian of New York City (born 1785).[9]

As abolitionist hostility to the Compromise of 1850 developed, large cities in the North became centers of devotion to "Unionism" and "law enforcement." Small towns and rural areas, less aware of the value of Southern ties and still dedicated to localism, were more likely to foster defiance. Men in major Northern cities whose business interests and political fortunes depended upon Southern connections and national tranquility took the lead in forming "Union committees" to assure Southerners of their patriotic intentions. They would enforce the law, remain faithful to the compromises of the Constitution, and maintain the Union. The leaders of this conciliatory movement could count on receiving support from racially prejudiced persons and from others who deplored agitation from whatever source it came and who were repelled by the radicalism and reputed impieties of certain abolitionists.

American writers were divided over the value of the Union and the merits of the Compromise. While Henry David Thoreau and Ralph Waldo Emerson sympathized with the abolitionist critique of national policy, Henry Wadsworth Longfellow, Smith Professor of Modern Languages at Harvard, became for a time virtually poet laureate of those who defended the Compromise. His much-admired poem, "The Building of the Ship," published in 1849, eulogized the American Union as freighted with the hopes of all mankind. Its popularity in the 1850s suggests that Longfellow had captured in its memorable stanzas the sentiment of those patriots who deplored abolitionist agitation:

... sail on, O Ship of State!
Sail on, O UNION, strong and great!
Humanity with all its fears,
With all the hopes of future years,
Is hanging breathless on thy fate![10]

Governor Enoch Lowe of Maryland echoed Longfellow in urging the worldwide importance of the American Union and the necessity for ending sectional discord. "Shall domestic feuds destroy our power," he asked, "when the eyes of all nations are turned to the star of our empire, as the harbinger of their deliverance?" Abolitionists, some of whom held a similarly grand view of the American mission, countered with the assertion that the United States never could fulfill its destiny to deliver the world from bondage until it had first freed the slaves within its own borders. Manifest Destiny could thus be turned to support the cause of either abolitionism or anti-abolitionism.[11]

Abolitionists implemented their vocal comdemnation of the Fugitive Slave Law with action. As soon as the Compromise of 1850 went into effect, abolitionist conventions in such widely separated places as Worcester, Massachusetts, Syracuse, New York, and the Western Reserve of Ohio proclaimed the intention of their members to defy the Fugitive Slave Law and encourage others to do the same. The advice soon was followed.

In February 1851, Frederick Jenkins, or "Shadrach," a black waiter in a Boston coffee house, was apprehended as a fugitive. A group of black men entered the United States courtroom in Boston where he was being held, surrounded the prisoner and hurried him to freedom before his amazed custodians realized what was happening. The rescue of Jenkins aroused consternation in Washington. President Millard Fillmore issued a proclamation calling upon all citizens and officials "in the vicinity of this outrage, to aid and assist in quelling this and all such combinations...." The secretaries of war and navy ordered military and naval officers to exercise more effective vigilance. Henry Clay introduced a resolution in the Senate requesting the President to disclose full information about the portentous event. Clay professed horror because the rescue had been accomplished, as he said, by a "band who are not of our people" and expressed anxiety that "the government of white men [was] to be yielded to a government by blacks." Secretary of

State Daniel Webster in a letter addressed to the Union Safety Committee of New York offered his opinion that the incident constituted "strictly speaking a case of treason."[12]

In due time one black and five white abolitionists were arrested and bound over for trial in Boston on charges of aiding in Jenkins's escape. Richard Henry Dana, Jr., a prominent Boston attorney, and John P. Hale, senator from New Hampshire, served as their defense lawyers. Perhaps anticipating a conviction, abolitionists challenged the impartiality of the American judicial system. A fair trial, they charged, would be impossible. "Our National Judges are, almost of necessity, political Judges," explained Francis Jackson, a prominent Bostonian and friend of Garrison.[13] But whatever prejudices the bench may have harbored proved insufficient to convict the defendants. All six eventually were exonerated.

As a number of Northerners declared unequivocally and to the accompaniment of generous fanfare their intention to render a key part of the recent political compromise a nullity, the United States government revealed the strategy it would use to maintain its authority. Secretary of State Webster carried the administration's message across the North: Resistance to the Fugitive Slave Law would be considered treason. In the spring of 1851, on a trip through central New York with President Fillmore, Webster elaborated his theme. He declared in a speech "to the young men of Albany" that resolutions passed by conventions in Ohio, New York, and Massachusetts denouncing the law were "distinctly treasonable," and that the rescue of Jenkins "was an act of clear treason ... and nothing less"—it was "Levying war against the Union."[14]

Abolitionists were hardly surprised to find Webster so aggressively denouncing them. Once they had thought him to be their partner much in the pattern set in the 1830s and 1840s by John Quincy Adams. But he ruined himself forever in their esteem when, on 7 March 1850, he argued before the Senate against restricting slavery in the territories. Webster's pro-compromise speech had been stunning in its effect. The antislavery congressman Horace Mann characterized him as a "fallen star! Lucifer descending from heaven!" As Mann explained, "We all had the greatest confidence in him. He has disappointed us all."[15] But surely disappointment was too mild a word to describe abolitionist reaction to Webster's evident defection. John Greenleaf Whittier, whose reputed Quaker gentleness did not in all instances extend to his rhetoric, scourged him with the merciless lines of his poem "Ichabod," and Garrison a few years later spent innumerable hours and incalculable energy in an unsuccessful effort to prevent the raising of a statue in Boston to the Senator's memory.

Webster's warnings that defiance of the Fugitive Slave Law would be prosecuted as treason had little deterrent effect on abolitionists. They continued to agitate against the law and to defy federal efforts to enforce it. In April 1851, authorities arrested Thomas Sims, a fugitive newly arrived in Boston, and after complex legal maneuvers returned him to his owner in Georgia. The provisions of the law had been fulfilled, but at astounding financial cost to the federal government and—what was more important—to the accompaniment of widespread publicity favorable to the antislavery cause. Public meetings held to protest the rendition of Sims heard addresses not only from such well-known abolitionists as Wendell Phillips, Charles L. Remond, and Theodore Parker, but also from the rising antislavery politicians, Horace Mann, John G. Palfrey, and Henry Wilson. A handful of antislavery politicians were capitalizing on the popular resentment aroused by the fugitive slave issue.[16]

In September 1851, Edward Gorsuch and his son Dickerson came from Maryland to Lancaster County, Pennsylvania, to recover four escaped slaves. There they met resistance from the small black community where the fugitives were harbored. In a battle with armed Blacks at Christiana, the elder Gorsuch was killed and his son wounded. During the affray, a deputy United States marshall ordered Caster Hanway and Elijah Lewis, both of whom

"Emminent Opponents of the Slave Power"

Outer circle, clockwise, John Quincy Adams, William Lloyd Garrison, Joshua R. Giddings, Cassius M. Clay, Benjamin Lundy, Owen Lovejoy, Gerrit Smith, William Cullen Bryant, Henry Ward Beecher. Inner circle, clockwise, John Greenleaf Whittier, Charles Sumner, Wendell Phillips were Quakers, to join a posse to round up the Blacks. Their refusal to follow the order was construed as giving aid to the fugitives. Accordingly, Hanway and Lewis, together with twenty-eight other persons thought to be involved in the affair, were arrested and charged with treason against the United States. After a well-publicized trial in federal court in Philadelphia, the jury deliberated only ten minutes before rendering its verdict for acquittal. Secretary of State Webster's strategy for enforcing the law had failed.[17]

Abolitionists were anything but humble in their victory. On the floor of Congress, Joshua Giddings defended the actions of Hanway and Lewis and of those persons who had aided the fugitives and asserted that the Gorsuchs had met a richly deserved fate. Giddings foresaw a multitude of similarly gory incidents ahead. "Thousands of agencies are at work," he declared, "preparing the minds of Southern slaves for that work which lies before them; a work which, if not accomplished by the voice of truth and justice, will be perfected in blood."[18]

The Christiana riot was unplanned, and the publicity it brought the antislavery cause was unanticipated. The same could not be said of the rescue of the fugitive Jerry at Syracuse, New York, in October 1851. A large antislavery convention was scheduled to meet in the city, and as a special feature of the occasion, abolitionist leaders decided to arrange a confrontation with the law. The Reverend Samuel J. May seems to have been a principal leader in the affair. "I have felt the strongest assurance that our Government was clearly in the wrong [with respect to the Fugitive Slave Law], and could not maintain its position except by the grossest abuse of its powers," May explained. "I have seen that it was necessary to bring the people into direct conflict with the Government, that the Government may be made to understand that it has transcended its limits and must recede."[19]

It is not at all clear that May achieved his purpose when members of the antislavery convention triumphantly rescued Jerry, for as a consequence of that exploit the United States government in no way retreated from its position.

But participation in the Jerry rescue undoubtedly stimulated the fervor of the abolitionists who had banded together to defy the law. The event apparently confirmed the
antagonism many of them already felt toward national
authority. In October of each year throughout the 1850s,
hundreds of abolitionists converged on Syracuse to com-
memorate the rescue and to renew the exhiliration that had
surrounded the affair in 1851.

The conjunction of these events in 1851—the Jenkins rescue in February, the rendition of Sims in April, the Gorsuch
murder in September, and the Jerry rescue in October—
gave Southerners reason to believe in the existence of an
abolitionist conspiracy to destroy their institutions by spir-
iting slaves to freedom. Nothing that happened afterward
removed the suspicion; incidents similar to those of 1851
continued to occur throughout the rest of the decade.
Scarcely a month passed without the newspapers reporting
a sensational rescue or attempt at rescue somewhere in the
North. Southern apprehensions were increased by the fact
that the abolitionist press portrayed those persons who
were tried and convicted for aiding fugitives as heroes and
martyrs. In a number of instances, books detailing their
experiences and their persecution achieved extensive circulation.[20]

While the underground railroad generally remained a
furtive enterprise, in a few places—especially in parts of
New England and in Ohio's Western Reserve—secrecy in
aiding fugitives no longer seemed essential. Some individuals gained notoriety for their persistent underground-rail-
road work. Harriet Tubman, a stouthearted black woman
who achieved near-mythic status, spirited many slaves to
freedom, as did William Still, a black abolitionist from
Philadelphia. Among Westerners, the Quakers Levi Coffin
of Cincinnati and Laura Smith Haviland of Lenawee
County, Michigan, were especially noteworthy for their
years of similar activity.

Perhaps the culminating incident in the fugitive-slave
drama occurred at Oberlin, Ohio, in April 1859, when federal marshals apprehended a fugitive who then was spir-

ited away by a mob of college students, faculty, and local
citizens. Thirty-seven of the "rescuers," including ordained
clergymen and Oberlin College professors and students,
were indicted and held in jail in Cleveland to await trial.
Their case, like the several that preceded it, became nation-
ally celebrated as abolitionists publicized the clash between their ideas of morality and the requirements of law.
Again the incident proved useful in creating hostility to
slavery and to Southern influence in government. At a mass
protest meeting in Cleveland, called by several antislavery
politicians, some ten thousand persons gathered to hear
Joshua Goddings and others denounce the Fugitive Slave
Act as unconstitutional and an act of piracy, and declare
their support for the prisoners and their own willingness to
resist the law.[21]

The uproar that accompanied enforcement of the Fugitive Slave Law did not mean that the law became a dead
letter. On numerous occasions fugitives were apprehended
and returned to their owners without the community being
aware of the event; in many places no abolitionist leadership existed to resist the return of fugitives. Despite the
sensational efforts at "rescue," the law was effectively enforced on the whole, especially in Pennsylvania and in the
states of the Old Northwest.[22] Yet so well publicized were
the dramatic instances when it was defied and so vocal
were abolitionists and antislavery politicians in denouncing it that the effect was otherwise. One might understandably, if mistakenly, conclude that abolitionists had
succeeded in nullifying the law. Such a belief became common in the South. There the impression was created that in
defiance of constitutional obligations Northerners were
united in purpose to help slaves escape. Thus the controversy over enforcement of the Fugitive Slave Law resulted
in still further antagonism between slaveholding and non-
slaveholding parts of the country, while it garnered new
sympathy in the North for the slave.

In the North, as a result of the controversy, competing
loyalties once again were brought to general attention: obe-

dience to law versus moral obligation; maintenance of the Union versus humanitarian principles; social tranquility versus justice. In sentiment, if not always in actual practice, the ideals of justice, humanitarianism, and morality appear to have gained the victory."Thus far we can find no man, republican or democrat, who would not violate the fugitive law," wrote the editor of the *Ohio State Journal* on 5 August 1859.

Resistance to the law elated some abolitionists, but its enforcement produced despair in others. A moment's consideration would show that the full power of the United States government had been placed at the disposal of slave-owners. Both fugitives and their defenders appeared to have been placed in a hopeless position. James G. Birney at that time abandoned faith that Blacks would soon be accorded justice within the United States. In a pamphlet published in 1852, he advised them to seek homes elsewhere. "Your presence here now can be of no service to your enslaved brethren," he wrote. "By remaining, you only destroy yourselves. Your submitting, suffering, ultimately dying here, can effect nothing on the hearts and determination of your oppressors. . . ." Birney found no reason to believe that the "principles of our government would prevail" and end slavery. He had lost faith in the very basis of the organized antislavery movement of which he had once been a key figure. Slavery eventually would disappear through changes in economic and social conditions, he predicted, not by the spread of moral and religious principles.[23]

Lewis Tappan could not concur with Birney's weary despair. Still less would he join him in advocating emigration of the Blacks. "If we give up the contest for the free colored people," Tappan wrote, "if they give it up, the cause of the slave is hopeless. The great battle for Freedom can not, it would seem, be successfully waged unless the colored people 'abide in the ship.' "[24]

Yet even some black leaders in the 1850s accepted Birney's analysis and also advocated emigration. They became increasingly embittered as they saw little evidence for believing that the campaign to end slavery and to achieve equal rights for black people would be successful. Colonization, which abolitionists and free Negroes had overwhelmingly rejected in earlier days, now became a subject of renewed interest. Henry Highland Garnet, H. Ford Douglass, Martin Delaney, and William H. Day, among other black abolitionists, supported a plan for colonization in Central America put forward by the white politician Francis P. Blair and endorsed by several prominent figures in the new Republican party.[25]

Perhaps of all abolitionists the Garrisonians were least likely to be discouraged by even the most dismal turn of events. Garrisonian abolitionists had long been in a frame of mind to expect the worst from existing political parties and from government. They had seldom found hope in the glimmers of righteousness that more sanguine observers had been able to detect in events. The optimistic statements that occasionally appeared in their writings only thinly disguised their knowledge that for all the years of antislavery activity public opinion with respect to Negro rights had not yet been revolutionized. For years they had denied the legitimacy of federal authority exercised under a Constitution that was, in Garrison's words, borrowed from the Prophet Isaiah, "a covenant with death and an agreement with hell." Nothing had ever happened to persuade them that their verdict was wrong.

On 4 July 1854, at an antislavery convention in Framingham, Massachusetts, Garrison publicly burned certain government documents, including a copy of the Constitution. Verbal symbols and an act of defiance merged in Garrison's sensational gesture.[26] Such acts on the part of abolitionists were altogether exceptional. They customarily restricted their opposition to the Union to rhetoric, and even their most extreme hostility was generally couched in terms of civility. With a few flagrant exceptions, New England abolitionists voiced their opposition to public policy in rhetorically chaste style and grounded it in exalted religious and philosophic principle. But their example was not everywhere closely followed. Out in western New York, Beriah Green, the cranky, tough, and inelegant preacher who in 1833 had chaired the convention that founded the American Anti-Slavery Society, expressed his distaste in earthy terms. "This hog-haunted, so called government I abhor as an atrocious conspiracy," he told Birney in April 1852, "and submit to its demands just as I would to the demands of a band of robbers."[27] Despite the contrast in mode of expression it was obvious that for the evangelical Green, as for the religiously unorthodox Garrison, the United States government by the 1850s had lost its moral authority.

Indignation over the Fugitive Slave Act had scarcely reached its height when installments of *Uncle Tom's Cabin* began appearing in the *National Era* in 1852. Harriet Beecher Stowe's novel conveyed to a large audience a sentimental critique of slavery that awakened new degrees of sympathy for the slave and hostility to the slave system. The audience for that message had been created both by abolitionist activity and Southern policy. When Richard Hildreth's pioneer antislavery novel, *The Slave: or Memoirs of Archy Moore,* was published in 1836, it aroused little interest and proved to be a financial failure. Its poor reception at that early stage of the antislavery movement could not be charged alone to inferior literary quality. Much happened between 1836 and 1852 to prepare the reading public to respond sympathetically to a fictional portrayal of the cruelties of slavery. Not least crucial was the agitation over fugitive slaves that erupted just before Mrs. Stowe's novel appeared.

Mrs. Stowe's book was the literary sensation of the era. Sympathy for the slave as embodied in the *"Uncle Tom* theme" soon became a part of popular culture. Within a few months waltzes, dioramas, and stage plays based on the novel had been produced. A critic who attended a performance of *Uncle Tom's Cabin* at the National Theater in Philadelphia reported with wonderment that "every sentiment of freedom elicited applause" from an audience "composed mainly of the very class which has mobbed the abolitionists for the last twenty years. . . ." According to another contemporary, theatergoers were "unconsciously accepting anti-slavery truth" as they heard actors "preach immediate emancipation" and as they watched "slaves shoot their hunters to wild applause."[28]

By the 1850s, the fugitive slave and his rescuer had become folk heroes. But the correspondence between drama—whether on the stage or as perceived in the exceptional actual event—and reality was, as always, less than perfect. The mind unavoidably associated the three pertinent black figures in American society: the fugitives, the Southern slaves, and the free Blacks; yet the identification of the three remained incomplete, and the value placed upon each varied. Popular indignation over the mistreatment of fugitives and the cruelties of slavery was not the equivalent of a willingness to end slavery immediately. Still less did such indignation necessarily indicate determination to shed prejudice toward Negroes who lived in the North. Absorption in the dramatic events of *Uncle Tom's Cabin* and of the slave rescues themselves did not signify a revolution in racial attitudes.

At Harvard Medical School, located not far from the office of the *Liberator* and the scene of the Jenkins rescue, white students in the winter of 1851–1852 petitioned Oliver Wendell Holmes, the school's Dean, to rid the class of its black members. At a meeting held at Holmes's residence, the faculty acceded to the white students' request by dismissing three black students. One of them was Martin Delaney, who soon would become a major abolitionist.[29]

It was one thing to sympathize with fugitives and to hate the institution of slavery. It was much more difficult to extend the same warmth and understanding and philanthropy to the Northern free Blacks. Legal and extra-legal proscriptions against free black people continued in the 1850s, despite abundant evidence of sympathy for fugitives and increasing signs of hostility toward slavery and the South. In spite of the opposition of both white and black abolitionists, nearly all the legal restrictions affecting black persons in the North remained on the statute books. Only in portions of New England were significant gains achieved in repealing them. There was no obvious drama or adventure or entertainment value in the plight of free Blacks. They were too near Northern Whites; their oppressed status was too much a part of Northern life for them to be made an object of philanthropy. Thus an abolitionist agent reported that in a community he visited in New Hampshire an audience easily could be gathered to attend a black-face minstrel show, but he found few persons willing to listen to a black abolitionist lecture on the wrongs committed against his people.[30]

The Northern resentment, awakened by events of the early 1850s, found part of its expression in political action. The Free Soil party, first organized in 1848 to support the Wilmot Proviso, was revived in time to make nominations for the election of 1852. The chief plank in its platform remained opposition to the spread of slavery into the territories, an antislavery goal since the Northwest Ordinance of 1787.

By passing the Kansas–Nebraska Act in 1854, Congress greatly expanded the Northern antislavery constituency. When by that action the Missouri Compromise was repealed, Congress opened the possibility for slavery to be extended into large areas from which it long had been barred. Anti-Southern politicians joined abolitionists in declaring that now all the compromises of 1850 were null and void. The sectional understanding so painfully arranged by politicians only four years earlier was wrecked. Harriet Beecher Stowe used part of her royalties from *Uncle Tom's Cabin* to organize opposition to the bill; 3,050 New England preachers signed a 200-foot-long petition, which Edward Everett presented to Congress. New York City merchants held protest meetings and organized to correspond with similar groups in other cities. Despite all these efforts the objectionable law was passed.[31]

The South, it could reasonably be charged, controlled national legislation. But that was not the whole of it. At just the time the Kansas-Nebraska Act was being passed, Federal authorities apprehended the fugitive Anthony Burns in Boston and, to the accompaniment of an enormous outpouring of popular resentment, returned him to slavery. Not least effective in provoking that resentment was the knowledge, hard for a citizen of Massachusetts to accept, that the "slave power," operating through the national government, had the capacity to reach far into a Northern state to enforce its will.

The organization of the Republican party in 1854, an amalgam of Free Soilers, antislavery Whigs and Democrats, and Know-Nothings, was the concrete political result of the widespread upheaval resulting from the Kansas-Nebraska Act. While the new party refrained from endorsing abolitionism, it nevertheless embodied a morally derived opposition to slavery and slaveholding society as well as a commitment to free labor. Thus it immediately became the political vehicle for implementing Northern economic and antislavery programs.

Despite their unrelenting criticism of what they regarded as the Republicans' half-way measures, abolitionists were inclined to support the party as offering the best available means for expressing antislavery opinion and for achieving at least limited antislavery goals. Even Garrison, who did not himself vote, conceded that the new party, for all its inadequacy, was the best antislavery instrument then available, and he welcomed each of its victories as marking an advance for the abolitionist cause.[32]

In New York, Samuel J. May endorsed the Republican presidential candidate, John C. Frémont, in 1856 on the ground that unsatisfactory as he was it still would be better to have a Republican than a Democrat in control of the government when the inevitable clash between North and South came. In Illinois, Representative Owen Lovejoy owed his political success in part to abolitionist support. The conservative *Detroit Free Press,* failing to distinguish between the varieties of abolitionists who traveled through Michigan, credited the Republican electoral victories in the fall of 1854 to the lecturing activities of the Garrisonians Stephen S. Foster and his wife Abby Kelley, and to the anti-Garrisonian Alanson St. Clair.[33]

It was commonly remarked in the 1850s, as in the previous decade, that persons converted to abolitionism were quick to try to make their principles felt in politics by working within one of the existing parties. But some abolitionists considered this course a lessening of their influence. The dispute continued between those on the one hand who would remain aloof from party entanglements altogether or at the most form independent third parties and those on the other hand who would seek to leaven the existing parties with abolitionist principles. One of Garrison's correspondents in western New York complained to him in 1854 that renewed interest in antislavery politics had led most antislavery men there to abandon disunionist, anti-government principles and to join either the Whig, Free Soil, or Know-Nothing party.[34] Within a few months they and others like them all across the North would enter Republican party ranks.

The Garrisonians generally remained skeptical of the value of this development, for they continued to maintain that the nation would not be prepared to take effective antislavery political action until a majority had undergone a moral reformation of which one result would be a new attitude toward the rights of black people. The accomplishment of that reform appeared still to be a long way off. The great requirement, wrote a New York abolitionist in 1854, remained a revival of "that Christianity which teaches man to recognize man as a brother although his skin may be black."[35]

Fugitive slaves had helped promote such brotherly accord by calling forth aid in their effort to free themselves. In escaping to the North, slaves became active participants in the sectional conflict, provoking Southerners to seek more effective protection for their property and their "rights," and driving abolitionists into ever more extreme positions.

Notes

1. Larry Gara, "The Fugitive Slave Law: A Double Paradox," *Civil War History,* 10 (September 1964): 229–40.
2. American and Foreign Anti-Slavery Society, *Annual Report . . . 1851* (New York: the Society, 1851), p. 55.
3. Lewis Tappan to John Scoble, 25 November 1850, in *A Side-Light on Anglo-American Relations, 1839–1858, Furnished by the Correspondence of Lewis Tappan and Others with the British and Foreign Anti-Slavery Society,* ed. Annie H. Abel and Frank J. Klingberg (Lancaster: Association for the Study of Negro Life and History, 1927), p. 258; Weld to Tappan, 9 April 1846, Weld-Grimké Papers (William L. Clements Library, Ann Arbor).
4. Massachusetts Anti-Slavery Society, *Nineteenth Annual Report . . . 1851* (Boston: the Society, 1851), p. 45.
5. August Meier and Elliot N. Rudwick, *From Plantation to Ghetto, an Interpretive History of American Negroes* (New York: Hill and Wang, 1966), pp. 113–15.
6. Timothy Smith, *Revivalism and Social Reform in Mid-19th Century America* (New York: Abingdon Press, 1957), pp. 204–24.
7. Abel and Klingberg, eds., *A Side-Light,* p. 272.
8. Massachusetts Anti-Slavery Society, *Nineteenth Annual Report,* p. 91.
9. For a survey of clerical views on race and the racial controversy, see John R. Bodo, *The Protestant Clergy and Public Issues, 1812–1848* (Princeton: Princeton University Press, 1954), pp. 112–49.
10. Longfellow had "prostituted his fine genius," said Garrison. Ibid., *Eighteenth Annual Report . . . 1850* (Boston: the Society, 1850), pp. 99–100.

11. The neglected relation between the reform movements and concepts of national destiny is alluded to in Don E. Fehren-bacher, *The Era of Expansion: 1800–1848* (New York: Wiley, 1969), p. 113. Owen Lovejoy, speaking of America's mission "to bless and save a world!" observed that "to my mind it is clear that God cannot make use of the instrumentality of this nation to accomplish his purpose of mercy to the world, nor even the church of this nation, reeking as it is with ... blood, and tread-ing with iron heel on the poor." *Western Citizen,* 20 January 1843.

12. Carleton Mabee, *Black Freedom; the Nonviolent Abolitionists from 1830 through the Civil War* (New York: Macmillan, 1970), p. 307; Massachusetts Anti-Slavery Society, *Twentieth Annual Report ... 1852* (Boston: the Society, 1852), pp. 10–11.

13. Massachusetts Anti-Slavery Society, ibid., p. 15.

14. *Works of Daniel Webster* (Boston: C. C. Little and J. Brown, 1851), II: 577–78.

15. Larry Gara, "Horace Mann: Anti-Slavery Congressman," *The Historian,* 32 (November 1969): 28.

16. Leonard W. Levy, "Sims' Case: The Fugitive Slave Case in Bos-ton in 1851," *Journal of Negro History,* 35 (January 1950): 39–74.

17. Massachusetts Anti-Slavery Society, *Twentieth Annual Re-port,* pp. 80–83; *Report of the Trial of Caster Hanway for Trea-son ...* (Philadelphia: King and Baird, 1852).

18. U.S., Congress, *Congressional Globe,* 32d Cong., 1st Sess., p. 775.

19 May to William Lloyd Garrison, 23 November 1851, in Wendell Lloyd Garrison and Francis P. Garrison, *William Lloyd Garri-son, 1805–1879; the Story of His Life Told by His Children* (New York: Century, 1885), III: 336; Massachusetts Anti-Slavery Soci-ety, *Twentieth Annual Report,* pp. 33–35.

20. "It would require a volume to attempt to recount even the most prominent of the other instances of the execution of the Fugi-tive Slave Law within the last two years." American Anti-Slav-ery Society, *Annual Report ... 1855* (New York: the Society, 1855), p. 40. See Joseph C. Lovejoy, *Memoir of Rev. Charles T. Torrey, Who Died in the Penitentiary of Maryland, Where He was Confined for Showing Mercy to the Poor* (New York: J. P. Jewett, 1847); Daniel Drayton, *Personal Memoir of Daniel Drayton, for Four Years and Four Months a Prisoner (for Charity's Sake) in Washington Jail* (Boston: B. Marsh, 1855); George Thompson, *Prison Life and Reflections ...* (Hartford: A. Work, 1854).

21. *Liberator,* 6 May 1859.

22. Stanley W. Campbell, *The Slave Catchers; Enforcement of the Fugitive Slave Law, 1850–1860* (Chapel Hill: University of North Carolina Press, 1970), pp. 110–47.

23. James G. Birney, *Examination of the Decision of the Supreme Court of the United States . . .* (Cincinnati: Truman and Spofford, 1852), p. 43.

24. Lewis Tappan to Andrew Scoble, 7 February 1852; Abel and Klingburg, eds., *A Side-Light*, p. 283.

25. Eric Foner, *Free Soil, Free Labor, Free Men; the Ideology of the Republican Party before the Civil War* (New York: Oxford University Press, 1970), pp. 274–75.

26. Garrisons, *Garrison*, III, p. 412.

27. Beriah Green to Birney, 6 April 1852, *Birney Letters*, II, p. 1144.

28. *Liberator*, 23 September 1853; 27 July 1855. For the novel's vogue in the Michigan backwoods see Birney to Harriet Beecher Stowe, 10 January 1853, *Birney Letters*, II, p. 1161. With the dramatization of the novel, said Joshua Giddings, "the theater, that 'school of vice,' has been subsidized to the promulgation of truth. . . ." U.S., Congress, *Congressional Globe*, 32d Cong. 2d Sess., Appendix, p. 29.

29. Floyd John Miller, "The Search for a Black Nationality: Martin R. Delaney and the Emigration Alternative" (Ph.D. dissertation, University of Minnesota, 1970), pp. 63–64.

30. *Liberator*, 7 January 1859.

31. For a review of the significance of the Kansas-Nebraska Act see Roy Franklin Nichols, "The Kansas-Nebraska Act: A Century of Historiography," *Mississippi Valley Historical Review*, 43 (September 1956): 187–212.

32. Garrisons, *Garrison*, III, pp. 443, 445–47; see also Henry C. Wright's comment in *Liberator*, 11 April 1856.

33. Samuel J. May to Henry C. Wright, 21 October 1856, *Liberator*, 31 October 1856; *Detroit Free Press*, 5 May 1855, quoted in ibid., 25 May 1855.

34. A. J. Simmons to Garrison, 17 December 1854, ibid., 5 January 1855.

35. On the small gains made in New England, see ibid., 24 August 1855.

CHAPTER NINE

An Abolitionist Revival

The fugitive slave issue reawakened the religiously inspired antislavery zeal that had been allowed to fade after
political abolitionists organized during the 1840s. Keeping
slavery out of the territories was no doubt as important as
Free-Soil and Republican politicians insisted it was; nevertheless, to abolitionists caught up in the furor aroused by
the new Fugitive Slave Act, it seemed a minor issue.

Abolitionists were concerned for individual human beings; politicians debated lifeless abstractions. A conviction
that free-soil principles inadequately expressed abolitionist goals led Garrisonians to new efforts to promote moral
reform. It also stimulated evangelicals to undertake enlarged abolitionist campaigns. An antislavery revival took
place in the 1850s as both groups of abolitionists responded
to the crisis produced by the new phase of the sectional
conflict.

Late in 1849, while debate over sectional compromise
stirred the nation, evangelical abolitionists in Ohio issued
a call for a Christian Antislavery Convention to meet early
the next year.[1] In April 1850, religiously oriented abolitionists from across the North—most of them Congregation-
alists and Presbyterians—converged on Cincinnati to
consider their responsibility in the national crisis. The fact
that so many antislavery reformers had become single-

mindedly absorbed in politics troubled them. Opposition to slavery, once primarily a religious cause and a moral duty, appeared in danger of becoming solely a matter of politics. In submitting to that secular transformation, abolitionism, they believed, risked losing its spirit and moral influence. In its concern for the growth of Southern power and the spread of Southern institutions into the West, it nearly forgot the slave himself. In a search for sectional advantage, it neglected the needs of black men. The Free Soil party, in their opinion, embodied only the shadow of antislavery principles. They were not convinced that the central plank of its platform, the nonextension of slavery, would speed the end of slavery in the South. Still less would it alter the shabby treatment free Blacks customarily experienced in the North.

Matters closer to home also disturbed the church-oriented delegates. They were chagrined that the major religious denominations, whose pulpits many of them occupied, had failed to take an unequivocal stand in favor of abolition. Furthermore, several important church agencies —the American Home Missionary Society, the American Board of Foreign Missions, the American Tract Society, the American Sunday School Union and others—were thought by abolitionist churchmen to have compromised the reform cause by their ambivalent antislavery stands.

The purposes of the Christian Antislavery Convention, then, were to restore a high level of moral fervor to the antislavery movement at a time of national crisis, to stimulate church-based antislavery action, and to revive the old effort to transform the churches themselves into avowedly abolitionist organizations. Those had been the goals of abolitionists in the 1830s. The clergymen who met at Cincinnati in the spring of 1850 had faith that they still might be attained.

Probably few if any of the delegates thought of themselves as followers of Garrison; indeed, as orthodox church leaders they were inclined to shun such association on account of his reputation as an apostle of "infidelity"; yet as firmly as any Garrisonian they were convinced that signifi-

"A Slave Caught Without a Pass"

cant political antislavery action must be preceded by the
moral regeneration of individuals. "[T]his question in its
primary and most important aspect belongs not to politics,
but to morals," said one of the convention speakers. "Political action can have no natural connection with it except to
carry out by appropriate legal forms a previous moral decision."[2] The delegates did not reject political antislavery action any more than Garrison did, but they shared his doubts
that the electorate had yet been morally prepared to make
such action effective.

Later, similar gatherings of clergymen in Cincinnati and
Chicago developed detailed plans aimed at restoring the
moral element to the antislavery movement and at rescu-
ing it from becoming solely a sectional struggle for control
of national power. The Negro himself, they believed, and
not slavery as an institution must remain central to abolitionism.[3]

By their insistence on the preeminently religious character of the antislavery movement, the Christian antislavery
conventions attempted to revive the evangelical attitudes of

the 1830s. Their example and urgings probably led additional clergymen to ally with abolitionist organizations and to preach antislavery sermons. They may also have helped move some of the Protestant denominations further toward specifically antislavery positions. In any event, such a course was followed in Congregationalist churches throughout the North during the 1850s.

The Presbyterians moved more slowly. Not until 1857 did the New School Presbyterian General Assembly unequivocally condemn slavery and bar slaveholders from membership. The Methodist church remained reluctant to endorse abolitionism; yet a Methodist preacher in 1859 probably was correct in assuring critics that even though the Methodist bishops resisted abolitionism, their influence on church members in this respect was slight. The Methodist church, like the Baptist, contained a large number of members who were far more sympathetic to the antislavery cause than were their official denominational spokesmen.[4]

But despite all efforts of evangelicals to persuade Northerners otherwise, it was in politics that the conflict between slavery and abolitionist principles was most evident in the 1850s, and it was on politics that most antislavery Northerners focused their concern. Even participants in the Christian antislavery conventions could not altogether neglect the ultimate goal of political antislavery action. Sometimes the connection was made all but explicit. The antislavery Baptist church in Lancaster, Indiana, for instance, published a call for two meetings in 1851—a statewide Christian convention to meet at Indianapolis on 28 May to be followed the next day by an antislavery political convention in the same city. The sponsors obviously took for granted that the membership of the two gatherings would be nearly identical. The resolutions adopted by both the Indiana conventions, as by most of those held elsewhere, proclaimed the obligation of abolitionists to exert moral influence in politics.[5]

The political aspect of the Christian convention movement became still more evident at Cincinnati in April 1852 in an evangelical-sponsored meeting judged by Frederick Douglass to be "the best convention ever held west of the Alleghenies." The newly constructed Concert Hall was jammed with the curious as well as the committed. Every seat was occupied; the platform and aisles were full. Each important element in the antislavery movement understood the potential of the occasion. Conservative antislavery politicians who endorsed no measure more extreme than barring slavery from the territories shared the platform with zealous out-and-out abolitionists who longed for the day when Congress would strike the death blow at slavery everywhere in the nation. Joining with them as fellow members of the convention were more austere men and women who had renounced political action in the interests of pursuing single-minded moral and religious agitation.

Frederick Douglass, once allied with the New England disunionists, had split with Garrison partly over the issue of political action. Now he traveled to Cincinnati to try to convince the assembled clergymen of the power and duty of the United States government to abolish slavery throughout the nation—in the states as well as in the territories. Douglass's strong urgings were not sufficient to bring the convention to endorse so advanced a policy, but neither did the members accept Charles C. Burleigh's Garrisonian-inspired resolution calling for dissolution of the Union. It soon became obvious that the majority of the convention rejected extremism of every sort. Despite its religious inspiration and predominantly clerical membership, the convention was committed to traditional political antislavery action with all its familiar limitations. The only questions left unresolved were the means and the occasion for such political action and the precise goals it should seek.

One of the key speakers at Cincinnati was George Julian of Indiana, a son-in-law and protégé of the antislavery veteran Joshua Giddings and soon to be the Free Soilers vice-presidential candidate. He had placed all his faith for antislavery accomplishment in politics. He now called upon the delegates to help overthrow the Whig and Democratic parties and to replace them with a new abolitionist party. The plea for radical politics constantly intruded upon the deliberations of those who hoped that moral regeneration of individuals would prove a sufficient means to reform the nation. The proceedings at Cinicinnati demonstrated once again the extreme difficulty of separating the moral reform urged by abolitionists—whether of the evangelical or the Garrisonian variety—from antislavery politics.[6]

At the start of their organized crusade in the 1830s, abolitionists generally adopted the states' rights constitutional position that slavery in the states was immune to Congressional interference. Abolition, they assumed, must be accomplished by the decision of individual slaveholders or, at most, by legislative action of the individual states.[7] When abolitionists took that stand, they apparently surrendered the means by which a Northern majority might directly use its power to end slavery. Their strategic error was apparent as soon as it became clear that the abolitionists' moral attack would never persuade Southerners themselves to act against slavery. Garrisonians in particular became captives of their own early developed states' rights political theory. They did not modify that theory to meet new situations. When the failure of their original strategy became obvious, they demanded dissolution of the Union.

Doubtlessly that audacious call seemed the more startling and repugnant to antebellum Northerners because it so closely resembled the threat of secession persistently voiced by spokesmen for the South. Yet some politically oriented abolitionists at the time were more sympathetic toward the doctrine and exhibited better understanding of its purpose than most commentators of a later day. William Goodell, an organizer of the Liberty party, readily agreed that the Garrisonians' slogan, "No Union with Slaveholders," was unrealistic and visionary. The esoteric no-human-government, no-association-with-evil-men theory on which it was based could never be accepted by more than a few Americans. But, he added, their slogan had a practical hard-headed aspect as well. When Garrisonians urged "the duty of dissolving the Union ... on the ground that the Union upholds slavery, they proposed a serious and intelligible question, and one that comes home to the conscience and interests of every northern citizen."[8]

Despite Goodell's appreciative explanation, the disunionist views put forward by Garrison and his followers were not much more widely accepted in the 1850s than they had been when first voiced a decade earlier. On the contrary, advocacy of them continued to evoke intense opposition—even mob violence—much as the doctrine of abolitionism itself had done in the 1830s.

When the Garrisonian Richard Glazier, Jr., spoke in Pontiac, Michigan, on two successive days in February 1856, his sentiments aroused mounting hostility. After officials locked him out of the courthouse, he delivered his third lecture at National Hall. There "rowdy malefactors" interrupted the meeting, and boys pelted him with corn and beans. At his next lecture he was threatened with still more menacing violence from which he escaped somewhat ignominiously only when a group of women escorted him home. Pontiac, concluded Glazier, was a city ruled by the "American triumvirate" of "democracy, Rum, and Religion."[9]

Black abolitionists who ventured to preach in the Garrisonian revival were still more likely to face hostility. A barrage of eggs and other missiles drove C. P. Depp from the lecture platform of the Baptist church in Monmouth, Illinois, early in 1856.[10]

Some Garrisonian lecturers believed that young men and women in the West listened more sympathetically to their radical sentiments than did older ones. Giles Stebbins found on his tour in 1853 that "the Old Line Democrats do not turn out much, but their families will." Conservatism, he predicted, "is in a fair way to die out with its ancient supporters."[11] Perhaps the disorder that broke out among pupils in a Detroit public school in 1856 illustrates the youthful abolitionist sympathies Stebbins discerned, or it may only suggest normal resentment of authority. When

Levi Bishop, president of the Detroit Board of Education, reprimanded the school principal for allowing a student to recite one of Whittier's antislavery poems, "The boys hissed Mr. Bishop . . . ," the *Liberator* reported. "It was difficult to produce order; and when the school was dismissed, one of the boys proposed three groans for Bishop, which was responded to with hearty good will."[12]

The hostile reaction so often encountered by calls for dissolution of the Union does not mean that it had no positive effect in altering public opinion. We can suppose that, as Goodell suggested, the frequently repeated expression of such radical programs did not in every instance lead to total rejection of the ideas that lay behind them.

In 1857, Caroline Putnam reported from the village of Jonesville, Michigan, that she and her fellow Garrisonian Sallie Holley met with little success in their efforts to persuade rural audiences to repudiate the government and the churches, but she then added that those same audiences generally accepted the idea of the sinfulness of slavery and, it followed, the sinfulness of a government and a church which tolerated slavery.[13]

The unacceptability of the specifics of the Garrisonian program never obscured the fact that the program proceeded from a conviction of the utter evil of slavery. Unable to ignore this fact, growing numbers of Northerners translated the Garrisonian plea for separation from the Union into the more acceptable and practical program of withdrawing governmental support from slavery and separating political parties from Southern domination. Accordingly, they were encouraged by the Garrisonian doctrine to seek a Union purified of its slaveholding elements rather than one wracked by dissolution. It was perhaps this rationale that in 1855 led a Methodist clergyman to speak at Aurora, Illinois, in support of a "Union for liberty, not for slavery." If the Union was to be preserved, he said, it must be made worth preserving.[14] This common sense attitude fostered by the Garrisonians eventually became Northern doctrine, and when civil war finally came it helped account

William Goodell

for popular acceptance of Lincoln's emancipation program.

The widely accepted and conservatively respectable antislavery theory that held slavery to be exclusively a states' rights matter was no more tolerable to many abolitionists than was the Garrisonians' radical disunionist approach. Some could not accept either the view that the Constitution was thoroughly pro-slavery or the view that it gave Congress no power over slavery in the states. It was difficult indeed in pre-Civil War America to discard a political theory based on state sovereignty, however effectively the theory hobbled antislavery effort. A number of abolitionists, nevertheless, overcame that difficulty. Some of them early abandoned precedent and called for the positive use of national power to end slavery wherever it existed.

Beginning in the late 1830s, Liberty party men started to express such views. In pamphlets published in 1845 and 1847, an eccentric Bostonian, Lysander Spooner, developed a thorough exposition of the theory that slavery was illegal and unconstitutional everywhere and that the people of the United States could constitutionally abolish it despite the opposition of the Southern minority.[15]

In his *Views of American Constitutional Law* (1844), William Goodell came to similar conclusions. He explained his theories further during the 1850s in a series of letters on "The Legal Tenure of Slavery" published in the widely read *National Era* and later in articles in his own journals, *The American Jubilee* and the *Radical Abolitionist.* According to Goodell the United States government was fully competent under the Constitution to destroy slavery in the states.

Goodell adhered to no narrow theory of national power. He offered a view of the rights of Negroes and of the obligations of government toward them that, for the 1850s, was truly breathtaking in its extent. "The Constitution was formed by 'the people of the United States,' (*all* of them), 'to secure the blessings of LIBERTY for (themselves) and (their) posterity,' without exception or distinction of race or color," asserted Goodell. "And hence, no portion of 'the people of the United States' can be constitutionally enslaved, and the declared *object* of the Constitution *requires* the Federal Government to 'secure the blessings of liberty' to each and all of them."[16]

Those abolitionist leaders who were governed by a concern for precedent and consistency could not accept Goodell's sweeping political theory that so conveniently located in the national government the instrument of abolitionist power. But antislavery lecturers now and then reported finding in their audiences a quite different attitude. Ordinary men and women, undeterred by the restraining subtleties of constitutional interpretation, took for granted that an antislavery political majority would find a way to end slavery however much theorists might object. Theory, they seemed to believe, must not prevent the nation from dealing with its pressing social problems; caution dictated by constitutional scruples must not make slavery immune from destruction.[17]

The Garrisonians spent less time than others in arguing how slavery might be abolished. Constitutional theory interested most of them no more than it interested the general public. They believed with the evangelicals that the important task was simply to persuade men and women that slavery must be ended. The "great thing needed," Abby Kelley contended at a convention of the Massachusetts Anti-Slavery Society in 1855, was "to get the people *ready* to do antislavery work; and when they get ready to do it, they will, of course, do it in their own way."[18]

Edmund Quincy, the aristocratic secretary of the Society, agreed. In 1851, he had written that the abolitionists' purpose should not be to develop programs for emancipation or to organize antislavery political parties but simply to change public opinion with respect to slavery. When that change had been accomplished, slavery would end, though the means that would be used to achieve abolition could not be predicted. "Numbers are not necessary in the beginnings of Revolutions," Quincy wrote. "Those beginnings are in the secret chambers of men's hearts, and not at the polls. . . . When the full time shall have come for the birth of this Revolution, men will not be wanting at ballot-boxes, in Senates, or on battle fields." When the goals were agreed upon, Quincy said, the means for attaining them would be found and shaped by circumstances that the future would provide.[19]

Politically oriented abolitionists were generally less flexible than Garrisonians in their advocacy of means. Those who believed Congress possessed Constitutional powers that it might use against slavery generally had assumed that those powers were limited to such indirect devices as barring slavery from the territories and ending the interstate slave trade. Abolitionists holding such views were likely to find the limited antislavery program of the new Republican party satisfactory. But a small group led by Goodell and Gerrit Smith did not so approve. They became impatient both with Free Soilers and Republican politicians, whose cautious and half-way antislavery measures they deplored, and also with the Garrisonians whose call for disunion they dismissed as impractical anarchism.

When most Liberty party voters swung support first to the Free Soil and then to the Republican party, Goodell and Smith formed the Liberty League. In June 1855, under their leadership a small group of abolitionists met at Syracuse and adopted resolutions declaring slavery unconstitutional everywhere. Among the other prominent members of the Syracuse meeting were the antislavery veteran Samuel J. May and the black abolitionists, Dr. James McCune Smith (who served as chairman of the sessions) and Frederick Douglass. The convention adjourned to meet again at Boston in October 1855, where it was joined by the Tappan brothers, Simeon S. Jocelyn (one of Garrison's early associates), Beriah Green, and a few others who, like them, had long been identified with evangelical abolitionism. There they formed the American Abolition Society and undertook sponsorship of a journal, the *Radical Abolitionist,* edited by Goodell. This tiny group, pledged to Congressional action against slavery wherever it existed, nominated Gerrit Smith as its presidential candidate in 1856.[20]

The society Smith and Goodell had founded was probably little noticed outside New England and western New York. Few antislavery politicians accepted its extreme position, and few antislavery Northerners regarded its platform as anything but impracticable as well as unconstitutional. Yet the point of view it represented gained a hearing. The evangelical ministers who joined the Society enjoyed considerable influence within their denominations, and even though they secured few endorsements for their particular program, they vigorously urged its acceptance, and from their prominent clerical positions maintained steady insistence that government must faithfully reflect religious principles. Voters who accepted that moralistic and religious position were likely to be Republicans.

Despite the support antislavery reformers gave the newly organized Republican party, some abolitionists remained openly critical of it and continued to doubt its abolitionist character. They understood that abolitionism was a program acceptable only to a minority; no political party intent on victory, as Republicans of course were, dared incorporate such a radical policy in its platform. A "party whose great aim is NUMBERS cannot abolish American slavery," declared Henry C. Wright. Arthur Tappan was still more blunt. The Republicans, he said in 1856, are "a white man's party united for selfish purposes." Gerrit Smith, expressing a similar verdict, noted in particular the fact that Republican-controlled state governments were doing little to remove discriminatory laws against Negroes from the statute books. "If the Republican party enjoys the confidence of the abolitionists," said Smith, "it is nevertheless not too much to say that it has not yet earned it." The need to win popular support kept Republican officeholders from acting in accord with antislavery principles, however praiseworthy Republican intentions may have been—or so believed the young Massachusetts abolitionist Thomas Wentworth Higginson, pointing to the example of Senator Henry Wilson, who, he complained, "sympathizes with revolution in his heart ... [yet] has to talk law and order in the Senate."[21]

Most abolitionists, save for doctrinaire disunionists and a few others like Smith and Higginson whom nothing less than perfection could satisfy, supported Republican candidates. Abolitionists generally felt little need to apologize for the Republicans' inconclusive policy toward slavery and racial injustice because they were convinced that the party would eventually move forward to occupy a more acceptable position. They placed their faith in the party's potential for future accomplishment, rather than in its declarations of limited present intentions. Probably Samuel J. May voiced the expectations of most abolitionists when he explained in 1856 that "the rank and file of the Republican party are much more anti-slavery than many of their leaders; and the tide is rising, and will rise to put these men into higher and truer positions than they now dare to take, or else put better men in their places."[22]

The Republicans' moderate antislavery program attracted support from voters of many convictions. Moderates on the slavery issue supported it because of its conservatism; radicals supported it because they expected it soon to abandon its moderation. Typical of the radical response to Republicanism was the course of a Wesleyan Methodist minister in Ohio who, in a debate with Garrisonian Andrew T. Foss, upheld Goodell's view that slavery was unconstitutional everywhere. At the same time he announced his support for Salmon P. Chase's candidacy for the United States Senate on a platform calling not for abolition but only for the nonextension of slavery.[23] The clergymen did not demand perfection in politicians but only the most advanced position that was politically feasible. He too would accept the half loaf Republicans then offered as a promise of more good things to follow.

Yet, from the abolitionists' viewpoint, these antislavery accomplishments came with distressing slowness. It had always been so. When sentiment against slavery broadened in the 1840s and found its focus in national politics, the older, religiously oriented antislavery societies lost much of their membership and, in the eyes of many, even their reason for existence. The Tappan-controlled American and Foreign Anti-Slavery Society proved even less effectual than the Garrisonian American Anti-Slavery Society. In 1853, when the Tappan organization was nearly ready to wind up its affairs (most of its members went into the American Abolition Society after 1855), Garrison gloated over the collapse of the rival society.

He pictured Lewis Tappan, its chief organizer, as sitting "like a second Marius among the ruins of a rotten Carthage, and [meditating] upon the mutability of human affairs."[24] It was a cruel simile, the more inappropriate for implying a constrasting humility in Garrison, a quality which in fact he conspicuously lacked. And if Garrison meant his remarks to suggest the prosperity of his own society, he was misleading to say the least. The income of the American Anti-Slavery Society in 1853 was reported to be only six or seven thousand dollars, a sum the executive committee had to stretch to support the society's printing and lecturing activities as well as to subsidize its newspaper, the *National Anti-Slavery Standard.* Part of even these meagre receipts came from English reformers.[25]

Despite the poor financial support for the New England-based abolitionists, they continued their agitation through the 1850s absolutely unabated. "Our cause is 'onward'—right onward," Garrison boasted in the *Liberator.*[26] While a myriad of other abolitionist newspapers flourished for a time and then quietly disappeared, Garrison's *Liberator* appeared faithfully each week for thirty-five years, presenting its relentless antislavery critique unimpaired. The Garrisonian *National Anti-Slavery Standard* was published weekly in New York from 1840 until 1870. Probably the circulation of neither of these newspapers ever exceeded 3000. The more moderate *National Era,* by way of contrast, had 25,000 subscribers in 1853. But the rather small circulation of the Garrisonian newspapers was no measure of the widespread attention and influence achieved by their editorial content.

In Pennsylvania there were two Garrisonian organizations, the Philadelphia Female Anti-Slavery Society and the Pennsylvania Anti-Slavery Society. The latter continued its work of sponsoring traveling lecturers and publishing the *Pennsylvania Freeman* throughout the 1850s. In Ohio, the Ohio American Anti-Slavery Society (later renamed the Western Anti-Slavery Society), provided a nucleus for persistent radical agitation, and circulated its newspaper, the *Anti-Slavery Bugle,* throughout the states of the Old Northwest.[27] A few new state-wide Garrisonian societies were founded in the 1850s, among them the New York Anti-Slavery Society and the Michigan Anti-Slavery Society.

Both the American Anti-Slavery Society and the Massachusetts Anti-Slavery Society in the 1840s and 1850s published numerous tracts and systematically sent lecturers through New England and into the Western states. In 1856, the executive committee of the American Anti-Slavery Society announced plans to hold 100 conventions in New England and the West, a repetition of a lecture campaign it had undertaken in 1843. The committee may not have come close to achieving its goal; but nevertheless, under its sponsorship in the mid–1850s, more than a dozen abolitionists— black and white, male and female—lectured across the North and as far west as Iowa. From scores of platforms, mostly in small towns and rural communities, they expounded the revived moral arguments against slavery, their condemnation of a society that tolerated it, and their demand for the destruction of institutions that maintained it.[28]

The Garrisonians' high-pitched argument, when accepted by persons not prepared to follow them in rejecting institutional remedies, commonly led to intensified anti-slavery political activity. But a few responded to the message differently. Those who caught the bitterness and near hopelessness of the lecturers' message and yet had no conception of the uses of political power saw no solution in orthodox, patient reform measures. For such persons, action confined within the narrow walls of legislation seemed utterly inadequate to remedy the long-sustained grievances and abuses depicted by the lecturers. They rejected society and its institutions as irremediably corrupt. For persons of such persuasion, violence became the only recourse.

Notes

1. The origins of the Christian anti-slavery convention movement
   are traced in William Goodell, *Slavery and Anti-Slavery; a History of the Great Struggle in Both Hemispheres with a View of the Slavery Question in the United States* (New York: W. Goodell, 1852), pp. 488–89.
2. *Minutes of the Christian Anti-Slavery Convention,* p. 13.
3. *National Era,* 15 May and 10 July 1851.
4. Ibid., 12 November 1857; American Anti-Slavery Society, *Reports for 1857–1858* (New York: the Society, 1859), pp. 147–54.
5. *National Era,* 15 May 1851.
6. *Cincinnati Gazette,* 20, 28, 29, 30 April 1852; *Cincinnati Journal and Messenger,* 24, 26 April 1852; Douglass to Gerrit Smith, 7 May 1852, in *The Life and Writings of Frederick Douglass,* ed. Philip S. Foner (New York: International Publishers, 1950–1955), II: 179.
7. This was the position written into the constitution of the American Anti-Slavery Society, but there were early dissenters. See Amos A. Phelps, *Lectures on Slavery and Its Remedy* (Boston: New England Anti-Slavery Society, 1834), pp. 194–95.
8. Goodell, *Slavery and Anti-Slavery,* pp. 526–27.
9. *Liberator,* 14 March 1856.
10. Ibid., 4 April 1856.
11. *National Anti-Slavery Standard,* 20 January 1853. John Smith, writing from western New York, said much the same thing. *National Era,* 26 August 1847. In contrast, Parker Pillsbury reported his unhappy experience with young listeners in *Liberator,* 23 October 1846.
12. *Liberator,* 2 January 1857.
13. Ibid., 29 May 1857.

14. Ibid., 20 July 1855.
15. *The Unconstitutionality of Slavery...* (Boston: B. Marsh, 1847). See also [Richard Hildreth], "Has Slavery in the United States a Legal Basis?" *Massachusetts Quarterly Review,* 1 (June 1848): 273–93; and "Relation of the Federal Constitution to Slavery," *The New Englander,* 3 (October 1845): 595–600.
16. *Radical Abolitionist,* 1 (August 1855): 1.
17. Giles Stebbins so reported from northern Illinois, *Liberator,* 20 July 1855, and Aaron Powell from Michigan, ibid., 25 January and 29 August 1856.
18. Massachusetts Anti-Slavery Society, *Annual Reports ... 1854, 1855, 1856* (Boston: the Society, 1856), p. 39.
19. Ibid., *Nineteenth Annual Report,* p. 83; Charles C. Burleigh expressed a similar sentiment at the Cincinnati Christian Anti-Slavery Convention. *Cincinnati Gazette,* 29 April 1852.
20. Ralph V. Harlow, *Gerrit Smith, Philanthropist and Reformer* (New York: Henry Holt, 1939), pp. 341–43; *Liberator,* 6 July and 31 August 1855.
21. *Liberator,* 11 April 1856; 13 February and 23 October 1857.
22. May to Henry C. Wright, 21 October 1856, ibid., 31 October 1856.
23. Ibid., 23 October 1857.
24. Ibid., 4 November 1853.
25. Massachusetts Anti-Slavery Society, *Annual Reports ... 1854, 1855, 1856,* pp. 13–14.
26. *Liberator,* 20 November 1854.
27. The story of the Western Anti-Slavery Society is told in Douglas Gamble, "Moral Suasion in the Old Northwest: Garrisonian Abolitionism, 1831–1861" (Ph.D. dissertation, Ohio State University, 1973).
28. American Anti-Slavery Society, *Annual Report ... 1856* (New York: the Society, 1856), pp. 52–53, 69; *Annual Report ... 1857–1858* (New York: the Society, 1858), pp. 187–88.

CHAPTER TEN

The Resort to Carnal Weapons: Politics and Guns

1854–1860

Nearly all abolitionists from the beginning of their agitation expected to confine their antislavery efforts to moral suasion and political action. Organized at a time when fears of slave uprising gripped the nation, the American Anti-Slavery Society specifically renounced all violent and coercive tactics. Some leading abolitionists, especially those of Quaker backgrounds, were confirmed nonresistants. But for others, pacifism was a chosen tactic dictated by circumstances of the time and not a matter of deep conviction. Such persons could change their mode of operations to meet new occasions and suffer no pangs of conscience in consequence.

Peaceful tactics obviously harmonized with the religious and philosophical tenets held by most abolitionists, but such methods also were dictated by the fact that abolitionists comprised only a tiny minority within the nation. Power, in the form of numbers and institutions, was controlled by the opposition. For abolitionists to resort to violence in the 1830s and 1840s, or even to countenance its use, would almost certainly have led them and their cause to disaster. When in the 1830s they folded their arms and called upon the nation to repent, they were mobbed. What would have been the consequence had they called instead for physical attack against slavery and slaveholders? The mobs that assailed even their most peaceful efforts brutally reminded them of the peril to which they were subject on account of their minority position.[1]

Circumstances ordinarily required even those who might be of militant persuasion to carry out their protests by peaceful means. A number of black residents of Boston, for example, were said to have moved to the suburbs in the early 1850s as a nonviolent protest against Boston's segregated schools.[2] Here and there an abolitionist quietly withdrew support from a government that he found evil. Thoroughgoing Garrisonians were likely to refrain from voting; some refused to pay taxes to a government whose policies they could not approve. On 12 January 1856, Samuel D. Moore of Ypsilanti, Michigan, issued the following notice, later published in the *Liberator:* "Know all men (and women) by this, that as the state of Michigan, through the General Government is pledged to sustain and protect the unrighteous system of chattel slavery, I hereby refuse of my own free will and consent to pay all taxes to sustain said State and National Governments."[3]

The move from such tempered opposition to still more direct forms of protest and thus toward violence seemed all but irresistible. As soon as abolitionists admitted the propriety of organizing to exert antislavery political power, the way was open for them to advocate the use of other kinds of coercion. A speaker at a Liberty party convention held at Marlboro, Ohio, on 1 August 1845, asserted in a statement reminiscent of Andrew Kopkind's frequently cited aphorism in the *New York Review of Books* ("Morality, like politics, starts at the barrel of a gun"), that he had "no confidence in moral power, except where it is backed up by the Ballot box and cartridge box, by the Bayonet's point and the *Cannon's* mouth."[4]

Except for Quakers, religiously oriented abolitionists ordinarily found in religious doctrine no insurmountable obstacle in the way of accepting such supplements to moral suasion. While admonitions to meekness and passivity could be found in the Bible, that book also contained unmistakable themes of violence. Both the Old and New

"The Runaway"

Testaments portrayed retribution for wrong doing and redemption from sin as taking place through blood and suffering. Bible-reading abolitionists were exposed to numerous examples of violence employed against transgressors and in the interest of righteousness. One might choose to ignore this element in Christianity and remain a nonresistant as Lewis Tappan, for example, consistently did. But by no means did all evangelicals follow Tappan onto pastures of peace. In 1843, for instance, the abolitionist students at the Missionary Institute, an evangelically oriented college at Quincy, Illinois, adopted as their class slogan the bellicose motto, "*Universal Freedom,* or *death on the battlefield.*"⁵

Counsel urging or at least sanctioning a slave uprising was even more likely to be heard. In the same year that Illinois students declared themselves ready for war, a young black clergyman speaking at a Negro convention in Buffalo, New York, called on slaves to rise in rebellion as Nat Turner had done in Virginia a dozen years earlier.

"Brethren, arise, arise!" cried the Rev. Henry Highland Garnet, who had studied at Beriah Green's Oneida Institute, "strike for your lives and liberties. Now is the day and hour." The convention failed to endorse Garnet's sentiments, but only by a vote of nineteen to eighteen.[6]

One of Garnet's acquaintances, John Brown, also grew increasingly militant in his views toward slavery in the 1840s. Soon he was quoting from Hebrews 9:22 that "almost all things are by the law purged with blood; and without shedding of blood is no remission." In 1849, Garnet's address to the Buffalo convention, together with David Walker's *Appeal,* a militant antislavery tract first published in Boston in 1829, appeared in pamphlet form, perhaps at Brown's expense.[7]

By the end of the 1840s, such advice as Garnet's received growing support in Negro conventions and in Negro newspapers and pamphlets. Some were losing faith that moral suasion, nonresistance, and even political action—the modes of antislavery action almost universally endorsed by white abolitionists—ever could destroy slavery. In 1849, Frederick Douglass, still at that date a loyal Garrisonian, told an audience at Faneuil Hall in Boston that he would "welcome the intelligence to-morrow should it come, that the slaves had risen in the South, and that the sable arms which had engaged in beautifying and adorning the South were engaged in spreading death and devastation there."[8]

Few white abolitionists could have motives as strong as Douglass and Garnet for sanctioning slave rebellion. Yet the logic of their ideology led some Whites also to accept rebellion as a just and rational response to oppression. Abolitionists often found in the events and ideas of the Revolutionary era justification for their hostility to slavery. No one could easily ignore—or fail to condone—the American revolutionary record: An oppressed people in the preceding century had taken up arms against their oppressors and had won their freedom on the battlefield. Not even Garrison, famed as a nonresistant, failed to note the implications of the fact that American independence had been achieved through violence and not by moral suasion or electoral politics. The example could not be hidden; the precedent it set for slaves was hard to explain away. "Is it wrong to resist oppression unto blood?" Garrison asked in 1837. "A voice from Bunker Hill cries, 'No!' The gory soil of Lexington and Concord thunders, 'No!' "[9]

Thus at an early date Garrison compromised his nonresistance and peace principles. On the one hand he opposed the use of force and violence; on the other he recognized the justice of their use by slaves. Some abolitionists found a way out of the dilemma when they recognized, as Abby Kelley did in 1857, that slavery itself was warfare.[10] Since slavery was maintained by force, it might justly be opposed in the same way. The rules of nonresistance that might have applied in other circumstances had already been nullified.

Abolitionists increasingly brought moral suasion into question as its accomplishments were judged wanting. Developments after 1850 did nothing to persuade either black or white abolitionists that peaceful abolition could be achieved. Several events contributed to the noticeable trend toward violence. The Fugitive Slave Act resulted not merely in verbal denunciation. It also brought open resistance to its enforcement, in some instances by violent means. As such instances multiplied, an acquiescence in force and physical resistance developed. Men became resigned to their use in the antislavery cause.

The struggle in Kansas between free state and slave state settlers thrust the fact of open warfare directly into the abolitionist consciousness. Events in Kansas inspired a belief that violence was inevitable, however much it might be deplored. "That spirit which desired the peaceful extinction of slavery has itself become extinct," wrote Abraham Lincoln on 15 August 1855; "... experience has demonstrated, I think, that there is no peaceful extinction of slavery in prospect for us." James G. Birney, now nearing the end of a lifetime spent in pursuit of peaceful abolition, wrote in 1856 in similar vein: "I regret that a civil war should rage but if slavery cannot be exterminated without one—& I don't see how it can be—I say let it come."[11]

When news of armed clashes in Kansas reached the East, some took for granted that the ultimate battle between slavery and freedom at last was underway. The war was likened to Armageddon, and no compromise could end *that* conflict. "This is the death-grapple between Slavery and Freedom, on the tempestuous ocean," announced Lydia Maria Child, "and one or the other must go down!"[12] Warfare in Kansas seriously weakened Mrs. Child's commitment to nonresistance, as it weakened that of others. She expressed disgust at news that a party of New England emigrants headed for Kansas had allowed themselves to be arrested and disarmed by authorities in Missouri. She was provoked at them "for *relinquishing their arms* without a struggle. . . . It makes this sacred struggle for freedom seem ridiculous."[13]

Unlike some other abolitionists, Garrison did not romanticize the free-state emigrants in Kansas. He was more skeptical than most about the depth of their commitment to abolitionist principles. He doubted that the Kansas settlers were the "friends of freedom without distinction of color. As a class, they did not go there to battle for freedom," he wrote. "They went to make money."[14] Garrison's realistic view was anything but general in the North, however, where the Kansas settlers were more often supported as being truly representative of Northern interests—as indeed they may have been.

The situation in Kansas doubtlessly was intricate and hard to comprehend, but in some quarters little effort seems to have been made to learn the truth about events happening there. It was enough to know that pro-Southern forces had attacked settlers from the free states. Confronted by such knowledge, abolitionists found it difficult to do otherwise than to accept the fact of war and to adjust policy and conduct to accord with the new situation.

In 1855, when the convention that organized the American Abolition Society met at Syracuse, it listened to an ap-

peal to supply aid for John Brown, who then was engaged
in adventures in Kansas, and a collection was taken to support him—"pistols and all," the *Liberator* reported.[15] The
Garrisonian Giles Stebbins found on his lecture tour in
southern Michigan in 1856 the general opinion that "slavery is beginning to lay hands on northern men, and people
are surprised and indignant."[16] A similar attitude in the
Northeast led to the creation of the New England Emigrant
Aid Society, supported by prominent abolitionists, to help
finance the Northern forces in Kansas and to encourage
more Northerners to move there.[17]

In some places men made actual preparations for war. In
1855 citizens in Grand Rapids, Michigan, formed a military
company "for the protection of Northern rights and Northern men." Its leaders announced their intention to organize
similar companies "in every city, town, and village north of
Mason and Dixon's line." Blacks in Cleveland and other
cities formed military companies at about the same time. In
1857, delegates to a Negro convention in Ohio resolved
"when practicable" to set up such groups to study military
tactics and "to become more proficient in the use of arms."[18]

As the sectional clash markedly sharpened in the mid–
1850s, metaphors of violence became conspicuous in abolitionist writing and oratory. The most vivid of these were
borrowed from the Bible. Parker Pillsbury took to incor-
porating in his lectures and applying to the abolitionist
cause a passage from the Parable of the Vineyard (Luke
20:18): "Whosoever shall fall upon that stone shall be
broken; but on whomsoever it shall fall, it will grind him to
powder."[19] George Sunter, Jr., a recent arrival from England, altered the phrases so as to apply them specifically
to Southerners. "The only available anti-slavery is the total
and everlasting destruction of all their idols," said Sunter,
"to break them to pieces, to grind them to powder, and
scatter them to the winds."[20] It was but a short step from
smashing idols to wishing to destroy those who worshipped
them. "To us, as Abolitionists, slaveholders, as such, have
no rights," asserted Henry C. Wright in 1857; "outlawed by

humanity, they are to be exterminated, as slaveholders, from the face of the earth."[21]

The abolitionists' desire for tangible accomplishment and their impatience after decades of peaceful but apparently fruitless effort were understandable. "The *Theory* of emancipation has been pretty well discussed," observed Alonzo J. Grover of Earlville, Illinois, in February 1857. "Twenty-five years of anti-slavery debate ought to have resulted at least in a programme of action.... Certainly, we are not going to continue the discussion twenty-five years longer without testing our theory by some practical experiments!"[22]

Grover, who had recently moved from Massachusetts to Illinois, professed to be a nonresistant Garrisonian, yet the "practical experiment" he proposed was an abolitionist-supported slave uprising. "Is it not time to endorse slave insurrections, and preach revolution?" he asked. The slave deserved aid from abolitionists, said Grover, in the form of "Lead and steel."

Such sentiments, once nearly unthinkable within the antislavery movement, became commonplace in 1857. In earlier days peace-minded abolitionists had defended their program as a means of avoiding a slave insurrection; now a number of them openly advocated revolt. The issue was thoroughly debated at the Massachusetts Anti-Slavery Society's convention in January 1857.[23]

Henry C. Wright, after carefully explaining that few abolitionists had ever adhered to the doctrine of nonresistance, declared that "resistance to tyrants is obedience to God; and the man who believes in fighting at all, is a traitor to his principles if he does not assert the right of the American slave to armed resistance." Every antislavery man, said Wright, resisted slavery and rebelled against it to the extent that he refused to recognize its legality and claims to permanence. There was no logical reason, then, why abolitionists might not carry their resistance further. "Every man must actualize his resistance and rebellion—his treason—by such means as he thinks right and most efficient." For

Wright as well as for much of the Garrisonian circle, resistance had come to mean advocacy of slave rebellion. "It is the right and duty of the people of the North, themselves being witnesses, to incite the slaves to insurrection," said Wright, "and to furnish them with arms and ammunition to carry out their purpose."

Wendell Phillips endorsed Wright's counsel. "If a negro kills his master to-night," he said, "write his name by the side of Warren; say that he is a William Tell in disguise.... I want to accustom Massachusetts to the ideas of insurrection; to the idea that every slave has a right to seize his liberty on the spot."

No doubt even some belligerent-minded abolitionists doubted that they could justly incite a racial war. Abby Kelley, a birthright member of the Society of Friends, supplied an answer to that objection. She assured her fellow abolitionists that "the question is not whether we shall counsel the slaves to forsake peace, and commence war; *the war exists already,* and has been waged unremittingly ever since the slave has been in bondage."

Garrison entered the discussion, not in doctrinaire support of nonresistance but in oblique endorsement of rebellion. "A man has no right to consent to be a slave," said Garrison. "He is bound in duty to seek freedom; and he must seek it in a manner accordant with his own ideas of right, deciding that point for himself." Parker Pillsbury concurred with Garrison but stated the idea more starkly: "It is as well a sin to be a slave as to hold a slave." Both Pillsbury and Garrison declared, in effect, that since no man had the right to enslave another, no man could rightly remain a slave. Slaves were duty bound to rebel and assert their right to freedom. Abolitionists had restated the eighteenth-century right of revolution and applied it to American slavery.

Of all the delegates who spoke at the Massachusetts convention, only Arnold Buffum, a Quaker who nearly a generation earlier had helped found the New England Anti-Slavery Society, and David Wasson, a much younger Unitarian minister, supported the claims of nonresistance as a conviction and not merely as a tactic. Their pacifistic views were disputed by two formidable figures: Abby Kelley, who thought it "sad that Mr. Wasson sees so justly the reality of a war in Kansas, and not in Carolina," and by Garrison himself who condemned Wasson's argument against slave rebellion as evidence of racial prejudice.

The despair of conventional approaches that led the Massachusetts abolitionists to see no peaceful way out of the impasse of the 1850s was far from being universal among antislavery men. Most still were reluctant to acknowledge the failure of their time-honored tactics. Numerous evangelicals as well as followers of Garrison continued to agitate the antislavery cause exclusively by means of moral suasion and politics as they had always done. They were not prepared to follow critics of those traditional approaches who argued that pro-slavery, anti-Negro interests would never surrender peacefully to electoral majorities or to persuasion.

Yet little in contemporary events appeared to warrant such optimism. In this instance, Gerrit Smith, who had been an abolitionist for twenty years, appraised the situation without illusion. By 1855, he had concluded "that the movement to abolish American slavery is a failure." To those optimists who found in the British example of peaceful abolition in her West Indian colonies proof that the United States could follow a similar course, Smith replied that the historical analogy was imperfect. The circumstances of the two countries were quite dissimilar. "England was not debauched and ruled by her slavery—but American slavery has left scarcely one sound spot in American character; and it is, confessedly, the ruler of America." Like so many others in the 1850s, Smith thought he detected in the conflict over slavery a logic that propelled the nation toward catastrophe. "It is but too probable," he predicted, "that American slavery will have expired in blood before the men shall have arisen who are capable of bringing it to a voluntary termination."

Smith's gloomy appraisal of the accomplishment and prospect of the antislavery movement did not lead him to abandon the cause to which he had devoted a large part of his energy and much of his considerable wealth for nearly a quarter of a century. His justification for continued effort was not, however, the prospect of success but a concept of religious duty that might have been voiced by the most otherwordly of evangelicals: "Notwithstanding we have failed, and will, in all probability, continue to fail, to accomplish our great work, we, nevertheless, cannot abandon it. We must persevere in it, if only to save our own souls."[24]

As the months passed, Smith, like members of Garrison's circle, increasingly put his trust for the eventual end of slavery in the slaves themselves. Now he opposed all moderate antislavery efforts and refused to support them. He became the complete come-outer. Even though he continued his own radical political activity, he seemed to have no faith in it. He decided that all the usual means of antislavery had demonstrated their futility and must be repudiated. In 1859, he even refused to take part in the annual celebration of the rescue of Jerry at Syracuse, an event that once had seemed to him as well as to many other abolitionists a symbol of vital antislavery accomplishment and a means of promoting abolitionism. Exhortation, agitation, politics—all were useless. Slave rebellion, Smith finally declared, was the only solution. A rebellion might be put down, Smith conceded, but its repercussions would nonetheless be so overwhelming that slavery would go down in failure with it.[25]

A clue to the source of Smith's ideas may be found in his association with John Brown. Since April 1848, when Brown first visited Smith's home at Peterboro, New York, contact between the two had been frequent and increasingly intimate. Smith had been the largest single financial contributor to Brown's exploits in Kansas. In February 1858, while spending several days at Smith's home, Brown revealed a new antislavery plan to his host and to Smith's other house guests, Edwin Morton and Franklin Sanborn, a member of the Transcendentalist circle at Concord, Massachusetts. Now as Brown developed a plan to carry war into the South itself, Smith declared that he was ready to "go *all* lengths to support him."[26]

A few months earlier Smith with his customary enthusiasm endorsed still another plan to end slavery. In its conservatism and bloodlessness it differed altogether from Brown's militant scheme. It was a proposal that would have appeared more reasonable had it been offered thirty years earlier before experience taught that few slaveholders were seeking for ways to end slavery. Now it seemed utterly anachronistic. It was a proposal to free the slaves with the approval of Southerners themselves. This approach had often been suggested—and as often rejected—in earlier, more innocent days. It seemed a waste of effort to bring it forward again.

The plan Smith endorsed was another proposal for compensated emancipation. "The Learned Blacksmith," Elihu Burritt, who had become famous for his tireless work on behalf of the peace movement, hoped to commit the federal government to use the proceeds from public land sales to buy and free slaves. Thus the whole nation would share in the expense of gradual emancipation.

Burritt organized a National Emancipation Convention at Cleveland in August 1857 to consider the proposal.[27] Some prominent clergymen endorsed the convention, but almost the only well-known abolitionist to attend was the ubiquitous Gerrit Smith. Surprisingly, the antislavery veteran John Rankin, whose abolitionism dated from the 1820s, also supported the plan, declaring that slaveholders had a moral right to be compensated for the loss of their slaves, a view held by almost no other abolitionist. Since the North had allowed Southerners to become enmeshed in the slave system, Rankin reasoned, it should bear part of the cost of doing away with it. Most of the abolitionist press ridiculed Burritt's proposal. Only the *National Era* saw some value in holding the convention. Editor Gamaliel Bailey rejected the plan, but in the spirit of the true agitator declared nevertheless that he welcomed the controversy the proposal was certain to create.[28]

Smith justified his own support for Burritt's seemingly impractical scheme by explaining that it would capitalize on the antislavery sentiment that then appeared to be growing in Maryland and other border states. If the plan persuaded even one state to end slavery, another would follow its example, and then another, until at last all the Southern dominoes collapsed and slavery would be swept from the nation.

Smith's enthusiasm was unwarranted. The unfavorable response to Burritt's proposal should have surprised no one. Few abolitionists gave it serious attention, having long ago rejected the notion that slaveholders should be paid for setting free their "stolen property." And outside of a cluster of supporters in Maryland, Southern response too was generally hostile. The *Richmond Enquirer* assembled an imposing array of pejoratives to help dispose of the plan. It was "ludicrous, chimerical, and factious, . . . presumptious, foolish, fanatical, and traitorous, evidence of abolition insanity," declared the editor.[29]

Despite the nearly total rejection of Burritt's plan, he was not so altogether misguided in proposing it as might appear. Apprehension did in fact grow among slaveholders in the late 1850s that some states in the Upper South would fall under Republican party control and adopt a policy of gradual emancipation. This prospect was not unthinkable so far as Maryland, Kentucky, and Missouri were concerned, for in those states the Republicans had secured a toehold by 1860, and local opponents of slavery began freely to criticize the institution. Southern fear of emancipation in the border states soon would serve as a powerful stimulus to the secession movement, for, it was thought, if Southerners could be persuaded to unite in defense of their common political cause, the wavering border states would loyally remain within the Southern orbit, and slavery would be saved.[30]

But Burritt's plan could not take advantage of any of these Southern anxieties. Few Southerners would support any antislavery proposal arising in the North. The lack of favorable response to the National Emancipation Convention plunged Smith into one of his periodic moods of despondency. Abolitionists were not interested in promoting compensated emancipation, and not one Southern newspaper, so far as he could learn, had endorsed the plan—"he was at a loss to know what further action to take." It was perhaps the rejection of what Smith regarded as the last conceivable hope of ending slavery peacefully and with the consent of the South that led him six months later to listen sympathetically when John Brown unfolded his scheme to destroy slavery by launching an attack against Virginia.[31]

Signs increased that abolitionists in growing numbers were ready to acquiesce in the use of violence. By the 1850s, even the Garrisonians' presumably peaceful tactic—dissolution of the Union—was accompanied by overtones of militancy bordering on violence. This fact became evident in the proceedings of the National Disunion Convention held at Cleveland in October 1857, two months after Burritt's fiasco in the same city. The committee of arrangements for the disunion meeting was headed by Garrison and a coterie of his New England associates, including Thomas Wentworth Higginson, Frank W. Bird, Wendell Phillips, and Daniel Mann, some of whom were not Garrisonian in ideology but rather were strong supporters of the new Republican party. Although New England abolitionists sponsored the affair (it had been preceded by a similar meeting held at Worcester, Massachusetts), support for it was much less regional.[32]

Some 6,033 persons from sixteen states signed the call for the convention. Of these, 4,200 were identified as qualified voters. Presumably the remainder were minors, disfranchised Blacks, and women. The considerable influence of Garrisonian lecturers and newspapers in the West is suggested by the fact that more than half the signers of the call lived in states west of New York and Pennsylvania: 1,757 were from Ohio, 496 from Michigan, 474 from Indiana, 181 from Iowa, 150 from Illinois.[33]

Just as Burritt's plan for compensated emancipation had been welcomed in some quarters on account of its agitational value, so some abolitionists unsympathetic with Garrison and his disunionist theories nevertheless believed the convention would be useful as a means of publicizing abolitionism. Gamaliel Bailey, editor of the politically oriented *National Era,* noted that the convention was endorsed by persons "hitherto associated with wise and practical movements."[34] William Jay, no longer a proponent of disunion as he had been a decade earlier, did not accept Garrison's invitation to attend the meeting, but neither did he altogether repudiate it. Its effect, he thought, would benefit the antislavery cause. The convention's call for dissolving the Union would not win much public acceptance, Jay predicted, but nevertheless the indictment of the North for its ties with slavery would help persuade additional persons to demand reform. Jay valued "such exposure, as tending, not to bring about dissolution, but to render it unnecessary."[35]

At the very last moment, the Eastern sponsors of the convention withdrew their support and announced postponement, ostensibly on account of financial problems growing out of the Panic of 1857.[36] But by the time their decision was made, Westerners were already on their way to Cleveland. They ignored the postponement, and the meeting proceeded as scheduled under the direction of Garrisonians who lived in the West or who happened to be lecturing there at the time.

The membership was nearly all of an extremist mood. Continuing warfare in Kansas and the Supreme Court's recent pro-Southern decision in the Dred Scott case had helped raise abolitionist indignation to a high pitch. Parker Pillsbury caught the militant spirit of those who answered the call to attend the convention. He wrote from Adrian, Michigan, on 26 October that abolitionists headed for Cleveland "with a purpose as earnest and holy as brought the farmers of New England to Lexington and Bunker Hill at the opening of the great Revolutionary Drama which it is left for us to complete." His own belligerency at that moment may have been aggravated by the fact that he and his black companions, Charles and Sarah Remond, had just ended a series of antislavery meetings in Lenawee County, Michigan. It had not been a pleasant experience for either the Remonds or Pillsbury. "The dire necessity for revolution was made most apparent," was Pillsbury's dry comment.[37]

As Pillsbury suggested, racial prejudice continued to plague Blacks and those white abolitionists who accepted their equality. William Wells Brown, a convention delegate, was refused dining room service at the Bennet House in Cleveland, although he was given a room there. Not until some of his fellow delegates—Aaron M. Powell, Susan B. Anthony, Andrew T. Foss, and Lucy Coleman—protested by refusing to eat at the hotel, was Brown accommodated.[38]

The delegates selected Marius Robinson, editor of the Ohio *Anti-Slavery Bugle* and one of the Lane Rebels of 1834, as its presiding officer. Addresses were delivered by Pillsbury, Charles Remond, Abby Kelley, Powell, and Charles C. Burleigh. The delegates branded "this Union a crime and curse, that should not exist a single hour"; and proclaimed their determination "come to us what may . . . in the name of Freedom and of God, to seek its destruction."

The tone of the resolution reflected a degree of defiance not often encountered in earlier abolitionist gatherings outside New England, but the most startling act of the convention was its adoption of a resolution endorsing slave rebellion: "It is the duty of the slaves to strike down their tyrant masters by force and arms," said the delegates, "whenever the blow, however bloody, can be made effective to that end . . . ; whenever we behold them in the battle-field of Freedom, we will give them every aid and comfort in our power."[39] In view of such sentiments, William Wells Brown's findings that "the colored citizens of Cleveland took decidedly more interest in the late convention than the whites" is not surprising.[40]

The aggressive spirit that marked the Cleveland meeting also swept through the convention of the Massachusetts Anti-Slavery Society in January 1859. One of the participants in the Boston meeting was Richard J. Hinton, a British-born newspaper correspondent just returned from reporting events in Kansas. He read the delegates a letter of greeting from John Brown in which Brown proclaimed the opening of "a new era in the Anti-Slavery movement." Hinton explained what Brown meant: "The rifle shot that laid low the first victim in Kansas, has rung the death-knell of slavery on this continent."[41]

Hinton advised the assembled Garrisonians, some of whom still were confirmed nonresistants, that "the terrible Logic of History teaches plainly that no great wrong was ever cleansed without blood." The particular lesson taught by events in Kansas, he said, was "the mode and manner by which the most vulnerable point of slavery, that of Insurrection may be reached. Kansas has done this and it has also educated men for the work."

Hinton pictured for the abolitionists scenes of horror and the use of weapons that they had designed their life's work to avoid: "For one, believing in the right of resistance for myself, I extend the same to my African brother and stand ready at any time to aid in the overthrow of slavery by any and all means,—the rifle or revolver, the dagger or torch."

Thomas Wentworth Higginson, the young Unitarian preacher who had long talked of revolution and who also was a confidant of Brown, favored a slave uprising just as Hinton did. He explained to the convention that a raid Brown recently conducted into Missouri to free slaves was "an indication of what may come before long." Once Higginson had sought to free slaves through the Underground Railroad. It was he who had led the Boston mob that, in 1854, tried unsuccessfully to free the fugitive Anthony Burns. He put such tactics behind him now. The principle of liberty was working among the great mass of slaves, he declared, creating in them the desire "not as formerly to go to freedom" by escape into the North, "but to have freedom come to them. And who knows how speedily a morning may arise to show us that it has come?"

Some members of the Boston convention may have been horrified at such predictions. Parker Pillsbury, however, welcomed the sanguinary prospect Brown's friends described. He accused the assembled abolitionists of naïveté in clinging to the old tactic of moral suasion. "Whoever expects to see slavery extinguished but in a Red Sea of blood, knows little of the philosophy of human experience and of human needs," said Pillsbury. He chided nonresistant abolitionists for being out of touch with their times. He also had words for those who were not philosophically opposed to force and yet declined to use it. They were "not up to the exigencies of this hour," he declared, "and the young men who are not training themselves in the art of war, are probably only prolonging a strife that must end at last either in complete submission to the Slave Power, or in scenes of blood at the very mention of which we well might tremble." Pillsbury still respected the philosophy of nonresistance, but he made clear his belief that persons who adhered to it were only a drag on the abolitionist cause.

Such bloody and martial sentiments shocked Garrison. Though he had wavered in his commitment to nonresistance and had declared his belief in the justice of slave rebellion, proposals for abolitionists themselves to go to war were another matter. He was not convinced that it would be better to end slavery in a holocaust than to see it continue; he did not believe that it would be better for Negroes to be dead than enslaved. "Where there is no life, there are no rights," he said. But aside from such crude weighing of values, there was a persistent, practical question that had to be raised. If we decide to take up arms and fight against slavery, Garrison asked, where should the battle begin? A conceptual problem had to be faced: the term "Free States" was not quite accurate. In one sense no such entity existed, as Garrison made clear. "If we fight with actual slaveholders in the South, must we not also fight with pro-slavery priests, politicians, editors, merchants, in the North?" he asked. "Where are we to begin?" And this was a problem Garrison also would have had to confront had his call for dissolution of the Union ever been seriously entertained. A geographic line that would neatly separate pro-slavery from antislavery forces could not be drawn.[42] This was the overpowering lesson taught by the antislavery controversy.

Garrison understood that the moral conversion of the North to the abolitionist cause was still far from complete. Anti-Southern sentiment was not the equivalent of abolitionism. Though polarization of the sections with respect to slavery was far advanced, he knew that the same could not be said about attitudes toward race. Slavery as an institution had become sectional; the racial attitudes that sustained it remained national.

Some clergymen, as appalled as Garrison by the rush to embrace violence, attempted to halt it by reawakening the old commitment to moral suasion. In March 1859, an Evangelical Anti-Slavery Convention met at Worcester, Massachusetts with some fifty clergymen from New York and New England in attendance. They declared their purpose to be the "total abolition of the vast system of American slavery, to be accepted as the providential Mission and Duty of the American clergy and the American churches in this generation." They left no doubt that in their minds this was a goal to be achieved peacefully. The clergy would mobilize to end slavery by the force of moral power, not through blood and fire. Out of these deliberations came the formation of the Church Anti-Slavery Society. Throughout the Civil War it acted as a pressure group attempting to move slow and reluctant politicians toward a policy of emancipation.[43]

Efforts to promote moral suasion in the face of a growing martial spirit were not confined to clergymen in the East. In August 1859, another in the long series of Christian Anti-Slavery Conventions met at the Congregational Church in Columbus, Ohio.[44] The gathering was in part a response to recently announced intentions of Southerners to revive the

African slave trade; partly it was an effort to speed the quickening movement within the Protestant churches to adopt abolitionist principles. The delegates made a special point of shying away from endorsement of coercion and violence; they even downgraded political antislavery action. A few months earlier, John Brown had told the Massachusetts Anti-Slavery Society that a new phase of the antislavery movement characterized by warfare had begun. In contrast, Henry Peck, an Oberlin professor of mathematics who recently had helped rescue a fugitive slave, informed the delegates at Columbus "that the leading feature of the new anti-slavery movement was prayer." He and his fellow delegates seem to have had the impression that their convention marked a new departure in antislavery activity, that they were leading the antislavery host from the inferior level of political abolitionism onto a higher moral and religious plane.

Antislavery political activity might be a "great means of good," Peck conceded, but prayer still remained "an appeal superior to the ballot-box." The convention directed its special criticism, however, not at politicians or would-be warriors but at the churches, for their half-hearted antislavery stand. The revival in prayer that the delegates advocated was expected to take place outside the churches as well as in them. "The Church! God save us from the Church! What had she ever done?" exclaimed the political abolitionist Joshua Giddings during one of the sessions.

In their adherence to prayer as the primary instrument of abolitionism, the clergymen at Columbus may have been as out of touch with the needs of their time as Pillsbury said nonresistants were, but their analysis of party politics demonstrated that they were nonetheless capable of shrewdly assessing the tactical problems facing abolitionists. The urgency that marked their deliberations resulted from their understanding of the limitations of political power to achieve moral ends. Like Garrison, they perceived that the Northern commitment to racial justice remained tentative and incomplete. Thus, the 1859 convention was as critical of antislavery political parties as its predecessors earlier in the decade had been, and as apprehensive of the results of emancipation if it were accomplished without an accompanying change in attitude toward human rights.

The delegates noted in particular the Republican party's "prevalent *tendency to overlook the claims of the oppressed themselves—the injustice and wickedness of slavery,* and to limit the public concern to questions of interest to the dominant race—the right and requirements of free labor." They were troubled by the secularism of antislavery politics. "We do not wish to undervalue the political antislavery which prevails," they explained, "but how little of it has even the semblance of repentance for wrong doing and of zeal for righteousness?"

The delegates thought they understood only too well the source of the Republican party's neglect of these matters. It sprang from the same racial attitudes that had always blocked abolitionist efforts. Closely allied to the politicians' "indifference to the claims of the oppressed," the clergymen charged, *"is the cold-hearted and repelling prejudice which exists against the coloured race,* both bond and free —a standing illustration of the truth discovered of old, that men hate those whom they have injured."

Evangelical abolitionists would try to change this situation by promoting a religious revival. Others would view it as hopeless and call for slave insurrection as the only recourse; a few, likewise despairing of ever altering racial attitudes, proposed emigration of the Blacks.

Despite the clergy's criticism of antislavery politics, they directed their critique, finally, not so much against Republican party leadership as against the Northern majority itself. Party strategists—Republicans and Democrats alike —took for granted that most voters rejected abolitionists and their program. They made little effort to help the electorate rise above racial bias. If victory was their aim, they perhaps had no other choice. Because of their limited antislavery stand, Republicans were condemned by their opponents as abolitionists and especially as advocates of Negro equality—charges they were quick to refute because they understood the ruinous effect such association would have in swaying a conservative, racially prejudiced electorate.

Almost everywhere in 1859 and 1860, but most conspicuously in Western states, Republican leaders acquiesced in the all but universal racial bias and took stands far removed from abolitionist positions. When a Democratic party newspaper warned in 1859 that Republican party success would encourage the Blacks in Canada to move to Ohio, William Dennison, the Republican candidate for governor, hastened to assure voters that the charge was false. The "Republican party is the white man's party," he declared, "and it labors for the prosperity and liberty of the white man." Republican candidates in most other states were attacked by similar allegations and attempted to repel them in the same way.[45]

The effort Republican spokesmen made to disassociate themselves from abolitionism was not completely successful, partly because abolitionists in the party and outside of it would not let it succeed. They were determined to make the Republican party an extension of the antislavery movement and as quickly as possible to transform it into an abolitionist instrument. Gamaliel Bailey, who reported these efforts in the *National Era,* wrote that the link between Republicanism and abolitionism was too close to be broken, no matter what the desire of some party leaders. "They cannot do it," was his comment; "the movements are one: the early Abolitionists were only the pioneers."[46] Bailey's history may have been faulty, but his political sense was shrewd. The Republican party had taken an antislavery stand, even if only a partial and weak one. Bailey and other abolitionists planned to hasten the time when the full implications of its position would be realized, and Stephen S. Foster assured voters that antislavery politicians aimed at total abolition.[47]

On 21 October 1859, in the First Congregational Church in Chicago, some two hundred abolitionists from across the North gathered to attend the Northwestern Christian Anti-

Slavery Convention in response to a call issued by the earlier Ohio convention.[48] The delegates intended to use the occasion to indict politicians for their lack of genuine concern for slavery. The Reverend Jonathan Blanchard declared that "he trusted in no political party," for the men who "plan political organizations cannot be governors and prophets at the same time." Yet Blanchard admitted that such considerations had not kept him from voting for Republican candidates. While the chief concern of the delegates in attending the meeting was the low moral level of politics and politicians, a still more urgent matter now demanded their attention.

Only a week earlier, on 16 October, John Brown and his small band of followers attacked the United States arsenal at Harper's Ferry, Virginia, in a futile attempt to start the slave uprising that Gerrit Smith, Thomas Wentworth Higginson, and Richard Hinton had earlier predicted was imminent. Brown bungled the operation, and the slaves did not respond as he had been led to expect they would. Brown and his men soon were captured and indicted for treason against the state of Virginia.

The evangelicals gathered at Chicago could not ignore so explosive an event. As abolitionists, they were involved in it. Conscience as well as public opinion required their comment. The delegates finally voted to "deplore" Brown's raid. But the resolution was adopted only over vigorous opposition and after impassioned debate. Among the most avid of Brown's defenders at the meeting was a black delegate, H. Ford Douglass of Chicago. The convention erupted into turmoil over the issue. According to a reporter for the *Chicago Tribune,* "Several of the speakers indulged in exceedingly strong and very foolish language" by justifying Brown's actions. "During the excitement ... the President of the meeting proposed that the Convention stop the debate and have a short session of prayer, which was done, and the convention then proceeded to business."

Brown's raid contributed to the crisis atmosphere that enveloped the South in 1860. Abolitionist criticism had long antagonized Southerners and created fear that it would someday produce direct antislavery aggression. Now it had done so. Even before Brown's raid, Southerners realized that they faced a formidable political menace. A Northern antislavery majority, the specter that had haunted the South since at least 1820, had attained reality. It was apparent, by late 1859, that Republicans were likely to carry the forthcoming presidential election. Southern patriots urged secession as the only recourse. Brown's raid played into the hands of those radicals who insisted on the necessity of the South's leaving the Union. They were not deterred from their plans by the fact that most Republican leaders repudiated Brown and disclaimed abolitionism. The Republican convention of 1860 wrote into the party platform a plank denouncing the Harper's Ferry raid, and Abraham Lincoln accepted Brown's execution as being just, "even though he agreed with us in thinking slavery wrong." Large anti-Brown rallies were held in New York and Boston, the site of earlier Unionist meetings. But whatever reassuring effect these events might have had for Southerners was counteracted by the far more numerous meetings in smaller towns across the North celebrating Brown's principles and exploits. Southerners could not ignore the fact that many abolitionists defended Brown and that a group of well-known Northern intellectuals and literary figures, including Ralph Waldo Emerson, Henry David Thoreau, and Henry Wadsworth Longfellow, justified his acts.[49]

The Michigan Anti-Slavery Convention at its meeting in Adrian in November 1859 resolved that "the recent attempt at Harper's Ferry ... was an act of humanity and heroism of so divine a character as that the memory of the brave men who attempted it will be held in admiration by American posterity when the names and fame of Lafayette and Kosciusko shall have long been forgotten."[50] Knowledge that eminent and powerful Northerners condemned Brown's act and disapproved abolitionism provided little comfort for Southerners, who were struck instead by such statements as the one made at Adrian. Brown's raid seemed to be an expression of a well-developed aim voiced by significant numbers of determined Northerners, and not the isolated act of a madman. It was against that background that Southerners responded to the Republican victory in the election of 1860.

Notes

1. The relative conservatism of abolitionist tactics is pointed out by Bertram Wyatt-Brown, "William Lloyd Garrison and Anti-slavery Unity: A Reappraisal," *Civil War History,* 13 (March 1967): pp. 5–24; see also John Demos, "The Antislavery Movement and the Problem of Violent 'Means,'" *New England Quarterly,* 37 (December 1964): pp. 507–26 and Louis Filler, "Nonviolence and Abolition," *University Review,* 30 (Spring 1964): pp. 172–78.

2. Carleton Mabee, *Black Freedom; the Nonviolent Abolitionists from 1830 through the Civil War* (New York: Macmillan, 1970), pp. 174–75.

3. Ibid., pp. 244–67; *Liberator,* 29 February 1856. Daniel Hise of Salem, Ohio, refused for seventeen years to vote, changing his practice only after the southern states seceded. Lewis E. Atherton, "Daniel Hise, Abolitionist and Reformer," *Mississippi Valley Historical Review,* 26 (1939): 349.

4. *Anti-Slavery Bugle,* 15 August 1845; Andrew Kopkind, "Soul Power," *New York Review of Books,* 9 (24 August 1967): 3. See Herbert Aptheker, "Militant Abolitionism," *Journal of Negro History,* 26 (1941): 438–84.

5. *Western Citizen,* 17 August 1843.

6. Mabee, *Black Freedom,* pp. 60–61.

7. Stephen B. Oates, *To Purge This Land with Blood: A Biography of John Brown* (New York: Harper and Row, 1972), p. 61.

8. Mabee, *Black Freedom,* pp. 60–66; Benjamin Quarles, *Black Abolitionists* (New York: Oxford University Press, 1969), pp. 223–35.

9. Massachusetts Anti-Slavery Society, *Fifth Annual Report ... 1837* (Boston: the Society, 1837), p. xxxv.

10. *Liberator,* 13 February 1857.
11. Abraham Lincoln to George Robertson, 15 August 1855, in *Collected Works of Abraham Lincoln,* ed. Roy P. Basler and others (New Brunswick: Rutgers University Press, 1953), II: 318; note Gerrit Smith's comment, "For many years I have well nigh despaired of the peaceful, blocdless abolition of American slavery." *Liberator,* 15 February 1856. On the general subject see Jane H. Pease and William H. Pease, "Confrontation and Abolition in the 1850s," *Journal of American History,* 58 (March 1972): 923–37.
12. Lydia Maria Child to Mrs. Ellis Gray Loring, 26 October 1856, Lydia Maria Child Papers (William L. Clements Library, Ann Arbor).
13. Child to Ellis Gray Loring, 3 July 1856, ibid.
14. *Liberator,* 4 February 1859.
15. Ibid., 6 July 1855.
16. Ibid., 11 July 1856.
17. Samuel A. Johnson, *The Battle Cry of Freedom; the New England Emigrant Aid Company in the Kansas Crusade* (Lawrence: University of Kansas Press, 1954).
18. *Liberator,* 20 July 1855; Howard H. Bell, "Expressions of Negro Militancy in the North, 1840–1860," *Journal of Negro History,* 45 (January 1960): 11–20.
19. *Liberator,* 29 February 1856.
20. Ibid., 7 March 1956.
21. Ibid., 13 February 1857.
22. Alonzo J. Grover to William Lloyd Garrison, 24 February 1857, ibid., 13 March 1857.
23. Much of the debate is quoted in *Liberator,* 13 February 1857.
24. Gerrit Smith to Wendell Phillips, 20 February 1855, ibid., 16 March 1855; Ralph V. Harlow, *Gerrit Smith, Philanthropist and Reformer* (New York: Henry Holt, 1939), pp. 336–37.
25. Harlow, *Gerrit Smith,* pp. 405–6.
26. Ibid., pp. 391–422; Oates, *To Purge This Land,* pp. 183, 227, 229, 269.
27. *Liberator,* 11 September 1857; *National Era,* 13 August 1857.
28. *National Era,* 3 September 1857.
29. Quoted in ibid., 13 August 1857.
30. Eric Foner, *Free Soil, Free Labor, Free Men; the Ideology of the Republican Party before the Civil War* (New York: Oxford University Press, 1970), pp. 120–21.
31. *National Era,* 10 September 1857; Harlow, *Gerrit Smith,* pp. 391–408.
32. Accounts of the Worcester meeting appear in American Anti-Slavery Society, *Annual Reports for 1857 and 1858,* pp. 90–98,

and Wendell Lloyd Garrison and Francis P. Garrison, *William Lloyd Garrison, 1805–1879; the Story of His Life Told by His Children* (New York: Century, 1885), III: 448–64.

33. *Liberator,* 25 September 1857.
34. *National Era,* 15 October 1857.
35. Ibid., 29 October 1857.
36. *Liberator,* 23 October 1857.
37. Ibid., 6 November 1857.
38. Ibid.
39. Ibid. Most resolutions were adopted by nearly unanimous vote. This one received only a majority. American Anti-Slavery Society, *Annual Reports for 1857 and 1858,* p. 183.
40. *Liberator,* 20 November 1857.
41. Ibid., 4 February 1859; this source records the proceedings of the Convention.
42. Note George W. Julian's later comment (18 February 1863): "The war is not a war of sections, but of ideas. . . ." George W. Julian, *Speeches on Political Questions, 1850–1871* (New York: Hurd and Houghton, 1872), pp. 205–6.
43. James M. McPherson, *The Struggle for Equality: Abolitionists and the Negro in the Civil War and Reconstruction* (Princeton: Princeton University Press, 1964), pp. 5, 39.
44. *Ohio State Journal,* 10, 11, 12 August 1859.
45. Ibid., 5, 12 August 1859; V. Jacque Voegeli (*Free but Not Equal; the Midwest and the Negro During the Civil War* [Chicago: University of Chicago Press, 1967]) documents the political turmoil produced by the issue of race.
46. *National Era,* 2 July 1859.
47. Foster soon became a staunch opponent of the Lincoln administration. McPherson, *Struggle for Equality,* pp. 99, 100, 102–3.
48. *Chicago Tribune,* 22 October 1859.
49. Mabee, *Black Freedom,* pp. 321–23; Steven A. Channing, *Crisis of Fear; Secession in South Carolina* (New York: Simon and Schuster, 1970), pp. 17–57, 92–93.
50. *National Anti-Slavery Standard,* 3 December 1859.

CHAPTER ELEVEN

"Trampling Out the Vintage"

THE CIVIL WAR AND AFTER

The election of 1860 brought the crisis Southerners had so long dreaded. Abraham Lincoln did not receive a single popular vote in ten Southern states; yet no one could deny that he had been constitutionally elected and now would be president of the United States. At last the executive branch of government would come under control of a political party immune to Southern influence and committed to the containment of slavery. In Lincoln's election the defenses Southerners had so painstakingly constructed for their special interests were shattered. Shortly thereafter the seven states of the lower South seceded from the Union.

They had little choice. The application that the new antislavery Republican party intended to make of its opportunities remained unclear. Lincoln himself was not an abolitionist, and the party he headed was not pledged to abolition. It is also true that despite the vague disapproval most Northerners felt for slavery, no general commitment prevailed to destroy it immediately. But such considerations carried little weight in the South, nor could they have, for they in no way diminished the South's peril.

The fact remained that Lincoln was head of a Northern-based party comprising voters whose wealth and status had no obvious ties to slavery, whose ideology supported a free labor system, and who were hostile to Southern society and Southern values. The Republican party's commitment to "free soil, free labor, and free men" and its theory of positive government forecast evil days for slavery and the Southern agricultural system. Secession was an act of desperation, but the alternative for the South was abject surrender and consent to its own destruction.[1]

While a few Northerners welcomed secession as good riddance, it was more commonly viewed as a calamity. Both before and after the electoral campaign of 1860, Republican leaders sought to maintain—and then to restore—the Union by giving abundant assurances that they did not intend to abolish slavery and did not seek racial equality. Throughout the secession winter of 1860–1861, fevered efforts were made to hold the Union together by removing some of the grievances that had impelled separation. While Republican congressmen almost unanimously voted against the Crittenden compromise proposals, which would have allowed slavery to extend into territories south of the old Missouri Compromise line of 36° 30', they were willing to placate the South in other ways. Republican leaders promised that henceforth the Fugitive Slave Law would be scrupulously enforced. As a goodwill gesture, three states hastily repealed their personal liberty laws, which had given Southerners such great offense in the 1850s and had served as partial justification for secession. Prominent Republicans, including Lincoln himself, endorsed a proposed constitutional amendment forever guaranteeing slavery in the states where it then existed. Congress passed the amendment and submitted it to the states for ratification.[2]

Such developments appalled abolitionists, who found in them confirmation for the contempt they had always held for politicians. They feared that a new series of compromises with the South would in effect surrender the victory just won at the polls by the antislavery, anti-Southern majority. But their alarm proved unwarranted, for Republicans stood firm against the extension of slavery—the central point in the party's antislavery program—and none of the North's other conciliatory political gestures con-

The Story of Peter Martin and the Loyalty of his Wife

vinced secessionists that Republican intentions were benign. Southern leaders understood that no legislation and
no assurances, however heartfelt and sweeping, could restore the prestige and power that Republican victory had
wrenched from them.

Abolitionists, however, did not view the flurry of political
activity pointing toward compromise as being doomed to
failure. Having slight faith in the moral steadfastness of
political leaders, they resolved to do all they could to rouse
publican opinion to resist concessions. Their newspapers
and lecturers condemned every effort at reunion if it were
accomplished at the price of maintaining slavery and restoring Southern influence. In this policy, they clashed with
influential Northerners who sought reconciliation at almost any price—and for whom the Union assumed a value

most any price—and for whom the Union assumed a value and interest paramount to any other consideration. The abolitionists' denunciation of compromise appeared to confirm the charge repeatedly made by the Democratic and conservative press: Abolitionists and Blacks were in some way responsible for provoking secession. The result was a new wave of hostility directed against both minority groups.[3]

At no time since the 1830s had abolitionists been subjected to such virulent mob violence as in the secession winter of 1860–1861. On 3 December 1860 an abolitionist meeting in Boston was stormed by a mob of "North end Roughs and Beacon Street Aristocrats" led by lawyers and merchants, who marched to the platform, removed the speaker, James Redpath—a partisan of John Brown—and took over the meeting. The abolitionists then moved to a nearby Negro Baptist church and continued their proceedings. Afterward, mobs assaulted Blacks who had attended the meeting and smashed windows in the Negro section of the city. This was only the first of a succession of similar incidents in Boston that winter. n January 1861, for the first time in its long history, a convention of the Massachusetts Anti-Slavery Society was broken up as several hundred opponents crowded into Tremont Temple, threw cushions from the gallery onto the abolitionists seated below, and finally drowned out the speakers with their clamor.[4]

Garrisonian lecturers throughout the West faced new ordeals as rioters assailed them. Mobs disrupted abolitionist meetings all across the state of New York. In Buffalo, no less a personage than former governor Horatio Seymour led the assault that drove abolitionists from their platform. In Ohio and Michigan, Parker Pillsbury, Josephine Griffing, and Giles B. Stebbins underwent trials similar to those endured by Henry B. Stanton and Theodore Weld during the first extensive abolitionist campaigns a quarter of a century earlier.[5] But no more successfully in 1861 than in 1835 did opponents succeed in silencing them. Indeed it may be that such attacks aroused more sympathy and gained a larger hearing for the abolitionist message than could otherwise have been attained. Yet the hostility continued well into the war. During the bloody draft riots that convulsed New York City in July 1863, mobs destroyed the property of prominent abolitionists and attacked and murdered Negroes. While such overt evidences of hatred for white abolitionists had become exceptional by 1863 and soon nearly disappeared, the same relief was not granted Northern urban Blacks, who continued to encounter abuse throughout the war years.[6]

Northern attitudes toward race changed slowly, almost imperceptibly; in contrast, attitudes with respect to proper governmental policy toward slavery changed quickly and radically with the advent of secession and war. In 1860–1861, as had so often happened in the past, Southern action played into the hands of abolitionists. By leaving the Union, slaveholders created the situation in which slavery could be destroyed. While some abolitionists at first welcomed secession as a means of freeing the nation from an insidious influence, most soon had second thoughts.[7] They supported Lincoln's determination to restore the Union. But to his starkly political aim of restoration they added a significant corollary: There must be no further compromise with the South, and the Union must be restored without slavery. Once again abolitionists asserted that if the Union were to be saved, it must be made worth saving. This sentiment, once endorsed by so few as to appear both eccentric and radical, now became widespread as a Northern majority began to view slavery as the root cause of secession and the ensuing war.

The abolitionists' determination to use the secession crisis as a means of ending slavery was immeasurably strengthened by the Confederate bombardment of Fort Sumter in April 1861. The differences that had separated the most radical and anti-institutional abolitionists from those who endorsed political action became muted. Abolitionists who had been pacifists and nonresistants a decade earlier now for the most part accepted war, not as a means of suppressing rebellion and saving the Union, but as a way to free the slaves. At one time, they had rejected the claims of government and of arbitrary power; now they called upon government to use its martial power to crush the South and reform its institutions.[8]

This potential use of war was not altogether new to anti-slavery thought. A few politically minded abolitionists in the 1840s had followed John Quincy Adams in recognizing that the introduction of armies in the South—whether required by slave uprising, invasion, or civil war—could bring the end of slavery. The war powers of Congress and the President, as Adams repeatedly pointed out, would sweep away all the barriers that peacetime states' rights issues raised against national interference with slavery.[9]

As fighting between North and South began, abolitionists insisted that the Union's war powers should be used to end slavery. Temporarily setting aside moralistic arguments, abolitionists presented the case for emancipation in thoroughly opportunistic terms. Emancipation, they said, was a measure essential for Union military victory. It would deprive the South of much of its labor force and would diminish the likelihood of the Confederacy's gaining diplomatic recognition and aid from foreign powers. They accompanied their plea for emancipation with an eventually successful campaign to arm Blacks and admit them to the Union armies. Such a course would strengthen the Union's military might, they argued, and provide the numerical edge needed for victory.[10]

With the Union committed to a war against the South, few indeed of the abolitionists withheld support from either the government or the Republican party. Even Garrison, whose pre-war career was inseparable from an anti-establishment, anti-government stance, now gave full allegiance to Lincoln's administration. He opposed those abolitionists who followed Stephen S. Foster in refusing to support the government unless it immediately proclaimed black freedom. He removed from the masthead of the *Liberator* the disunionist statement it had long borne: "The

United States Constitution is 'a covenant with death and an agreement with hell,' " and he replaced it with what he hoped would become governmental policy during the conflict: "Proclaim Liberty throughout all the land, to all the inhabitants thereof." He accompanied that ringing slogan with a quotation from John Quincy Adams on the power of the President, the military commanders, and Congress to end slavery in time of war.[11]

But Lincoln hesitated to adopt so revolutionary a course, in part because he understood that his aim of promoting reconciliation between the sections would be impossible to achieve if the abolitionists' advice were followed, and in part because he doubted Northern support for it. Congress concurred with Lincoln's conservative policy. On 22 July 1861, the day after the Union disaster at the first Battle of Bull Run, it passed the Crittenden Resolution declaring "this war is not waged . . . for any purpose . . . of overthrowing or interfering with the rights or established institutions of . . . [Southern] states.[12]

Once again abolitionists resorted to their traditional tactic of trying to persuade the electorate to accept their views and thereby force officials to move toward emancipation. They undertook a widespread propaganda campaign in 1861–1862 conducted in part through Emancipation Leagues they had recently established in Northern cities as a substitute for the still unpopular antislavery societies. Again agents circulated antislavery petitions. Once more such experienced warhorses of abolitionism as Wendell Phillips and Frederick Douglass traveled the lecture circuit to whip up popular sentiment for abolition; Garrison even managed to persuade Theodore Weld to come out of his long retirement and speak again in the antislavery cause.[13] Abolitionist lecturers again found themselves listened to intently. Halls and churches long closed to them were now open.

This time the radical antislavery message matched the shifting Northern mood. As military operations expanded and the extent of national peril became apparent, the blame for secession and war, at first placed on abolitionists and Negroes, gradually was shifted in the public mind onto the South. With that transfer came a more deeply felt, pop ular hostility toward slavery. Slavery, secession, and war were linked and commonly deplored as a Southern trinity of evil. Even Northerners who saw the purpose of the war as limited to the restoration of the Union and who had little concern for racial justice came to realize that to reincorporate the South with its slaveholding aristocracy intact would solve no national problem. Slavery and the Republic, they concluded, could not exist together.

At the door of the planters, it was generally agreed, must be laid responsibility for those Southern policies and characteristics that some Northerners for forty years had found objectionable: its rigid states' rights political philosophy, its attempt at nullification and its frequent threats of secession; its willingness to abridge civil rights in the defense of slavery; its opposition to tariffs, banks, internal improvements, and homestead acts; its aggressive efforts to expand slavery into the West; its propensity for violence; the arrogant demeanor and despotic tendencies that Northerners thought they detected in the Southern character. Slavery, Republicans commonly charged, lay at the roots of all these long-standing grievances, just as slavery was judged responsible for secession and war. All were associated with the slaveholding planters. Slavery must be abolished then not so much because it was the just course to follow as because it was the most direct way to destroy the power of the planter class. If this were not done and the planters resumed their customary position in government, the restored Union would suffer from the same Southern-inspired troubles that so long had plagued it. Further, some persons believed, America could never play its destined world-role as leader and champion of liberty if slavery were perpetuated within its own borders.[14]

Such motives for abolition bore slight resemblance to the moral and religious imperatives that had inspired abolitionists during their long crusade. The new kind of antislavery had little to say about the rights of black people and about justice for freedmen. It was, finally, an emancipation policy derived from enmity generated by the strategic errors of slaveholders rather than from a recognition of the evils inherent in slavery itself. Its purpose was threefold: To punish and humble the mighty malefactors in the South, to promote the supremacy of small-scale capitalism and middle class society, and to serve the needs of an impersonal national interest. The welfare of Blacks was of secondary consideration.

Commentators at the time recognized that concern for morality and justice, as abolitionists understood those terms, was not uppermost in accounting for the new antislavery sentiment. "This is not now a question of the right to hold slaves, or the wrong of so doing," observed Charles G. Leland, editor of the Unionist *Continental Monthly,* during the first year of the Civil War. "So far as nine-tenths of the North ever cared, or do now care, slaves might have hoed away down in Dixie" forever had the South not seceded. Frederick Douglass offered a similar analysis. "Much as I value the present apparent hostility to Slavery at the North," he told an audience at Cooper Institute in February 1863, "I plainly see that it is less the outgrowth of high and intelligent moral conviction against Slavery, as such, than because of the trouble its friends have brought upon the country." In a more complex analysis, the transcendentalist author and editor George William Curtis observed that "there is very little moral mixture in the 'Anti-Slavery' feeling of this country. A great deal is abstract philanthropy; part is hatred of slaveholders; a great part is jealousy for white labor; very little is consciousness of wrong done and the wish to right it." But the relative absence of moral considerations in no way impeded the rise of opposition to slavery.[15]

The Union government, urged on by the newly invigorated anti-Southern and antislavery sentiment—opportunistic though it was—moved quickly toward adopting an emancipation policy. In the first months of 1862, Congress provided for compensated emancipation in the District of Columbia and prohibited slavery in the territories. It passed confiscation acts making the property (including slaves) of rebels subject to seizure. At the same time, the decision of thousands of individual slaves to flee their owners and to seek refuge as "contrabands" with the advancing Union armies forced authorities to develop a policy respecting their status. Slavery could not be evaded as a war issue, whatever the discomfiture of conservatives.

On 22 September 1862, following the Union victory at the Battle of Antietam, Lincoln issued a preliminary Emancipation Proclamation "as a fit and necessary war measure," declaring all slaves in areas still in rebellion on 1 January 1863, "then, henceforth, and forever free." His motives were mixed. In part, the proclamation was simply a political measure aimed at dividing the Confederacy by persuading some Southern states to return to the Union and depriving the rest of black manpower. In part, it may have been aimed at persuading European liberal opinion to halt the movement to aid the Confederacy. In part, it may have been a political response to the Radical Republicans in Congress, who, strongly swayed by abolitionist ideals, demanded greater energy in prosecuting the war and more tangible evidence that it was being fought to end slavery. But the proclamation also evidenced Lincoln's own advancing antislavery sentiment and his awareness of the swelling popular demand that this become an antislavery war, that the base of Southern power be altered, and the cruel anachronism of slavery be swept from America. For the creation of such sentiments abolitionists—unwittingly aided by slaveholders themselves—could take much credit.[16]

Though Blacks generally greeted the Emancipation Proclamation as the advent of freedom, abolitionists, struck by the document's deficiencies, were more skeptical. The Proclamation left slavery intact in the loyal border states and left the Fugitive Slave Law in force elsewhere. In its legalistic phrases, there appeared no hint that government acknowledged further responsibility toward Blacks than merely releasing them from slavery. The absence of any provision for the civil rights of the freedmen and any commitment to the ideals of racial justice troubled abolitionists, who were convinced that without these things emancipation would be a hollow accomplishment.

Thus at the convention of the American Anti-Slavery Society in 1863, part of the order of business was criticism of Lincoln's emancipation policy on the ground that it represented merely the letter and not the spirit of abolitionism. Such purists as Stephen S. Foster, his wife Abby Kelley, and Frederick Douglass led in warning of the fragility of black freedom achieved only out of military and political necessity. In their opinion, the abolitionist campaign should be acknowledged a failure, for it evidently had been unable to instill a sense of righteousness into the Northern majority.

Garrison and his close associate Oliver Johnson were more optimistic.[17] Once nothing less than the very highest standard of rectitude would have satisfied them, but with the outbreak of war both men had retreated from the perfectionism that had characterized their earlier years. Garrison now considered it unnecessary and even impertinent to inquire closely into the motives that led men to advocate and endorse emancipation. Acceptance of the principle of emancipation was all that mattered to him. Johnson too thought it a sign of abolitionist success rather than of failure that so many persons in the North had come to see emancipation as coinciding with their worldly interest. He ridiculed his colleagues who joined Foster in judging no act good unless it were performed by a thoroughly regenerate person. "Saints—perfect people—do not travel in regiments," observed Johnson, "and if I thought the slaves could not be emancipated before the masses of the people are brought up to the standard of absolute justice and righteousness, I should expect them to grind in the prison-house for centuries." This was common sense, but however much abolitionists might justifiably rejoice in Lincoln's emancipation policy, some of them remained troubled to find him and so many others doing the right thing for what appeared to be the wrong reason.

Abolitionist skepticism was reinforced by evidence that undisguised racism still exercised power over even many champions of emancipation. Despite nearly universal Northern support for a free-labor system and growing eagerness to punish the plantation South by destroying its economic base, it was evident that Northerners also feared and resisted racial equality. Lincoln himself made several proposals for black colonization between 1860 and 1863, actions that could only incense abolitionists who had rejected such policy more than thirty years earlier and could not conceive of a genuine opponent of slavery endorsing it now.[18]

Republican leaders repeatedly found it politically expedient to assure their constituents that emancipation would not end "white supremacy" or promote racial mixing. Nothing in the Republican program, they explained, would encourage Southern Blacks to move into the North, and nothing in it endangered the system that confined Northern free Blacks to an inferior caste position. When shortly after the war the Fourteenth and Fifteenth Amendments provided a basis for the freedmen's civil and political rights, politicians soothed apprehensive Northerners with the assurance that those measures would help keep Blacks contentedly in the South. In short, slavery could be extinguished and a measure of protection could be accorded the freedmen without altering Northern social arrangements. Even during the crusade-like atmosphere generated by the war experience, every step toward emancipation and the extension of rights to all Americans encountered stubborn resistance and warnings of impending ruin. "Conservatism always believes the heavens will fall when justice triumphs," commented Indiana's radical congressman, George W. Julian.[19]

Yet it may be that politicians misjudged the moral growth made by their constituents and thus underestimated the impact of abolitionist efforts in altering attitudes toward slavery and race. Racism and undiluted social conservatism, while still forces of significant power, at least temporarily ceased to dominate the Northern mind by the end of the Civil War. These ideas had been weakened by a tentative commitment to equality and racial justice. The shift in attitude was not made easily and, as it turned out, proved to be temporary. Men and women in the Civil War era who had come to accept the abstract truth of the abolitionists' condemnation of slavery and racism, but who yet retained culturally determined prejudices, experienced the anguish characterized by William Faulkner in his Nobel Prize acceptance speech as "the human heart in conflict with itself." They knew what was "right" with respect to race—abolitionists had taught them that lesson—but at the same time other of their values and interests required Blacks to be kept far from them and in an inferior, exploited position. While only a few persons could shed the ancient presuppositions of their culture and become full-fledged abolitionists, many more suspected that the abolitionists were right, adopted part of their principles as their own, and underwent a painful, interior ordeal in consequence.

Wartime politicians necessarily took Northern ambivalence (which of course they themselves also experienced) into account in developing policy, for however near to abolitionist views individual Republican political leaders came, they always felt themselves restricted in the antislavery measures they prudently could advocate by knowledge that large parts of the voting public lagged considerably behind in sentiment.[20] In virtually no instance did governmental racial policy meet abolitionist expectation. Abolitionists loathed such catering to popular prejudice and continued their own efforts to lead both the majority and its elected officials to what they regarded as higher, more consistent positions.

In some instances they succeeded. Aware of the inadequacies of the Emancipation Proclamation, for example, abolitionists campaigned to embody emancipation in the Constitution. The Thirteenth Amendment abolishing slavery passed Congress on 31 January 1865 and was ratified before the year ended. Garrison regarded that event as consummating his life's work and as completing the mission of the antislavery societies. At the end of 1865, he set the type for the final issue of the *Liberator* with his own hands and on 29 December 1865, announced that after thirty-five years it had ceased publication. He also recommended disbanding the antislavery societies. Abolitionists, he advised, might henceforth either work as individuals to promote racial justice or join new specialized organizations formed to aid the freedmen. Whether the old antislavery societies were obliged to aid the freedmen became an object of impassioned debate among abolitionists. The American Anti-Slavery Society was divided over the issue. One faction insisted that with ratification of the Thirteenth Amendment the society should dissolve. Others, agreeing with Parker Pillsbury's declaration that "our work is not yet quite done; at least mine is not done, nor will it be done till the blackest man has every right which I, myself, enjoy," managed to keep the society alive until 1870.[21]

The dispute over the proper postwar role of organized abolitionism does not mean that Garrison or any significant number of his associates retreated from what they regarded as their responsibilities toward the freedmen. They remained faithful to one of the oldest themes in antislavery thought, dating from the manumission societies of the 1790s and continuing through the organizations established in the 1830s: the abolitionist obligation to prepare Blacks for freedom and to aid them after their release from slavery. The dual aims of emancipation and equal rights for Blacks always were inseparable in abolitionism. Postwar concern for the welfare of Blacks is easily depreciated as paternalism. Yet for all its limitations, it seems obvious that the concern proceeded from a sense of duty to aid those whom society had wronged and that it reflected awareness of at least some of the complex social problems involved in emancipation.

In general, abolitionists considered freedmen's aid to be the function of individuals, churches, and of voluntary societies. But they did not exempt government from its full share of responsibility. Abolitionists took the lead in insisting that the national government must extend tangible forms of aid to the freedmen. In this instance they moved far beyond motives of mere benevolence. To their minds governmental benefits for the newly emancipated slaves were not required by philanthropic duty alone but above all by the demands of retributive justice. They viewed such aid as just reparation for centuries of wrongs inflicted upon an unoffending people. The national obligation would not be discharged, abolitionists insisted, until the freedmen had been trained and otherwise helped to assume a place of equality in American society. Thus abolitionists urged creation of the Freedmen's Bureau in 1865, supported its relief activities among both Blacks and needy Whites, and moved into the South to work under the Bureau's authority.[22]

Understanding, too, that freedom required an economic base if it were to have substance and permanency, abolitionists agitated for the distribution of land to the freedmen. Such a boon was not provided by Congress, however; except for the most radical Northern political leaders, few abolitionists supported extensive land confiscation, and much of the relatively small amount of land that had been distributed to former slaves was soon returned to its former white owners by President Andrew Johnson.[23]

Abolitionists approached the new task of aiding the freedmen with enthusiasm and dedication. Now their decades-long commitment to equal rights emerged clearly and unentangled by any other consideration. They joined Northern free Blacks to seek repeal of restrictive state laws that still impinged on the rights of black citizens. They worked to pass Federal legislation to protect the rights of Blacks in Southern states. They agitated for black suffrage. They personally moved into the South to aid the freedmen. Many worked in the South under commission from the American Missionary Association, the abolitionist agency organized in the early 1840s by the Tappan brothers. Others, in perhaps still greater numbers, represented the newly formed freedmen's aid societies. Names long familiar in the abolitionist movement—Garrison, Whittier, Child, Jocelyn, Redpath, McKim, among many others—now appeared as supporters of the new cause of freedmen's aid. Quakers, who had made a prewar career of assisting fugitive slaves through underground railroad activity, occupied conspicuous places in the new phase of antislavery activity.[24]

Abolitionist work among the freedmen started long before the war was over. When Union armies seized the sea islands off the coast of South Carolina late in 1861, the Whites fled, leaving behind nearly 10,000 slaves. Abolitionists recognized this situation as an opportunity for philanthropy and social experimentation on a large scale. With the encouragement of Lincoln's radical Secretary of the Treasury, Salmon P. Chase, several private benevolent societies undertook the task of aiding the freedmen. Soon teachers, missionaries, physicians, and labor superintendents, many of them abolitionists, were in the islands. "The Port Royal Experiment," as it came to be called, was regarded by abolitionists as a model that would demonstrate the capacity of slaves for freedom and the ability of reformers to educate and mold them into productive members of society. In these ways, the effort at Port Royal was reminiscent of Benjamin Lundy's project thirty years earlier to form a free labor colony in Mexico.[25]

The Port Royal freedmen industriously worked the land for wages, as abolitionists always had predicted emancipated slaves would do; they showed eagerness and ability to learn to read and write. Judged by such accomplishment, the experiment in social and economic reconstruction succeeded; yet its example was followed almost nowhere else, and eventually the Port Royal freedmen were betrayed and the experiment was abandoned when President Johnson's postwar amnesty program dispossessed the freedmen of their land.

Such disappointments, bitter though they were, did not mark the end of abolitionist commitment in the South.

They continued for decades after the war to work through both the American Missionary Association and the freedmen's aid societies to provide education for Southern Blacks. They helped establish public schools throughout the South and served in them as teachers. A number of Southern colleges—which eventually became an important source of the twentieth-century civil rights movement—owed their origins to abolitionists. Among the institutions founded or at least supported by abolitionists were Atlanta, Fisk, and Howard Universities, and Berea, Tougaloo, Talladega, Morehouse, and Spelman Colleges. Abolitionists seemed equal to any racial emergency. When an exodus of freedmen in the late 1870s took thousands of Southern Blacks into Kansas, abolitionists, led principally by the Quaker Elizabeth Comstock, organized large-scale relief efforts, extending even to England.[26]

Such postwar activities on the part of abolitionists represented, as always, the concern of only a Northern minority. As the practical difficulties the achievement of equality would entail and the long-term sacrifices its implementation would require became obvious, the majority's tentative commitment to the welfare of the freedmen wavered. Rather quickly, Northern determination to support the elevation of Blacks weakened and then nearly disappeared in the more compelling realities of postwar politics and economic growth.

That development, some abolitionists believed, was predictable. They related it to their discovery that they had failed to work that change in moral values which from the start of their crusade had been one of their two goals. Henry C. Wright, one of Garrison's close associates, observed at the end of the war that though slavery as a legal institution was dead, "its spirit and its results" lived on in the form of oppression and racial prejudice. In May 1865, Charles Lenox Remond, the black abolitionist, ventured the guess that if a referendum were then held on granting entire equality to his race, the proposal would be defeated by a margin of ten to one. Soon afterward, Stephen S. Foster repeated the apprehensions for the Negro's future that he had expressed in the midst of the war: Because abolition had been accomplished by force and not as a consequence of moral conviction, its gains would not last. Such gloomy views became rather common, especially among those abolitionists who had always insisted that a revolution in moral values must precede abolition and who measured their achievement by the degree of popular resistance that prevailed to the elevation of the freedmen.[27]

The Reconstruction effort of direct federal intervention in Southern political and social affairs soon was abandoned; and following the Presidential election of 1876, the Southern states were allowed to resume management of race relations with little outside interference. Thereafter, the status of the freedmen rapidly deteriorated. Observing this distressing development, Frederick Douglass, for one, was not surprised. "Liberty came to the freedmen of the United States, not in mercy, but in wrath," he explained, "not by moral choice, but by military necessity.... Nothing was to have been expected other than what has happened."[28]

Abolitionists protested strongly against the Northern abandonment of Reconstruction. National protection for the freedmen still was necessary, they insisted, and agitation for equal rights must continue. Abolitionists gathering as late as 1874 considered a resolution declaring "that so long as the freedmen are excluded from the public schools, equal seats in the railroad cars and churches, and places of amusement and hotels, our work is not done."[29]

But such calls for action were little heeded beyond abolitionist circles. The numbers of persons willing to continue agitation for equal rights and governmental protection dwindled, and their efforts aroused diminishing response. However sharp their own awareness of the nation's needs might be, abolitionists in the postwar years could have little realistic prospect for further accomplishment. By the 1870s, their program stood by itself, representing only the demands of benevolence and principle. Unlike the antebellum period, their program now coincided with no evident class or sectional or national interest. Without the motive power such interest would provide, their principled appeal could not succeed.

For most Northerners, the Civil War and Reconstruction settled the racial question. With the Union armies victorious and the Union restored, a mood of national self-congratulation replaced the guilt that characterized earlier years. After the ratification of the three Reconstruction amendments, one could believe that the American system had once more succeeded, that it had achieved a beneficent solution to its most difficult problem. The historical record also could be interpreted in such a way as to show that the antislavery movement had triumphed. Yet the relationship between the end of slavery and the long crusade of the abolitionists was anything but clear and direct. The overwhelming fact of secession and war, with the consequent impact of the Union armies, intruded to prevent the application of a simple cause-and-effect formula to the relationship. Neither did emancipation clearly proceed from the revolution in values advocated by a generation of abolitionists. Emancipation, far from being the result of a morally transformed America, as its early proponents anticipated, served rather to justify prevailing values and to reinforce the dominion of the ruling order.

Despite these ambiguities, the antislavery movement's reputed success in destroying an ancient, entrenched institution provided inspiration for later nineteenth-century reformers who sought to eradicate other evils. Following the Civil War, some abolitionists directed their efforts toward such reforms as woman suffrage and temperance. Susan B. Anthony, who as a young woman had been a Garrisonian disunionist as radical as any, now joined with other veterans of the crusade, including Elizabeth Cady Stanton, wife of the abolitionist veteran Henry B. Stanton, to lead the new women's suffrage movement. Of special concern to some— the "new abolitionists," as they sometimes were called— was the elimination of prostitution.[30]

Yet few abolitionists after the war continued the same incisive criticism of institutions, practices, and beliefs that had characterized their movement in pre-Civil War days. Wendell Phillips, with his strictures against the exploitation of industrial labor, was perhaps the best known of the abolitionists consistently to do so. Others occasionally made statements reflecting continued resistance to the course of American development. In 1863, Theodore Weld condemned what he termed the "dragon-brood" of slavery: "aristocracy, caste, monopoly, class legislation, exclusive privilege and prerogative, all legalized oppression of the weak by the strong, with whatever obstructs 'Liberty, Equality, Fraternity.'" Weld's catalog of the nation's ills appeared to promise an enlarged crusade on his part, but his words must be taken as an expression of radical attitude only, for he never acted on the basis of them.[31]

George W. Julian, as incisively as Weld, saw the direction the abolitionist impulse might take in postwar America. "The abolition of poverty is the next work in order," he declared, "and the Abolitionist who does not see this fails to grasp the logic of the Anti-Slavery movement, and calls a halt in the inevitable march of progress."

"African slavery," said Julian, "was simply one form of the domination of capital over the poor. . . . The system of Southern slavery was the natural outgrowth of that generally accepted political philosophy which makes the protection of property the chief end of Government." Julian called upon the "working classes" to "wage war against the new forms of slavery which are everywhere insidiously entrenching themselves behind the power of combined capital, and barring the door against the principle of equal rights."[32]

Such insights were shared by few, however, and insofar as Julian's conception of the abolitionist impulse persisted and was expressed in action at all, it became diffused in moral reform and in various forms of populism. No more successfully than abolitionists before them could men like Julian transform the character of their age.

Notes

1. Eric Foner, *Free Soil, Free Labor, Free Men; the Ideology of the Republican Party before the Civil War* (New York: Oxford University Press, 1970), pp. 313–17. A general treatment of secession is in Dwight Lowell Dumond, *The Secession Movement, 1860–1861* (New York, Macmillan, 1931). Steven A. Channing, *Crisis of Fear; Secession in South Carolina* (New York: Simon and Schuster, 1970), pp. 286–93, emphasizes racial fears as a cause of secession.
2. Political maneuvers during the secession period are described in Kenneth M. Stampp, *And the War Came; the North and the Secession Crisis, 1860–1861* (Baton Rouge: Louisiana State University Press, 1950) and David M. Potter, *Lincoln and His Party in the Secession Crisis* (New Haven: Yale University Press, 1942).
3. James M. McPherson, *Struggle for Equality: Abolitionists and the Negro in the Civil War and Reconstruction* (Princeton: Princeton University Press, 1964), pp. 29–45.
4. Wendell Lloyd Garrison and Francis P. Garrison, *William Lloyd Garrison, 1805–1879; the Story of His Life as Told by His Children* (New York: Century, 1885), IV: 5–9.
5. *National Anti-Slavery Standard,* 5 January and 9 February 1861; Giles Stebbins, *Upward Steps of Seventy Years . . .* (New York: United States Book Co., 1890), p. 214.
6. A. Hunter Dupree and Leslie H. Fishel, Jr., eds., "An Eye-Witness Account of the New York Draft Riots, July, 1863," *Mississippi Valley Historical Review,* 47 (December 1960); V. Jacque Voegeli, *Free but Not Equal: The Midwest and the Negro During the Civil War* (Chicago: University of Chicago Press, 1967), pp. 88–90; Jacob C. White to Joseph C. Bustill, 19 August 1862,

Carter G. Woodson Collection (Manuscript Division, Library of Congress).

7. David Potter, *The South and the Sectional Crisis* (Baton Rouge: Louisiana State University Press, 1968), pp. 219–42.

8. McPherson, *Struggle for Equality*, pp. 45–61.

9. Dwight Lowell Dumond, *Antislavery: The Crusade for Freedom in America* (Ann Arbor: University of Michigan Press, 1961), pp. 369–70.

10. McPherson, *Struggle for Equality*, pp. 52–133, 192–94.

11. Ibid., pp. 99–104.

12. U.S., Congress, *Congressional Globe,* 37th Cong., 1st sess., pp. 222–23, 265.

13. McPherson, *Struggle for Equality*, pp. 75–106.

14. George W. Julian, *Speeches on Political Questions, 1850–1871* (New York: Hurd and Houghton, 1872), pp. 154–80; Frederick P. Stanton, "Consequences of the Rebellion," *Continental Monthly*, 3 (January 1863): 36.

15. *Continental Monthly*, 1 (February 1862): 114; *New York Tribune,* 7 February 1863.

16. A general account of the Emancipation Proclamation and its background is in John Hope Franklin, *The Emancipation Proclamation* (Garden City: Doubleday, 1963).

17. For the debate see *Proceedings of the American Anti-Slavery Society at Its Third Decade . . .* (New York: the Society, 1864), pp. 70–73, 78–81, 111.

18. Charles H. Wesley, "Lincoln's Plan for Colonizing the Emancipated Negroes," *Journal of Negro History*, 4 (January 1919): 7–21.

19. *Chicago Tribune,* 11 June 1874; the ambiguities in northern racial policies are forcefully stated in C. Vann Woodward, *American Counterpoint: Slavery and Racism in the North-South Dialogue* (Boston: Little, Brown, 1971), pp. 140–83.

20. The advice given a leading Republican during the war suggests the prevailing perception of the problem: "Humanity to the Black has as yet no power in an election . . . we must be wise enough in the wisdom of this world to guide public opinion in the right direction instead of running a foolish tilt against it." Simeon Nash to John Sherman, 17 June 1864, John Sherman Papers (Manuscript Division, Library of Congress).

21. McPherson, *Struggle for Equality*, pp. 287–307; Parker Pillsbury, *Acts of the Anti-Slavery Apostles* (Concord, N.H.: Clague, Wegman, Schlecht, 1883), p. 501; Garrisons, *Garrison*, IV, pp. 157–61.

22. McPherson, *Struggle for Equality*, pp. 178–91.

23. Lawanda Cox, "The Promise of Land for the Freedmen," *Mississippi Valley Historical Review*, 45 (December 1958): 413–40.

24. James M. McPherson, "The Antislavery Legacy: From Reconstruction to the NAACP," in *Towards a New Past; Dissenting Essays in American History,* ed. Barton J. Bernstein (New York: Pantheon Books, 1968), pp. 140–42.
25. Willie Lee Rose, *Rehearsal for Reconstruction; the Port Royal Experiment* (Indianapolis: Bobbs-Merrill, 1964); *Genius of Universal Emancipation,* 13 (November 1832): 7.
26. McPherson, "The Antislavery Legacy," p. 141; John G. Van Dusen, "The Exodus of 1879," *Journal of Negro History,* 21 (April 1936): 111–29.
27. Carleton Mabee, *Black Freedom; the Nonviolent Abolitionists from 1830 through the Civil War* (New York: Macmillan, 1970), pp. 371–72; *Liberator,* 26 May and 2 June 1865.
28. McPherson, *Struggle for Equality,* p. 431.
29. *Chicago Tribune,* 12 June 1874.
30. Evidence of these interests may be found in *Commemoration of the Fiftieth Anniversary of the Organization of the American Anti-Slavery Society in Philadelphia* (Philadelphia: T. S. Dando, 1884), pp. 33–34, 48, 51; see also David J. Pivar, *Purity Crusade; Sexual Morality and Social Control, 1868–1900* (Westport: Greenwood Press, 1973).
31. Angelina Grimké Weld and Sarah Grimké to "Beloved Friends," 1 December 1863, *Proceedings of the American Anti-Slavery Society at Its Third Decade* ... (New York: the Society, 1864), p. 11. The style of the letter is that of Weld rather than of the Grimké sisters.
32. *Chicago Tribune,* 11 June 1874.

Epilogue

In 1874, some Chicago abolitionists, led by the veteran anti-slavery editor Zebina Eastman, invited their fellow crusaders from all over the country to attend a reunion. Besides renewing old friendships, Eastman explained, the antislavery veterans would use the occasion to review their achievements and thereby attempt to find meaning in their antislavery past.[1]

As might have been expected, the assembled abolitionists indulged in a good deal of sentimental reminiscing and self-congratulation, but two more significant themes ran through their proceedings: wonderment at the manner in which slavery had ended and sorrow over the fact that abolitionists had not been able to transform the majority's values and racial practices.

Some even suggested that abolitionists had not been directly responsible for emancipation, an interpretation at variance with most popular and historical opinion. Neither moral suasion nor electoral politics had ended slavery, the speakers agreed: "The perplexing Gordian knot has been cut by the sword." Slavery was destroyed by revolutionary violence, said John Greenleaf Whittier, "not, as we hoped, through the peaceful ways of argument, appeal, and constitutional legislation." A Northern majority had never fully accepted the abolitionist program, observed Francis Gillette, a Liberty party leader: "Nothing less terrible than the thunderbolts of war could arouse the country and break the chain of slavery."

Amos Dresser, who as a youth traveling in Tennessee forty years earlier had been whipped because of his abolitionist associations, now offered his comrades a word of counsel. The abolitionists' purpose, he reminded them, had been not merely to end slavery as an institution but also to bring about a reordering of values—to eradicate "the caste and prejudice from which [slavery] sprang and on which it fed" and to destroy "all institutions and customs which did not recognize and respect the image of God, and a human brother in every man."[2]

Even as Dresser spoke, abolitionists, surrounded by evidence of their triumphs, received public honor for having been in the forefront of a great humanitarian crusade.[3] They were popularly credited with having been responsible for ending slavery, but, as Dresser understood, this was a distortion of history, misleading in its implication that abolition came from moral reform and not as a consequence of secession and war. It detracted not at all from the moral grandeur of the abolitionists to recognize that their victories were incomplete and in part illusory and their honors thus not altogether deserved.

"We will thank God," said Dresser, "that so far as the statute is concerned slavery is no more, and the odious word 'white' is, or is about to be, erased from both the constitutions and the statutes of each State." But despite this accomplishment, Dresser was not convinced that the abolitionist revolution had achieved its aim. "There yet remains a great work to be done to eradicate the spirit of slavery and the spirit of caste so deeply rooted in the heart," he concluded.[4] This, the purpose of the abolitionists from the beginning, had not yet been accomplished. Perhaps in truth it never could be accomplished, at least through human agency. Nevertheless the ideal remained vivid, even in what appeared to be the darkest of hours.

At the end of the nineteenth century and the beginning of the twentieth, when legal discriminations multiplied in

the South and a wave of terror marked by mobs and lynch-
ings swept much of the country, Northern Blacks under the
leadership of W. E. B. DuBois organized the Niagara Movement to resist the forces of violence and oppression. In doing so, they deliberately associated their campaign with the
antislavery movement and with the American Revolutionary tradition of equal rights. One of their meetings was held
at Faneuil Hall in Boston, another at Oberlin, another at
Harper's Ferry—all sites important to the American radical
past.[5]

The relationship between the antislavery movement and
the new campaign for black rights extended beyond sym-
bolism. Some of the leading figures responsible for merging
the Niagara Movement into the National Association for
the Advancement of Colored People had obvious ties with
abolitionism. Oswald Garrison Villard, a grandson of the
founder of the *Liberator,* joined with Mary White Oving-
ton, a white social worker who was the daughter and grand-
daughter of abolitionists, to advocate organizing the
national society. Among the fifty-two white signers of a call
for a national conference to be held on Lincoln's birthday
in 1909 to discuss the race problem were at least fifteen
former abolitionists or their children. As James McPherson
has said, "The NAACP was literally as well as symbolically
a revival of the abolitionist crusade."[6]

Despite the enlarged efforts of early twentieth century
reformers to combat the forces of racism, advances toward
racial equality came with tantalizing slowness. But following the Second World War, a reinvigorated drive against
discrimination began. The prime movers were Blacks who
had concluded that without their own initiative American
racial practices were not likely to be changed.

The new black activism coincided with national uneasi-
ness at the disparity between professed American principles of equality and opportunity and the actuality of
segregation and discrimination. "A gap between our
recorded aspirations and actual practices still remains,"
said the United States Commission on Civil Rights in its
report, *Freedom to the Free,* issued in the centennial year

of the Emancipation Proclamation.[7] Ever since the American Revolution, black leaders and white reformers had been making the same point to no stunning effect. That it was heeded more seriously in the 1950s and 1960s may in part be explained by developments in national and international politics which bore little relation to refinements of the American conscience. The civil rights movement coincided with Cold War rivalries when Communist spokesmen held up American democratic pretensions to ridicule before the non-white peoples of the rest of the world, whose support the United States sought. The movement came, too, shortly after a large-scale migration of Blacks into Northern cities made them a political force that no longer could be disregarded.[8]

The fact that the climax of the new movement for civil rights also coincided with the centennial of the Civil War, while no doubt accidental, was nevertheless of considerable significance for advancing the cause. It became a source for rebuke in countless editorials and speeches that the promises of the Civil War era, whose anniversaries were then being commemorated, had not been kept. "One hundred years of delay have passed," said President John F. Kennedy in an address to the nation on 11 June 1963, "since President Lincoln freed the slaves, yet their heirs, their grandsons are not fully free. They are not yet freed from the bonds of injustice; they are not yet freed from social and economic oppression."[9] Civil rights leaders specifically associated their efforts with those of the abolitionists of a century before, regarded their own work as a continuation of the reconstruction process that ended prematurely in 1876, and identified the target of their crusade as latter-day slavery. Segregation "is nothing but a new form of slavery covered up with certain niceties of complexity," declared the Reverend Martin Luther King, Jr., perhaps the most charismatic of all recent Black leaders. The year of the centennial of the preliminary Emancipation Proclamation was marked by particularly dramatic racial confrontations, especially in Mississippi, where United States marshalls were called upon to guard the admission of James Meredith to the University of Mississippi at Oxford. The meaning of this and similar events appeared starkly in the last dispatch filed from Oxford by Paul Guihard, the French reporter who was killed during rioting on the university campus: "The Civil War has never ended."[10]

New civil rights legislation was enacted in the 1960s at both state and national levels. Segregation virtually disappeared, and many of the barriers to black participation in political, economic, and educational affairs were lowered. But despite the large achievements of the civil rights movement, its failures spawned extreme bitterness as great numbers of Blacks realized it left important aspects of their lives unchanged. If their legal rights were now for the most part those enjoyed by other Americans, their economic problems remained.[11] Reformers seemed once more to have reached a dead end. Radicals recalled the abolitionist conviction, repeatedly expressed in the preceding century, that legislative changes were superficial, that a fundamental change in values and institutions must take place if the American race problem ever were to be solved.

The black protest movement in the 1960s and 1970s confronted not only implacable racism and class interest but also the fact that the Northern urban ghetto had in some respect replaced the antebellum Southern plantation as a restrictive social and economic institution. Emotions, interests, and institutions continued to obstruct implementation of professed national ideals as the bicentenary of the American Revolution drew near.

Notes

1. Larry Gara, "A Glorious Time: The 1874 Abolitionist Reunion in Chicago," *Journal of the Illinois State Historical Society,* 65 (Autumn 1972): 280–92.
2. *Chicago Tribune,* 10, 11 June 1874.
3. Wendell Lloyd Garrison and Francis P. Garrison, *William Lloyd Garrison, 1805–1879; the Story of His Life Told by His Children* (New York: Century, 1885), IV: 136–52.
4. *Chicago Tribune,* 11 June 1874.
5. Franklin, *From Slavery to Freedom,* pp. 445–48.
6. James M. McPherson, "The Antislavery Legacy: From Reconstruction to the NAACP," in *Towards a New Past; Dissenting Essays in American History,* ed. Barton J. Bernstein (New York: Pantheon Books, 1968), p. 150.
7. United States Commission on Civil Rights, *Freedom to the Free, 1863–1963, Century of Emancipation* (Washington, D.C.: Government Printing Office, 1963), p. 2.
8. Ibid., pp. 205–7; August Meier and Elliot N. Rudwick, *From Plantation to Ghetto, An Interpretive History of American Negroes* (New York: Hill and Wang, 1966), p. 220.
9. *New York Times,* 12 June 1963.
10. Ibid., 3 October 1962, p. 30. On King and the civil rights movement, see Franklin, *From Slavery to Freedom,* pp. 623–52.
11. Meier and Rudwick, *From Plantation to Ghetto,* pp. 246–47.

Essay on Sources

Here are listed some of the most important standard and recent works relating to the abolitionists. My reliance on them obviously is heavy. Also mentioned are archival and specialized materials that were especially useful in preparing this book.

Much of the scholarship on the abolitionists takes the classic work of Gilbert H. Barnes, *The Antislavery Impulse, 1830–1844* (New York, 1933), as its point of departure. Of the two detailed modern histories of the antislavery movement one, Dwight Lowell Dumond, *Antislavery: The Crusade for Freedom* (Ann Arbor, 1961), follows Barnes in emphasizing abolitionism in New York, Pennsylvania, and the West. The other, Louis Filler, *The Crusade Against Slavery, 1830–1860* (New York, 1960), is less comprehensive than Dumond on events before 1830 and, unlike Barnes and Dumond, stresses New England abolitionists. More general and much shorter are Elbert B. Smith, *The Death of Slavery: The United States, 1836–65* (Chicago, 1967), and Russell B. Nye, *William Lloyd Garrison and the Humanitarian Reformers* (New York, 1955). The scope of Betty Fladeland's *Men and Brothers: Anglo-American Antislavery Cooperation* (Urbana, 1972) so far exceeds the limits indicated by its title as to warrant placing it among the comprehensive histories of abolitionism.

Readers interested in parallels between abolitionism and

more recent radical movements should consult three essays by Bertram Wyatt-Brown, "Abolitionism: Its Meaning for Contemporary American Reform," *Midwest Quarterly* 8 (October 1966): 41–55; "New Leftists and Abolitionists: A Comparison of American Radical Styles," *Wisconsin Magazine of History* 53 (Summer 1970): 256–68; and "The New Left and the Abolitionists: Romantic Radicalism in America," *Soundings* 54 (Summer 1971): 147–63. Howard Zinn, "Abolitionists, Freedom-Riders, and the Tactics of Agitation," in *The Antislavery Vanguard, New Essays on the Abolitionists,* ed. Martin Duberman (Princeton, 1965), is interesting for the same reason. But as a check on uncritical present-mindedness, Aileen Kraditor's cautionary essay, "American Radical Historians on Their Heritage," *Past and Present* 56 (August 1972): 136–53, is highly recommended.

An amazing quantity of facts about antislavery thought and activity before 1831 is brought together in two old but still useful books: Mary Stoughton Locke, *Anti-Slavery in America from the Introduction of African Slaves to the Prohibition of the Slave Trade, 1619–1808* (Boston, 1901) and Alice Dana Adams, *The Neglected Period of Anti-Slavery in America, 1808–1831* (Boston, 1908).

David Brion Davis, *The Problem of Slavery in Western Culture* (Ithaca, 1966), the first of a projected three volumes on antislavery movements in England, France, and the United States, provides a cultural explanation for the emerging eighteenth-century concern about slavery. Other aspects of slavery and antislavery during the colonial and early national periods are treated in these works: Thomas E. Drake, *Quakers and Slavery in America* (New Haven, 1950); Lawrence Towner, "The Sewall-Saffin Dialogue on Slavery," *William and Mary Quarterly,* 21:3rd ser. (January 1964): 40–52; Bernard Bailyn, *Ideological Origins of the American Revolution* (Cambridge, Mass., 1967); Staughton Lynd, *Class Conflict, Slavery, and the United States Constitution* (Indianapolis, 1967) and *Ideological Origins of American Radicalism* (New York, 1968); Donald L. Robinson, *Slavery in the Structure of American Politics, 1765–1820* (New York, 1971); Arthur Zilversmit, *The First Emancipation: the Abolition of Slavery in the North* (Chicago, 1967); and Robert McColley, *Slavery and Jeffersonian Virginia* (Urbana, 1964).

The thesis that slavery and its defense were inseparable from the antebellum South's culture and society is argued in two books by Eugene Genovese, *The Political Economy of Slavery: Studies in the Economy and Society of the Slave South* (New York, 1967) and *The World the Slaveholders Made: Two Essays in Interpretation* (New York, 1969). In contrast, Charles G. Sellers, "The Travail of Slavery," in *The Southerner as American,* ed. Charles G. Sellers (Chapel Hill, 1960), finds Southerners burdened and guilt-ridden by their peculiar institution. The importance of cotton exports—and hence of slavery—to the national economy is emphasized in Douglass C. North, *The Economic Growth of the United States, 1790–1860* (Englewood Cliffs, 1960). Philip S. Foner, *Business and Slavery: The New York Merchants and the Irrepressible Conflict* (Chapel Hill, 1941), is a localized study with a similar theme. David Brion Davis presents class interest as a pro-slavery determinant in *Was Thomas Jefferson an Authentic Enemy of Slavery?* (Oxford, 1970).

The fragility and limited extent of Southern antislavery activity are suggested in Gordon E. Finnie, "The Antislavery Movement in the Upper South Before 1840," *Journal of Southern History* 35 (August 1969): 319–42. But for the persistence of such activity see Patricia Hicken, "Gentle Agitator: Samuel M. Janney and the Antislavery Movement in Virginia, 1842–1851," *Journal of Southern History* 37 (May 1971): 159–90. Clement Eaton, *Freedom of Thought in the Old South* (Durham, 1940), traces the decline of Southern liberalism under the impact of slaveholding interests. The last major Southern debate over slavery is the subject of Joseph C. Robert, *The Road from Monticello; Study of the Virginia Slavery Debate of 1832* (New York, 1970). Glover Moore, *The Missouri Controversy, 1819–1821* (Lexington,

Ky., 1953), is the standard work on that milestone in abolitionist history. Richard H. Brown, "The Missouri Crisis, Slavery, and the Politics of Jacksonianism," *South Atlantic Quarterly* 55 (Winter 1966): 55–72, analyzes sometimes-neglected implications of the Missouri controversy. Important for a similar reason is William W. Freehling's work on a later crisis, *Prelude to Civil War; the Nullification Crisis in South Carolina, 1816–1836* (New York, 1966).

The motivation of the abolitionists for undertaking their crusade in the 1830s has interested a number of students. The much-discussed theory that abolitionists belonged to a displaced elite was formulated by David Donald in *Lincoln Reconsidered* (New York, 1956), pp. 19–36. A number of essays soon challenged Donald's view: Martin Duberman, "The Abolitionists and Psychology," *Journal of Negro History* 47 (July 1962): 183–91; Betty L. Fladeland, "Who Were the Abolitionists?" *Journal of Negro History* 49 (April 1964): 99–115; and Larry Gara, "Who Was an Abolitionist?" in *The Antislavery Vanguard, New Essays on the Abolitionists,* ed. Martin Duberman (Princeton, 1965), pp. 32–51. Gerald Sorin provides a book-length refutation in *The New York Abolitionists; a Case Study of Political Radicalism* (Westport, 1971). That none of these works dissuaded Donald is suggested by his essay, "The Proslavery Argument Reconsidered," *Journal of Southern History,* 37 (February 1971): 3–18. Bertram Wyatt-Brown makes an important contribution to the theme of motivation in "Prelude to Abolitionism: Sabbatarian Politics and the Rise of the Second Party System," *Journal of American History,* 58 (September 1971): 316–41.

The hostility encountered by abolitionists is described in Lorman Ratner, *Powder Keg: Northern Opposition to the Antislavery Movement, 1831–1840* (New York, 1968) and in Leonard L. Richards, *"Gentlemen of Property and Standing": Anti-Abolition Mobs in Jacksonian America* (New York, 1970). For a localized study see Linda K. Kerber, "Abolitionists and Amalgamators: The New York City Race Riots of 1834," *New York History* 58 (January 1967): 28–40.

James B. Stewart describes the effect of opposition on ideology in "Peaceful Hopes and Violent Experiences: The Evolution of Reforming and Radical Abolitionism, 1831–1837," *Civil War History* 17 (December 1971): 293–309.

The racial attitudes that obstructed the attainment of abolitionist goals are analyzed in Winthrop Jordan, *White Over Black: American Attitudes Toward the Negro, 1550–1812* (Chapel Hill, 1968) and George M. Fredrickson, *The Black Image in the White Mind: The Debate on Afro-American Character and Destiny, 1817–1914* (New York, 1971). Racial prejudice and the plight of Northern Blacks are the themes of Emma Lou Thornbrough, *The Negro in Indiana; A Study of a Minority* (Indianapolis, 1957) and of Leon Litwack, *North of Slavery: The Negro in the Free States, 1790–1860* (Chicago, 1961).

The political impact of racial prejudice is treated in V. Jacque Voegeli, *Free but Not Equal: The Midwest and the Negro During the Civil War* (Chicago, 1967); Eugene H. Berwanger, *The Frontier against Slavery; Western-Anti-Negro Prejudice and the Slavery Extension Controversy* (Urbana, 1967); and James A. Rawley, *Race and Politics; "Bleeding Kansas" and the Coming of the Civil War* (Philadelphia, 1969). On this point see also C. Vann Woodward, *American Counterpoint: Slavery and Racism in the North-South Dialogue* (Boston, 1971). William H. Pease and Jane H. Pease, "Antislavery Ambivalence: Immediatism, Expediency, Race," *American Quarterly* 17 (Winter 1965): 682–95, argue that abolitionists themselves were racially biased. Also critical of abolitionists but for different reasons is Larry Gara, *The Liberty Line: The Legend of the Underground Railroad* (Lexington, Ky., 1961.).

Eric Foner, *Free Soil, Free Labor, Free Men; the Ideology of the Republican Party before the Civil War* (New York, 1970), shows how antislavery mingled with politics after 1840. In some respects, Foner does for the antislavery North what Genovese's work did for the pro-slavery South. Foner's interpretation, which is closely related to the writings of Barnes and Dumond cited above, contrasts with the neo-

Beardian thesis of Larry Gara, "Slavery and the Slave
Power: A Crucial Distinction," *Civil War History* 15 (March
1969): 5–18; and with the Marxist-oriented thesis of Marga-
ret Shortreed [George], "The Antislavery Radicals: From
Crusade to Revolution, 1840–1868," *Past and Present* 16
(November 1959): 65–87. Julian P. Bretz, "The Economic
Background of the Liberty Party," *American Historical Review* 34 (January 1929): 250–64, emphasizes the economic
influences that led abolitionists toward political organization. In a similar way Russel B. Nye, *Fettered Freedom;
Civil Liberties and the Slavery Controversy, 1830–1860*
(East Lansing, 1949), traces the involvement of abolitionism with other libertarian issues. The irrational aspects of
abolitionism are treated in David Brion Davis, *The Slave
Power Conspiracy and the Paranoid Style* (Baton Rouge,
1969).

Aileen Kraditor analyzes ideological conflicts in *Means
and Ends in American Abolitionism: Garrison and His
Critics on Strategy and Tactics, 1834–1850* (New York,
1969). Kraditor's view of Garrison's political sagacity appears also in James B. Stewart, "The Aims and Impact of
Garrisonian Abolitionism, 1840–1860," *Civil War History*
15 (September 1969): 197–209. Other major efforts to probe
abolitionist ideas are David B. Davis, "The Emergence
of Immediatism in British and American Antislavery
Thought," *Mississippi Valley Historical Review* 44
(September 1962): 209–30 and Anne C. Loveland, "Evangelicalism and 'Immediate Emancipation' in American Antislavery Thought," *Journal of Southern History* 32 (May
1966): 172–88.

Abolitionist activity in the 1840s and 1850s has been less
systematically studied than in the 1830s, but important con-
tributions are made by Jane H. Pease and Willian H. Pease,
"Confrontation and Abolition in the 1850s," *Journal of
American History* 58 (March 1972): 923–37; Carleton Mabee, *Black Freedom; the Nonviolent Abolitionists from 1830
through the Civil War* (New York, 1970); John Demos, "The
Antislavery Movement and the Problem of Violent

'Means,' " *New England Quarterly,* 37 (December 1964): 501–26; and Lewis Perry, *Radical Abolitionism; Anarchy and the Government of God in Antislavery Thought* (Ithaca, 1973). Benjamin Quarles, *Black Abolitionists* (New York, 1969), contains much material on the 1840s and 1850s, though its main purpose is to emphasize cooperation between black and white abolitionists. The deep rifts between the two groups have not yet been fully explored.

James M. McPherson, *The Struggle for Equality: Abolitionists and the Negro in the Civil War and Reconstruction* (Princeton, 1964) and Willie Lee Rose, *Rehearsal for Reconstruction; the Port Royal Experiment* (Indianapolis, 1964), cover abolitionist activity during a period historians of antislavery have too often slighted. For abolitionism in still later decades see James M. McPherson, "The Antislavery Legacy: From Reconstruction to the NAACP," *Towards a New Past; Dissenting Essays in American History,* ed. Barton J. Bernstein (New York, 1968), pp. 126–57 and William B. Hixson, Jr., *Moorfield Storey and the Abolitionist Tradition* (New York, 1972). John S. Rosenburg, "Toward a New Civil War Revisionism," *American Scholar* 38 (Spring 1969): 250–73, offers a gloomy appraisal of the Civil War period and of abolitionist accomplishment.

Jane H. Pease and William H. Pease, *Bound with Them in Chains; a Biographical History of the Antislavery Movement* (Westport, 1972), approaches abolitionism through a study of some of its less well-known figures. Among the many biographies that contribute to an understanding of abolitionism and antislavery are Ralph V. Harlow, *Gerrit Smith, Philanthropist and Reformer* (New York, 1939); Benjamin Quarles, *Frederick Douglass* (New York, 1968); Benjamin P. Thomas, *Theodore Weld, Crusader for Freedom* (New Brunswick, 1950); Betty L. Fladeland, *James G. Birney: Slaveholder to Abolitionist* (Ithaca, 1955); David Donald, *Charles Sumner and the Coming of the Civil War* (New York, 1960) and *Charles Sumner and the Rights of Man* (New York, 1970); Irving H. Bartlett, *Wendell Phillips, Brahmin Radical* (Boston, 1961); Merton L. Dillon, *Elijah P.*

Lovejoy, Abolitionist Editor (Urbana, 1961) and *Benjamin Lundy and the Struggle for Negro Freedom* (Urbana, 1966); Martin Duberman, *Charles Francis Adams, 1807–1886* (Boston, 1961) and *James Russell Lowell* (Boston, 1966); Frank O. Gatell, *John Gorham Palfrey and the New England Conscience* (Cambridge, Mass., 1963); Walter M. Merrill, *Against Wind and Tide: A Biography of Wm. Lloyd Garrison* (Cambridge, Mass., 1963); John L. Thomas, *The Liberator, William Lloyd Garrison: A Biography* (Boston, 1963); Richard H. Sewell, *John P. Hale and the Politics of Abolition* (Cambridge, Mass., 1965); Gerda Lerner, *The Grimké Sisters from South Carolina: Rebels against Slavery* (Boston, 1967); Edward Magdol, *Owen Lovejoy, Abolitionist in Congress* (New Brunswick, 1967); Tilden G. Edelstein, *Strange Enthusiasm; a Life of Thomas Wentworth Higginson* (New Haven, 1968); Bertram Wyatt-Brown, *Lewis Tappan and the Evangelical War Against Slavery* (Cleveland, 1969); William E. Farrison, *William Wells Brown* (Chicago, 1969); Stephen B. Oates, *To Purge This Land with Blood; a Biography of John Brown* (New York, 1970); James B. Stewart, *Joshua R. Giddings and the Tactics of Radical Politics* (Cleveland, 1970); and Richard H. Abbott, *Cobbler in Congress: The Life of Henry Wilson, 1812–1875* (Lexington, Ky., 1971).

Histories and reminiscences written by abolitionists themselves provide valuable insights into the movement of which they were a part. Among the most interesting of these are William Goodell, *Slavery and Anti-Slavery; a History of the Great Struggle in Both Hemispheres with a View of the Slavery Question in the United States* (New York, 1852); Samuel J. May, *Some Recollections of the Anti-Slavery Conflict* (Boston, 1868); and Parker Pillsbury, *Acts of the Anti-Slavery Apostles* (Concord, N.H., 1883).

A guide to the abolitionists' own published works is Dwight Lowell Dumond, *A Bibliography of Antislavery in America* (Ann Arbor, 1961). This is supplemented by the extensive notes and bibliographical essays in Filler, *The Crusade against Slavery* (noted earlier), which lists writings both by and about abolitionists. More recent publications are described in Merton L. Dillion, "The Abolitionists: A Decade of Historiography, 1959–1969," *Journal of Southern History* 26 (November 1969): 500–522.

Important collections of abolitionist writings include Gilbert H. Barnes and Dwight Lowell Dumond, eds., *The Letters of Theodore Dwight Weld, Angelina Grimké Weld, and Sarah Grimké, 1822–1844,* 2 vols. (New York, 1934); Dwight Lowell Dumond, ed., *Letters of James Gillespie Birney, 1831–1857,* 2 vols. (New York, 1938); and Philip S. Foner, *The Life and Writings of Frederick Douglass,* 4 vols. (New York, 1950–1955). William Lloyd Garrison's letters are now being published under the editorship of Walter M. Merrill and Louis Ruchames, *The Letters of William Lloyd Garrison* (Cambridge, Mass., 1971).

Wendell Lloyd Garrison and Francis P. Garrison, *William Lloyd Garrison, 1805–1879,* 4 vols. (New York, 1885–1889), contains much source material extracted from Garrison's correspondence and from the *Liberator.* William H. Pease and Jane H. Pease, *The Antislavery Argument* (Indianapolis, 1965), reprint a variety of abolitionist writing and also include a compact history of the antislavery movement. Louis Ruchames, *The Abolitionists; a Collection of Their Writings* (New York, 1963), emphasizes Garrison's circle.

Records of several antislavery societies are available either in the original or in reprint editions. Especially useful in preparing this book were the *Minutes* of the American Convention for the Abolition of Slavery and the *Annual Reports* of the American Anti-Slavery Society, the American and Foreign Anti-Slavery Society, and the Massachusetts Anti-Slavery Society. The manuscript records of the New York Society for Promoting Manumission in the New-York Historical Society (New York City,) and the papers of the Pennsylvania Society for Promoting the Abolition of Slavery in the Historical Society of Pennsylvania (Philadelphia) also were consulted.

Abolitionist newspapers and journals provided many of the quotations and specific examples incorporated in this book. Of particular use were *The Emancipator (Complete), Published by Elihu Embree, Jonesborough, Tennessee, 1820* (Nashville, 1932); the *Genius of Universal Emancipation;* the *Liberator;* the *National Anti-Slavery Standard;* the *Anti-Slavery Bugle;* the *National Era;* and the *Western Citizen.*

Additional sources not otherwise noted that proved especially useful for this book were the manuscript letters of Lydia Maria Child and the Theodore Dwight Weld, Angelina Grimké Weld and Sarah Grimké Papers, both at the William L. Clements Library, the University of Michigan, Ann Arbor; the Joshua Giddings Papers at the Ohio Historical Society, Columbus; the Lewis Tappan Papers and the Salmon P. Chase Papers, both in the Manuscript Division, the Library of Congress; and the Salmon P. Chase Papers at the Historical Society of Pennsylvania.

Index

Abolition, 145, 254–55. *See also*
Emancipation

Abolitionism: converts to,
51–52, 57–59, 79n; and
evangelicalism, 14n, 29–30;
and Jacksonian democracy,
25; opposition to, 44–46, 64,
66–67, 74–75; and politics, 25;
and racial prejudice, 19; and
radicalism, 26, 29–30; split in
ranks of, 121, 124. *See also*
Antislavery movement

Abolitionists: arguments and
theories of, 57, 72–73, 83–84,
133, 150–56, 204; and
churches, 60, 119–20, 158–60,
200–202; and the Civil War,
251–53; and Confederation
Congress, 15; and
Constitutional Convention,
15–16; disagreements among,
53–54, 113–26, 131–32,
227–28; and Fugitive Slave
Law, 175–80, 199; and
Illinois convention
movement, 23; literary
themes of, 84–85; and
Mexican War, 160–65; and
Missouri Compromise,

23; opposition to, 44, 76, 99;
and party politics, 129–31,
146–47, 194–95, 199–200, 211,
248–50; and post-Civil War
reform, 265–66; post-war
reunion of, 271–72; programs
and goals of, 11–12, 16,
21–22, 40, 42–43, 56, 69–70,
84, 100; and race, 69–73,
260–63; radicalism and
eccentricities of, 29–30, 77,
107, 113–18; in
Reconstruction, 261–64; in
Revolutionary era, 6–7, 10;
rhetoric of, 57, 114, 190–91,
226; and theology, 28–30; and
violence, 219–20, 221–26,
234–37, 241–42

Abolitionists, black, 52, 71–72,
81n, 192–93, 205, 221–22

Adams, Charles Francis, 161,
168

Adams, John Quincy, 103, 105,
106, 153, 252, 253

Adams, Samuel, 6

Adrian, Michigan, 36, 242

Allan, William T., 58, 66

Alton, Illinois, riots in, 94–95

Alton Observer, 93–94

Bird, Frank W., 232
Birney, James G., 59, 64, 68, 98,
116, 145, 189; and churches,
157, 160, and Garrison,
123–24; and politics, 130, 147;
and slavery, 153, 166; and
violence, 223–24
Black culture, 73
Black laws, 69, 192–93, 211
Black mutual benefit societies,
21
Blacks, free: aid for, 63, 69, 73;
and antislavery societies, 49,
52, 53, 54, 71; arming of, 252;
in Baltimore, 36, 39; and
civil rights movement, 273;
and colonization, 20, 60, 61,
168, 190; and discriminatory
laws, 69, 144, 261; and
disunionism, 232, 234–35;
education for, 21–22, 32n, 52,
263; and Emancipation
Proclamation, 256; and Free
Soil Party, 168; and fugitive
slave issue, 175, 176, 179,
182; and W. L. Garrison, 36,
39, 51; at Harvard Medical
School, 192; B. Lundy's plans
for, 42–43, 105; militancy of,
222, 225; in Northern cities,
39, 63, 220; Northern fears
of, 149; and Quakers, 8, 73;
and suffrage, 53–54; violence
against, 63, 250, 251
Blair, Francis P., 190
Blanchard, Jonathan, 241
*Book and Slavery
Irreconcilable, The*
(Bourne), 14n, 38
Bourne, George, 14n, 38
Brown, John, 222, 225, 229,
230, 232, 235, 241–42
Brown, William Wells, 234
Buffum, Arnold, 227

"Building of the Ship, The"
(Longfellow), 181
Burleigh, Charles C., 114, 203,
217n, 234
Burns, Anthony, 194, 235
Burritt, Elihu, 166, 230, 231,
232
Business: and slavery, 25, 26

Calhoun, John C., 101
Cass, Lewis, 167
Chandler, Elizabeth Margaret,
36
Channing, William H., 163
Chase, Salmon P., 127, 142,
262
Cheever, George Barrell, 180
Chicago, Common Council of,
179
Chicago, First Presbyterian
Church of, 135
Chicago Tribune, 241
Child, Lydia Maria, 50, 91, 98,
110n, 171n, 224
Christian antislavery
convention movement,
199–202, 237–39
Christiana, Pennsylvania, riots
in, 184, 186
Church Anti-Slavery Society,
237
Churches: abolitionism and,
60, 117–19, 121, 126, 238; and
American Anti-Slavery
Society, 56–57; black, 21; and
Christian antislavery
convention movement,
200–202; come-outerism in,
150, 156–59; and slavery,
9–10, 26–27
Cincinnati, Ohio, 62–63, 158,
199
"Civil Disobedience"
(Thoreau), 59

Emancipation: compensated,
230–31; gradual, 8, 9, 11, 22,
36, 60, 230; obstacles to,
10–11; in South, 5. *See also*
Abolition
Emancipation Leagues, 253
Emancipation Proclamation,
83, 256, 273–74
Emancipator, 89
Embree, Elihu, 23
Emerson, Ralph Waldo, 162,
172, 242
Enlightenment, 11, 12, 28
Errett, Russell, quoted, 171n
Evangelical Anti-Slavery
Convention (1859), 237
Evangelicalism, 9, 14n, 29–30,
51, 62
Evangelicals, 44, 56–57, 144,
228, 241
Everett, Edward, 193
Expansionism, 149, 182, 197n

*Facts and Opinions Touching
... the American
Colonization Society*
(Stebbins), 61
Faulkner, William, 259
Fee, John G., 158
Fifteenth Amendment, 258
Fillmore, Millard, 182
Finney, Charles G., 29
Fiske, John O., 180
Fitch, Charles, 99
Foss, Andrew T., 212, 234
Foster, Abby Kelley. *See*
Kelley, Abby
Foster, Stephen S., 114, 163,
195, 240, 246n, 257, 263–64
Fourteenth Amendment, 258
Franklin, Benjamin, 6, 16
Freedmen, 263–64
Freedmen's aid societies, 249,
262, 263
Freedmen's Bureau, 261

Freedom Association (1845),
179
Freedom's Journal, quoted,
32n
Free labor, 42–43, 142, 194
Free Presbyterian Church,
158
Free produce movement, 56,
79n
Free Soil Party, 167–69, 193
French Revolution, 11
Friends of Humanity, Baptist,
157
Fugitive Slave Law (1793),
134, 169, 175
Fugitive Slave Law (1850):
abolitionist reaction to,
175–79, 188, 199; enacted,
175; enforcement of, 188–89,
197n, 223, 248
Fugitive slaves, 175–76, 178;
and abolitionists, 134–35,
148, 191, 194, 195, 199; as
heroes, 192; rescues of,
182–83, 184–87, 235. *See also*
Underground railroad

"Gag rule," 101, 102
Garnet, Henry Highland, 190,
222
Garrisonians, 59, 145, 151; and
constitutional theory, 190,
209; and politicians, 146–47;
and violence, 215
Garrison, William Lloyd, 49,
117, 158, 257, 260; and
antislavery schisms, 122–24;
and the clergy, 60, 117–20;
and colonization, 36, 60–61;
and the Constitution, 132,
156, 190; converts of, 50; and
founding of *American
Anti-Slavery Society,* 52,
54–55; and *Genius of
Universal Emancipation,* 36,

38; and immediatism, 36, 38;
and Kansas, 224; and
Liberator, 36, 260; and H. W.
Longfellow, 190n; and B.
Lundy, 36, 42; and Mexican
War, 168; and
non-resistance, 53, 222–23,
236–37; opposition to, 79, 90,
120, 123; and politics, 59,
122, 147, 167, 194, 252; and
race, 72; radicalism of,
114–18; rhetoric of, 49–50;
and L. Tappan, 213; and D.
Webster, 184
Gates, Seth M., 103, 153
General Association of
Connecticut, 117
*Genius of Universal
Emancipation,* 30, 35–36, 38,
39, 40
Ghetto, 275
Giddings, Joshua, 127, 186,
188, 198n, 238; and
abolitionists, 146; censure of,
128–29; and disunionism,
153; and "gag rule," 103; and
slave power, 143–44; and
Texas, 149–50
Gillette, Francis, 271–72
Glazier, Richard, Jr., 205
Goodell, William, 142, 157, 166,
204–5, 208–10; *Views of
American Constitutional
Law,* 208
Gorsuch, Dickerson, 184
Gorsuch, Edward, 184, 186
Great Awakening, 9
Green, Beriah, 54, 157, 191,
210
Griffing, Josephine, 250
Grimké, Angelina. *See* Weld,
Angelina Grimké
Grimké, Sarah, 72, 84, 95, 114,
118, 131
Grover, Alonzo J., 226–27
Guihard, Paul, 275

Hale, John P., 183
Hall, James, 63
Hamilton, Alexander, 6
Hammond, James, 101
Hanway, Caster, 184, 186
Harper's Ferry, Virginia, raid
at, 241, 273
Harvard Medical School, 192
Haven, Gilbert, 179
Haviland, Laura Smith, 187
Higginson, Thomas
Wentworth, 211, 232, 235
Higher law doctrine, 133, 135,
139n, 166, 179–80
Hildreth, Richard, 191
Hinton, Richard J., 235
Hise, Daniel Howell, 160, 244n
Holley, Myron, 130
Holley, Sallie, 206
Holmes, Oliver Wendell, 192
Hone, Phillip, 92
Hosmer, William, 139n

"Ichabod" (Whittier), 184
Illinois, 51, 157, 168, 233;
antislavery contest in, 23–24;
election of 1858 in, 165;
fugitive slave issue in, 134;
prejudice in, 69, 74, 80n
Immediate emancipation:
abolitionists' explanation of,
66–67; adherents of,
categorized, 50–51; and
American Anti-Slavery
Society, 55, 64; defined,
36–38; at Lane Seminary, 62;
and *Liberator,* 39; and New
England Anti-Slavery
Society, 49; as radical
slogan, 150
Imperialism, 3
Iowa Anti-Slavery Society, 164

Jackson, Andrew, 90, 101, 104
Jackson, Francis, 183